Learning Spaces in Africa

With a key UN Sustainable Development Goal for 2030 being to make basic education available to all the world's children, *Learning Spaces in Africa* explores the architectural, socio-political and economic policy factors that have contributed to school design, the main spaces for education and learning in Africa. It traces the development of school building design, focusing on Western and Southern Africa, from its emergence in the 19th century to the present day. Uduku's analysis draws attention to the past historic links of schools to development processes, from their early 19th century missionary origins to their re-emergence as development hubs in the 21st century. *Learning Spaces in Africa* uses this research as a basis to suggest fundamental changes to basic education, which respond to new technological advances, and constituencies in learning. Illustrated case studies describe the use of tablets in refugee community schools, "hole-in-the wall" learning and shared school-community learning spaces. This book will be beneficial for students, academics and those interested in the history of educational architecture and its effect on social development, particularly in Africa and with relevance to countries elsewhere in the emerging world.

Ola Uduku is Professor of Architecture at the Manchester School of Architecture, UK. She completed MPhil and PhD degrees in Architecture at the University of Cambridge focusing on School Design in Nigeria and has taught at Liverpool, Strathclyde and Edinburgh universities. She has written on and researched extensively into the history of school design and its influence on education in Africa and has research interests in contested urbanism, West African modernist architecture, passive design and thermal comfort in the tropics.

Learning Spaces in Africa
Critical Histories to 21st Century Challenges and Change

Ola Uduku

LONDON AND NEW YORK

First published 2018
by Routledge
2 Park Square, Milton Park, Abingdon, Oxon OX14 4RN

and by Routledge
711 Third Avenue, New York, NY 10017

Routledge is an imprint of the Taylor & Francis Group, an informa business

© 2018 Ola Uduku

The right of Ola Uduku to be identified as author of this work has been
asserted by her in accordance with sections 77 and 78 of the Copyright,
Designs and Patents Act 1988.

All rights reserved. No part of this book may be reprinted or reproduced
or utilised in any form or by any electronic, mechanical, or other
means, now known or hereafter invented, including photocopying and
recording, or in any information storage or retrieval system, without
permission in writing from the publishers.

Trademark notice: Product or corporate names may be trademarks
or registered trademarks, and are used only for identification and
explanation without intent to infringe.

British Library Cataloguing-in-Publication Data
A catalogue record for this book is available from the British Library

Library of Congress Cataloging-in-Publication Data
A catalog record for this book has been requested

ISBN: 978-1-4094-3303-3 (hbk)
ISBN: 978-1-315-57674-9 (ebk)

Typeset in Sabon
by Apex CoVantage, LLC

This book is dedicated to my daughter Esmé and to my partner Bob who have both in different ways spurred me to get this task done.

Contents

List of figures and acknowledgements		viii
Foreword		x
PROFESSOR SIMON McGRATH		
Acknowledgements		xiv
1	A background to school planning and design in Africa	1
2	School design in Africa: the background	26
3	Historical school case studies	51
4	African schools in the 21st century: context and background	77
5	Contemporary school design case studies	97
6	Conclusions: education futures in Africa	116
	Afterword	140
	Bibliography	143
	Index	157

Figures and acknowledgements

Cover Baptist Academy, Obalende Lagos Architects J. Godwin and G. Hopwood

1.1	Nsibidi – Southeastern Nigeria Secret Society Script	2
1.2	Islamic School, Northern Nigeria	3
1.3	Hope Waddell College, Calabar, Nigeria	5
1.4	Katsina College, Katsina, Nigeria	6
1.5	Achimota College, Legon, Ghana	8
1.6	Government Technical College, Takoradi, Ghana	10
2.1	Etching of Early Girls' School in Lagos	27
2.2	St Gregory's College Lagos, Nigeria	29
2.3	Wusasa College, Nigeria	30
2.4	Umuahia Regional Library, Nigeria	32
2.5	Vukani School, Khayelitsha, Western Cape, South Africa	36
2.6	School Feeding Programme, Kontonkoshie, Ghana	42
3.1	Typical School Plan	54
3.2	Lovedale College, Eastern Cape, South Africa	56
3.3	Kings College, Lagos, Nigeria	58
3.4	Adisadel College, Cape Coast, Ghana	60
3.5	Federal Government College, Sokoto, Nigeria	63
3.6	Typical 'DET' School, Langa, South Africa	66
3.7	International School, Ibadan, Nigeria	68
3.8	Aga Khan Academy, Mombasa, Kenya	69
4.1	Mawuli School, Ghana	81
4.2	Mawuli School, Ghana	81
4.3	Noraid School Zambia image from Forms of Freedom Exhibition, Kenya, 2016	82
4.4	School Tema Ghana School Design Project, Pat Wakely	83
5.1	Dwabor School, Cape Coast, Ghana	99
5.2	Kailahun School, Prototype Design Sierra Leone	101
5.3	Dalweide School	105
5.4	Inkwenkwezi School, DuNoon, Cape Town, South Africa	106
5.5	Umbano School, Rwanda	109
5.6	Mubugu School, Rwanda MASS Design	110

Figures and acknowledgements   ix

6.1	Refugees Using Tablets in Classroom	123
6.2	'Hole in the Wall' Learning, India	127
6.3	Floating School Makoko Iagos	130
6.4	Dwabor School	134
BM1.1	Africa ICT Project	142

I would particularly like to thank:

John Godwin, GHK Associates; Farrokh Derakhshan and Anise Ladha, the Aga Khan Foundation; Tessa Amoah, UNHCR; Ilze Wolff and Lauren Oliver, Wolff Architects; Iain Jackson, Liverpool University; Dominic Bond and Abigail Jago, Sabre Charitable Trust; Shaun McLeod and Africa ICT school Design Team, Edinburgh University, 2013; and finally William Martinson, and Frank Gaylard; Artefacts, for allowing me to make use of their images, 'pro-bono' for this publication. My thanks to Thatcher Bean, from MASS Design for putting me in touch with Suzanne Tóth-Pál from Iwan Baan Photography who provided the MASS Umbano School image, which is formally acknowledged here.

Foreword

Education remains one of the most pressing issues for development globally. Although there was a commitment to ensure that all Africans achieved full primary schooling by 1980, the latest round of international development targets, the Sustainable Development Goals (SDGs), now offers 2030 as the new deadline. Indeed, in the discussions that have followed the SDGs, there are concerns that even though that target looks achievable at the level of attendance, perhaps one-third of children will not be supported to meeting even the most minimum acceptable learning standards. Though the right to quality education has long been accepted as a core part of international human rights law, many millions of African children will continue to be denied this right for at least another generation.

In the discussions that surrounded the development of SDG4 on quality education and lifelong learning for all, and subsequent considerations of how to deliver on this, a range of aspects of such delivery have taken centre stage. New ways of testing what children have learnt and new assessments of an emerging global core education are being developed. Technological solutions have found favour as many times in the past. Teachers have returned to the stage as acknowledged important actors in delivering quality education, notwithstanding the attempts by some on the political right to portray them more as problem than solution.

Yet, in all of this education discussion, the question of what constitute appropriate, conducive learning spaces remains waiting in the wings. Although we know the importance of the built environment on how we think, behave and work, the issue of the nature of the spaces in which we learn has not been a significant part of the recent debates of the education and development community about how we are to achieve quality learning for all.

It is this gap that the present book, on *Learning Spaces in Africa*, goes a long way to identifying and then filling. It is important reading if we are to fully grasp both the challenge and possibilities of achieving the long-missed goal of giving all children, both in Africa and globally, the opportunity to get a good quality education.

Foreword xi

Ola Uduku is absolutely correct to insist on the importance of understanding the historical development of schooling and schools as a central factor in imagining how quality education might be thought about in the future. As she illustrates in both words and pictures, the current pervasive model of schooling and schools was not inevitable, but it has spread with incredible effectiveness across the globe. From the late 19th century, the school was one of the most visible signs of both Christian mission and colonial administration in the built environment of African communities, a bringer of industrial time discipline to locations where the factory has still not penetrated today.

The very success of the modern, Fordist school system and its instantiation in school buildings places severe limitations on what it is possible to imagine for future education approaches. It is hard to conceive of a way to move beyond this model, given all the investment sunk into the modern school and its bricks and mortar.

As Ola shows, more recent history has seen a dramatic turn in education governance that has served to make school design even less of a policy issue than it once was. She charts how the third-quarter of the 20th century saw major UNESCO and World Bank interest in educational planning stretch to the question of school architecture as many national school systems expanded quickly through the main era of decolonisation and modernisation. School building was heavily regulated in many systems, with the state often actively discouraging local involvement in design and planning decisions. With the arrival of neoliberalism and educational decentralisation in the 1980s, the importance of national planning was severely eroded. More recently, the phenomenon of 'private schooling for the poor', often with considerable donor and philanthropic support, has further eroded any sense of there being national or international standards for school buildings.

As she notes in Chapter 4:

> Despite more than 150 years of educational provision across most of sub-Saharan Africa, the contemporary school classroom remains close in design conception and use to its Victorian predecessor. Learning concepts, methods and theories have changed and begun to influence national curriculums and educational content. In general school design however remains wedded to the past, which harks to the symbolism of Western education as it was delivered via the missions and colonial government to an initial elite group of indigenous citizens.

What then can be done to bring sound educational and architectural principles together in order to support quality learning for all by 2030? The book has a number of interesting and important things to contribute to answering this question.

Advances in learning technologies and understandings of learning processes have progressed without the mass of schools catching up. This is

xii *Foreword*

hardly surprising, given the infrastructural investments required. Nonetheless, examples of innovative design for learning can be found and the consideration of some of these is the key future-looking contribution of the book. In reality, it is difficult to predict what new technologies will become pervasive in schools and how school design can best respond. What is clear is that schools and schooling are being reshaped, even in the poorest settings, by the rise of new technologies. The book offers some examples of how certain technological developments are influencing the construction of new learning spaces. Whilst the cutting edge here is very exciting, Ola also reminds us of the need to think about how we might design new and redesign existing schools to be more effective learning spaces as technologies do shift.

School gardens and kitchens are another example focused upon in the book. In Britain, there have been well-publicised campaigns to address the poor nutritional quality of school food, linking this to healthy diets and, increasingly, to wider issues of cooking skills and organic growing. In parts of Africa, concerns have been more about inadequate intake of calories and micronutrients. Not only are these linked to stunting but also to reduced educational attainment. Thus, school feeding schemes have received significant attention from organisations such as the World Bank. As in Britain, increasingly these have been linked to an awareness about growing, in particular, the opportunities for the community and local entrepreneurs to be involved in the supply of food to schools. As Ola shows, school design becomes an important element of this. Policies to get children eating better and even perhaps more involved in growing nutritious foodstuffs have frequently failed because schools lack the necessary facilities to grow, cook and/or serve food.

The Sustainable Development Goals place education within a wider setting of thinking about sustainable development. A third important strand of this book is a consideration of sustainable school design that also promotes wider notions and practices of sustainability. The case studies in Chapter 5 are good examples of how schools can be designed more sustainably. This must be grounded in the use of appropriate materials that are sustainably sourced and in designs that promote sustainable energy and water use. However, the examples also stress the importance of community involvement, a necessary component if schools are to be maintained long after the architects and builders have departed the stage.

Ola concludes by suggesting that we are entering a new era for thinking about school design in Africa. After the disruptions of the neoliberal era, the rise of new non-state actors and with the potentials of new learning technologies, the start of the SDG era is an important point at which to consider how architecture and education can better talk to each other. Whilst there is little scope for tearing down the modern school and building anew, it is apparent that there are opportunities for thinking innovatively about learning spaces that can better meet the needs of learners and communities, on the one hand,

Foreword   xiii

and the possibilities of technological change, on the other. Ola suggests that, as in mobile telephony, Africa's historical disadvantage in school development may offer an opportunity for a leap forward.

For those concerned with imagining and delivering quality education for all by 2030, there is an urgent imperative to engage with new thinking about the learning spaces to support this. This book is an important step towards opening up a much-needed debate in this area.

Simon McGrath
UNESCO Chair in the Political Economy of
Education, University of Nottingham, UK

Acknowledgements

I would like to thank a number of people without whom I would have not been able to complete this book project. First, my supervisor Robin Spence, who has been instrumental in guiding my post-graduate career from my first doctoral research inquiry to Cambridge as a very young architect in the late 1980s to his continued interest, support and encouragement in my academic life in the present day. Also Costa Criticos, who welcomed me to his then academic world at the University of Natal, Durban, supported my early research on school design in South Africa, and was instrumental in the planning and co-organisation of the international *Learning Spaces in Africa conference* in Durban in 1996. These initial encounters form a significant contextual background to the evolution of this book which partly shares this past conference title.

Writing this book has been a journey which in some ways has mirrored my post-graduate career. I am particularly grateful to my academic friends and colleagues in Cambridge, Zaria, Cape Town, Johannesburg, Liverpool, Strathclyde and Edinburgh University whom I have encountered along the way. Particular thanks to Janet Owers, Koen Steemers, Nick Baker, Dean Hawkes and those at the Martin Centre, and also to Keith Hart, Paula Pitman and Alicia Fentiman at the African Studies Centre, both being part of my academic family in Cambridge. In Liverpool, I should particularly like to thank Iain Jackson, my once student and now research collaborator, and also acknowledge the support I received from Simon Pepper, David Dunster and Gideon Ben-Tovim. Thank you also to my Liverpool-era colleagues Victor Flynn, Zachary Kingdon, Dmitri Van Den Bersselaar and Tunde Zack Williams. In Scotland, I should like to thank my friends at Strathclyde and Edinburgh universities, in particular Ombretta Romice and Felicity Steers, who have been both colleagues and good friends in Glasgow. In Edinburgh, my thanks to academic colleagues in ECA and ESALA, particularly the coffee club; Miles Glendinning, Ian Campbell and Alistair Fair, and my former teaching colleagues; Gillian Treacy, Lisa Moffitt, Tahl Kaminer, Soledad Garcia Ferrari, and Harry Smith, who have both stimulated and encouraged my inquiry and debate. My special thanks also to Paul Jenkins and Leslie Forsyth, who supported my initial research and teaching efforts at ECA-ESALA.

Acknowledgements xv

My special thanks to Rachel Collie, whose help with image formatting was invaluable. I also acknowledge with thanks the firms and individuals who have allowed me to reprint the photographs used throughout the text. My special thanks to Professor John Godwin and Gillian Hopwood for allowing me use their image of Baptist Academy on the front cover of the book. Thank you also to my editor Aoife for seeing this book through.

I would also like to thank my African and internationally based friends with whom I have discussed my work over time: Pamela Nichols, Angela Tait, Hannah Le Roux, Johan Lagae, Antoni Folkers, Joe Addo, Chris Cripps, my 'aburo' Remi Vaughan Richards, Berend van der Laans, Leon Tikly, John Godwin, Alan Davies and Elsbeth Robson. I would also like to acknowledge the research interest shown from my new colleagues at Manchester, particularly Tom Jefferies, Sally Stone, Lukasz Stanek, Stephen Walker and Albena Yaneva, who have already made me feel welcome. Also, in particular I would like to acknowledge my students past and present who have constantly kept me on my toes and encouraged critical inquiry, which in turn has helped me stay invested in ensuring that nurturing the next generation is as fundamental to academic life as research, leadership and outreach.

My family have remained central to me in my academic and personal life; without their support, material and emotional, and their continued presence through 'Uduku-meantime' calls at all hours this would not have finally come to fruition. I would like to remember specially those members who are no longer with us, my sister Chinwe, and father Dr Walter Uduku. I also would like to remember my late patrilineal and matrilineal grandparents; S. O. Uduku and W. Da Costa, who were of the early 20th century generation who understood how important it was to 'know book', as they had directly encountered the pre-colonial and post-colonial education legacy, a central part of this book's research. To my mother and my siblings Okechukwu, Ngozi, and Oluchi thank you for your ever-present support.

1 A background to school planning and design in Africa

Introduction

This chapter sets the background to this book by giving a brief account of the evolution of Western education in Africa and its influence on school design. It focuses mainly on its development in English speaking, former British colonies in West and Southern Africa. Drawing from research sources, it traces the involvement of Africans in Western education, from the children of the elite coastal traders to the mass education movements in the mid-20th century. Giving examples from schools in Nigeria, Ghana, Kenya, Tanzania and South Africa, it contextualises and compares the evolution process which took place across key Anglophone countries in sub-Saharan Africa.

Introduction – early schools in Africa: pre-Western education systems in Africa

Historically, Africa has often been portrayed in the public media and the local imagination as being the dark continent in which there has only been a limited and recent spread of formal Western education.[1] Factually, the continent has had a long and engaging encounter with European or Western education systems that now stretches back more than two centuries.[2] Prior to the transatlantic trade, traders from Europe were involved in commercial activities with indigenous coastal groups who engaged with the European merchants and developed trading systems for the transactions that took place. Whilst in these early days there was no established school system, often children of African traders and kings were sent to Europe for a proper 'Western' education.[3]

This is not to say that there were not historic indigenous education practices, usually associated with initiation rituals, that existed and still do so in different regions in Africa. The 'fattening' house system, for example, remains a traditional practice amongst the Efiks in southeastern Nigeria. The practice involves the sequestering of pubescent girls to a private dwelling and living area, where they are schooled in the arts of cookery and other domestic affairs for a month, whilst fed food to 'fatten' them. At graduation from the school, or fattening house, the graduates are presented as brides to men in the local community. Similar education ritual practices take place

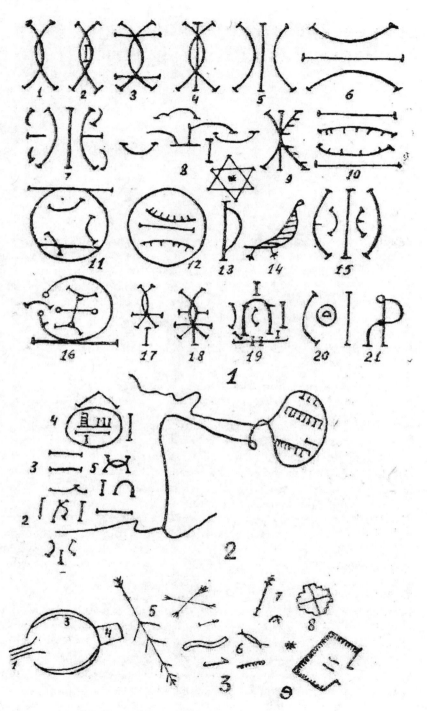

Figure 1.1 Nsibidi – Southeastern Nigeria Secret Society Script
Creative Commons Licence

amongst southern African groups such as the Xhosa and the Zulu have initiation rituals for males coming of age which again involves the youths being removed from their local village settings and taught the 'ways of manhood' over a period before being circumcised and then being reintroduced into their society as men.[4]

Also of note were the initiation and membership activities of traditional secret societies in Africa. In southeastern Nigeria and southwestern Cameroon, the *nsibidi* script was created by the Ekpe or Leopard Society; where teaching of the character script and other society rules would take place at the shrines or meeting places of these societies (see figure 1.1). This has been taken to the New World and has links to the *Abakua* Society in Cuba, who continue with this tradition, calling the writing system *anaforuwana*.[5] Again in these cases, a specific and designated space for the instruction and preparations of the initiates beforehand for these ceremonies would be constructed, albeit of an only temporary status.

The arrival of Islam from the 7th century affected education provision in North African or the 'Maghreb' countries,[6] the regions to the northernmost parts of West Africa,[7] and parts of East Africa facing the Indian Ocean seaboard.[8] In these regions the historic *madrasa* school system been established and retained popular prominence even with the advent of Christianity and the missionary based education systems (see figure 1.2). The *madrasa*

Figure 1.2 Islamic School, Northern Nigeria
Author's own image

4 *School planning and design in Africa*

school currently remains in place in most of the described Islamic regions of Africa. It is usually designed and built as an attachment to existing local mosques and has the primary function to provide Koranic learning to boys, overseen by local Islamic teachers or imams.[9] On occasion the *madrasas* are established structures, built separately from the main mosque, and do have architectural merit in their own right.

Africa did have a number of institutions such as these described that provided a form of pedagogy and instruction within societal groups. Many of these pre-Western education institutions have survived to the present day often taking place in parallel to the now official 'Western' education school systems. Their centrality to the educational experience has changed; traditional initiation ceremonies now take place at weekends or during school holidays. In many countries such as Nigeria and Ghana, most *madrasa* schools have been incorporated into Western education programmes in collaboration with local Islamic teachers.[10] In other states, *madrasas* now run as evening or weekend classes for pupils who attend Western-style schools during the week. Thus, the significance of these pre-Western educational systems has diminished in socio-cultural importance. This is in contrast to the critical importance now afforded to the acquisition of Western-style education. For most African societies, this is linked to the understanding that Western education is now crucial for progress in all forms – social, economic and cultural – at both individual and community level in contemporary Africa.

The continued persistence of these historic or traditional knowledge practices for religious and cultural reasons, however, demonstrates that societies are often able to negotiate their engagement with traditional and modern systems – in this case, knowledge acquisition – that enables access to future development and the modern world (through Western education) and a stake in historical-religious cultural practices (through initiation ceremonies and *madrasa* schools), which forms their continuing link with important traditional systems.[11]

The arrival of the missions

By the mid-19th century, only a small proportion of the African elite were able to send their children abroad to acquire a Western education, or had the wherewithal to employ private tutors. For most Africans, this period saw the introduction of formal Western education through the activities of the plethora of missionary groups and societies involved in bringing Christianity to Africa. A number of authors have written definitive texts on the early Christian missions in Africa. There are also first-hand archival accounts of the establishment and building of 'missions' written by these missionaries and their associates. In West Africa, the writings of the Presbyterian missionaries Mary Slessor and Hope Waddell give an insight into the challenges and successes of setting up these institutions.[12] In Southern Africa, similar memoirs exist in relation to the setup of Lovedale, in the Eastern Cape, South

School planning and design in Africa 5

Africa, the Buxton School at Frere Town and Rabbai near Mombasa, East Africa and elsewhere.[13]

The development and design of mission schools in Africa was directly linked to missionary exploration and establishment on the continent. The 'mission' was often the same semantic term used for the church, school and dispensary, and as such was central to both proselytising and also community development in the town and villages in which they were situated.[14] However, usually the location of the mission settlement was physically set apart from the local village homestead. In Eastern Nigeria, as Achebe narrates in his historic-fiction novel *Things Fall Apart* and corroborated in Waddell's Presbyterian Mission Calabar diaries, the location of the mission settlement was physically set apart from the villagers' dwellings, as there was significant local resistance to the new 'missionary religion and its converts'.[15]

Missionary school design was thus initially an addition to the general construction related to missionary church infrastructure including missionary housing, dispensaries, small cabinetworks and the like in Africa. The first coastal missions had building materials transported from countries, such as the UK, in prefabricated forms and occasionally as ships' ballast.[16] Initially, classes were conducted by the missionary or catechist within the church until school premises could be built.[17] In the case of the Methodist mission in Badagry, Nigeria, the first missionary school was a prefabricated house with the school master's house above, as was the Hope Waddell (Presbyterian Mission) College in Calabar (see figure 1.3).

Figure 1.3 Hope Waddell College, Calabar, Nigeria
Author's own image

6 *School planning and design in Africa*

Away from the coast, the first mission schools were built using local materials comprising local earth wattle and daub for walls, and grass thatch for roofing. There are existing photographic records that document these schools.[18] A significant school built of earth or *'tubali'* in the local Hausa language, in West Africa was Katsina College. This was in direct keeping with the local Islamic architectural style of the city and Hausa region in general (see figure 1.4).[19] As local building materials, such as clay and structural stone, were discovered and building skills such as carpentry and brickmaking and laying were taught and developed, school buildings became constructed as more substantial infrastructure.

At their height, in the late 1940s to mid-1950s, missionary schools were well-run institutions that received grant aid funding from the colonial government's education office and also denominational funding. This meant they had both well-paid teaching staff, and well-built and -maintained classrooms and other school infrastructure. Thus with the historically established early coastal missions and sources of government and missionary funding a network of schools – from small village schools to large, well-established secondary institutions and teaching colleges – emerged whose architecture and style, as well as academic results, were of equivalent status to the later government-funded colleges.[20]

The string of Ghanaian coastal colleges including Adisadel (CMS) Mfantispim (Methodist) and St Augustine's College (Roman Catholic) showcase

Figure 1.4 Katsina College, Katsina, Nigeria
Author's own image

the best of this legacy.[21] A number of these missions also set up teacher training colleges, or seminaries in the case of the Catholics, which were generally at higher secondary level. Of note is Fourah Bay College, Freetown, Sierra Leone, which is the only African tertiary institution and has its origins from this Christian (CMS or Anglican) denominational legacy.[22]

The colonial schools

By the mid-19th century, much of Africa had been claimed by various European powers. The British controlled trading across a swath of Southern and East Africa and had protectorate territories in West Africa. There were further ambitions of explorer entrepreneurs such as Rhodes pursuing their aim to run a route from the South African Cape to Cairo in Egypt. After the historic 1884–1885 Berlin conference resulting in the carving up of Africa, the missionary impact in Africa was also to reach its height by the early 20th century with all major religious denominations having established mission stations across much of the continent. The early 20th century also say the setup of a colonial administrative apparatus that ensured that institutional infrastructure such as schools, clinics and administrative offices were built in all cities and towns across its African colonies.

This resulted in a network of (colonial) government primary and secondary schools that were built to augment the existing missionary school network, and indeed to bring Western education to Islamic areas in northern Nigeria, Ghana and also in East Africa in areas such as Mombasa and Zanzibar. Primary and secondary schools outside the major cities were generally basic affairs, built and designed to the colonial Public Works Department (PWD) specifications.

Thus from the early 20th century, African schools could be run and owned by religious missionary bodies such as the Catholic church, the Church Missionary Society (CMS) or the Methodist church, or by the colonial government. By the mid-20th century, some communities and towns in the southern parts of West Africa, home town associations were able to raise funds for the building of schools, and then to negotiate to hand over the running and administration of these institutions to religious groups.[23] All forms of schools, whatever their ownership, were entitled to receive funding through the grants-in-aid system from the colonial government. This was subject to these schools meeting required standards in building and teaching, as well as attainment in examinations.

As a general rule, African cities and large towns such as Freetown Accra, Cape Coast, Lagos, Calabar, Mombasa, Cape Town, and Dar es Salaam were more likely to have historic religious founded schools as well as government and often privately run 'colleges', whilst smaller towns and villages were more likely to have basic mission schools and the home town association-funded schools discussed.

8 *School planning and design in Africa*

Figure 1.5 Achimota College, Legon, Ghana
Courtesy Iain Jackson

In most administrative capital cities in Anglophone Africa, however, aside from this primary and secondary school network, the colonial administration built a series of exemplar secondary schools that were set to become the premier educational institutions in each country. King's College, Lagos; Achimota College, Legon, Ghana (see figure 1.5); Nairobi School, Kenya and Wynberg Boys High School South Africa demonstrate this. These schools were not only academic exemplars, but were also designed and built to have direct architectural symbolism and association with the Colonial administration. King's College and Achimota College demonstrate this in different ways in their symbolic locations and landscapes, and also use of physical elements such as the clock tower as a visual identifier of both the institution and the organisational legacy of the colonial school and ultimately the British administration.[24]

Pre- and post-independence national schools and higher education

At the end of the Second World War (hereafter, WW2), nationalists in British colonies in Africa as elsewhere in the Empire began to agitate for self-rule or 'independence'. It would take two more decades, until the early 1960s, for most colonies to achieve this aim. Much has been written about this period,

School planning and design in Africa 9

and the efforts made by the colonial administration to improve and develop the infrastructure in the colonies.[25] Investment in educational infrastructure was crucial to this legacy.

The early 20th century Phelps-Stokes Reports had reported on the state of primary and secondary education in Africa covering both its teaching and infrastructure provision, and this had been addressed through the colonial government's commitment to the construction of the government colleges and teaching institutions discussed in the previous section.[26] In West Africa, the 1945 and 1959 Asquith and Ashby commissions' respective reports on Higher Education in Africa resulted in the establishing of the University of Ibadan in Nigeria.[27] This was followed by an act by the newly independent Ghana establishing the University of Ghana, at Legon (1961), and the University of Science and Technology (1961) in Kumasi. Fourah Bay College, Sierra Leone, as stated earlier had however been the earliest higher institution (f. 1827)[28], having started out as a CMS-founded teaching and theological college. It however also benefited from significant expansion to its estate in the period of tertiary education expansion in the 1960s. All of the early higher education campuses were designed by young British architects, mainly to tropical architectural premises discussed in the next chapter.[29]

Elsewhere in Africa, Makerere University in Uganda was founded in 1963, whilst the former university colleges in Nairobi and Dar Es Salaam also attained full university status.[30] South Africa's Universities of Cape Town, the Witwatersrand and Natal had been founded prior to WW2 to respond to the educational needs of the established settler population and a few African and Asian students who were able to enrol up until their prohibition from passing of educational apartheid laws from 1948 through the early 1990s.[31]

Further to these developments in tertiary education in West Africa, the emerging indigenous governments in southern Nigeria and Ghana, with the blessing of the colonial government, initiated mass school building programmes to improve access to education at primary and secondary level. The Ghanaian First and Second National Schools Building Programmes resulted in the construction of a number of new schools and the expansion and upgrading of school infrastructure across the then Gold Coast, largely designed by the architects Maxwell Fry and Jane Drew.[32] The new 'modernist' style of many of these schools had its origins in a number of sources; the emerging UNESCO international school design guidelines, the historic Overseas Building Notes and earlier-written design primers such as Fry and Drew's 'village housing in the tropics'.[33]

Also instrumental to postwar school design was the setting up of tropical research institutions which covered disciplinary areas such as health and housing. There had historically been medical-aligned institutions such as the London and Liverpool Schools of Tropical Medicine and Hygiene, founded separately to promote study of tropical disease and health, which was critical to British colonial interests in the tropics and also to trade interests.[34] The crossover of institutional research from being primary medical in focus, including environmental and eventually building-architecture, however, happened after WW2, and was a major factor in the founding of the AA Tropical School.[35]

In this same post-WW2 period, the establishment of the Building Research Establishment's Overseas Research Section resulted in the creation of *the Colonial Building Notes* pamphlet series.[36] These pamphlets were given to PWD staff, missionaries and others involved in designing and building social infrastructure in the colonies. This encapsulated basic information on the principles of 'tropical' design, covering ideal ventilation and shading strategies, as well as appropriate material selection and best construction methods. A number of these notes focused on school design.[37]

The significant investment in the school building programme by the colonial government not only resulted in the promotion of 'tropical' design in schools, but also the promotion of the use of new building materials and techniques as showcased not only at tertiary level at locations such as Fry and Drew's Ibadan campus, but also at institutions such as Cubitt's Technical College Takoradi (Fry and Drew) (see figure 1.6) and the Ansar Ud Deen School, Lagos (Architects Co-Partnership).

Despite this post-WW2 period up until the early 1960s being the apex of school design innovation in Africa, this legacy remains largely unrecorded.

Figure 1.6 Government Technical College, Takoradi, Ghana
Author's own image

The schools built during this period were designed to then new environmental research findings from the Building Research Establishment (BRE), as promoted in their colonial (later renamed overseas) building notes, and from institutions such as the London School of Tropical Medicine and from research stations elsewhere in the world. Actual classroom sizes were largely determined in collaboration with the UNESCO school design programmes which also worked in association with the BRE.

In much of Africa, the mainly British architects involved in designing these schools were involved in developing design responses to climate, and with the significant investment in school building by the then colonial welfare office, these schools were designed to very high construction and environmental standards.

Unfortunately, the number of primary and secondary schools built were unable to meet the local population's demand for the free education places. Subsequent mass school building schemes would also have neither the funding nor the architectural design commitment to match these projects, many of which remain as exemplars of this apex of school design in Africa.

The mass and technical and vocational education initiatives (TVIs) of the 1980s + the World Bank's education drive

Alongside the move to build more primary, secondary and tertiary institutions was the evolution of a technical education movement. This took place from the 1960s, when education policy research confirmed that not enough investment was being made in technical and vocational education. This was to the detriment of society, particularly in newly emerging countries in Africa, which were in danger of educating more doctors than those with the technical and scientific skills to support science and engineering tertiary degrees.[38] Also, vocational education had become the poor relative of formal reading, writing, arithmetic and science.[39]

In West Africa, Nigeria attempted to run trial, or 'demonstration', comprehensive secondary schools that were to offer both an academic and technical educational stream, with help from the USA via USAID funds two 'model' comprehensive schools were set up in the early 1960s in Aiyetoro, Western Nigeria, and Port Harcourt, Eastern Nigeria.[40] The schools still exist, but the imported technical equipment and other machinery for the schools from the USA were never replaced, and the comprehensive curriculum was superseded by the Nigerian National Education Policy, which was more attuned to the erstwhile inherited colonial 'three Rs' curriculum. However, in other countries, such as Ghana and Kenya, some schools were designed to have vocational departments, in which carpentry, woodwork and other technical trades, and sometimes a domestic science or catering stream, normally gendered for boys and girls respectively, were taught.[41]

In South Africa, Rhodesia and other schools in the region, education was segregated. Schools for mixed race or 'coloured' pupils were more likely to

12 *School planning and design in Africa*

have a vocational curriculum than schools for 'white' pupils.[42] Schools for blacks in South Africa – up until the native education policy introduced by the national government in 1976 – largely followed the historic academic 'three R's curriculum.[43]

By the mid-1970s, further international focus was given to the view that technical education was important for the 'developing world' as research papers on Technical Education became policy issues for organisations such as the Commonwealth Education Secretariat and the World Bank, the latter providing funding for the teacher training and infrastructure for vocational education.[44] Few African states committed to changing their educational systems to fully embrace technical education, preferring instead to create national education systems which incorporated a technical stream, or option, that often lacked the trained teachers or infrastructure to deliver nationally.[45]

The World Bank and education in Africa

Prior to the establishment of the World Bank, its predecessor the International Bank for Reconstruction and Development (IBRD) had been involved in negotiating and brokering financial grants and soft loans to emerging countries to provide capital with which to build schools, libraries, community centres and other social infrastructure for Africa's newly independent nations.[46] This was done in association with the United Nations Educational Social and Cultural Organisation (UNESCO), the United Nations (UN) body most associated with international education and education policy.

In some projects, such as the Nigerian model schools project (c. 1960–69), the IBRD provided the funding but the consultancy arrangements were through the UNESCO educational design department, with the British architectural firm RMJM acting as consultants to UNESCO. There had also been UNESCO funding for the design and provision of divisional libraries and regional libraries in the Eastern Region of Nigeria, the design commission going to James Cubitt Architects.[47]

Libraries were seen to have a dual purpose, as both book lending repositories and also as locations for evening classes and other community activities. In Ghana, the American architect Max Bond was commissioned directly by then President Nkrumah's office to design a series of libraries across the country as a symbol of educational advancement and public engagement. In effect, only one building – the Bolgatanga Library – was completed prior to the collapse of the regime.[48]

The education conferences and debates

Whilst UNESCO's economic power waned from the 1970s as the emergent World Bank became the developing world's main infrastructure financier, and former colonial or new socio-political ties ensured that some African nations could negotiate for or be given bilateral loans, the organisation retained its

School planning and design in Africa 13

status as having the foremost, most influential international policy voice on education. This meant it was able to initiate international missions promoting education and schools development, in Haiti (1947) and Afghanistan (1948) and later on debates on education; framing the global and future aspirations of the time. The first of these debates was held in 1970, and made a global call for Education for All by 1970.

As this target was not reached, the Jomtien Conference in 1996 aspired to have universal access to basic education by 2000. This target was not reached, either, and subsequently at the World Education Forum in Dakar, Senegal, education was promoted as one of the Millennium Development Goals (MDGs) with access to basic Education being an MDG to attain by 2015.[49] Although access to basic education was increased across the world, the 100% target was not attained, and the current Sustainable Development Goals has again set targets for global access to education for all children which are yet to be attained.

African countries have the most children who have no access to schooling. This is despite the numerous educational missions and consultancy activities that African countries continent have received and engaged with over the years. The continent thus remains the main target for the implementation of the current MDGs in respect of education and other basic development goals. These policies are driven by supranational bodies such as the World Bank and UN bodies. The link between the implementation of these policies at the local level can often be tenuous or contentious. The implications of these policies were important. Schemes such as the 1980s sweat equity school programmes – in which poor villages were expected to contribute to school building with labour – have not always been successful, in some villages the schools to be built using sweat labour were never built.

The World Bank's involvement in education funding was at its height in the 1980s during the African continent's structural adjustment era. With the downturn of world economies influenced by the oil crisis and collapse of commodity prices from the mid-1970s, much of the global economy faltered from the 1970s to the mid-1980s. Africa's countries fared particularly badly, as most were dependent on commodity prices, which had lowered dramatically in response to the depressed global costs, running their economies. The crisis heightened for African countries as they also had to finance the repayment of development loans negotiated at a period when interest rates were low and projected commodity prices were expected to remain high. Thus, as countries in Africa had to renegotiate their debt and request financial assistance, the World Bank set economic stringency requirements, structural adjustment programmes (SAPs) that were to be met before loans and debt renegotiation could take place.

As a result, public investment in education was cut, as World Bank SAP advisers encouraged countries to focus on investment in teacher education and support community self-build programmes for school buildings, which needed limited if any capital investment, thus cutting investment into

14   *School planning and design in Africa*

educational infrastructure. With this shift in focus, education policy in Africa changed from what had been up until the 1980s a national government approach to improving education via investment in both school buildings and teacher training to a focus of capital investment nearly exclusively on the latter.[50]

Thus by the mid-1990s, the reduced government investment in school infrastructure, and the limited progress in boosting teacher education and placement in more rural, hard-to-reach- African schools, resulted in a clear drop in educational investment and much slower progress towards achieving the initial goal of achieving basic education for all by 2000 or indeed by 2015, and to the target being moved to the educational SDGs discussed earlier.[51]

School design and the rise of the 1980s neoliberal consensus

From the 1980s as the new educational policies were being initiated, the neoliberal consensus led by the Republican administration in the USA and conservative regimes in Europe further influenced educational policy, emphasising a more liberal market approach to education and effectively the opening up of investment in schools and their infrastructure to private players.[52] The total monopoly on education that most post-independence governments had since the 1960s thus now was open to private education investors, from religious groups to corporate educational companies. This resulted in the re-emergence of many religious schools, which could as with other private non-government investors set up private schools that were now able to operate in the deregulated education environment.

Since educational deregulation came in to place in the late 1980s in most of Africa, all schools have been expected to comply with regulatory guidelines covering school curriculum, teachers' qualifications, and classroom space design requirements. The regulation and enforcement of these standards, however, is difficult to assess. Education standards across a range of different school types are more difficult to define and hard to enforce.[53] This has resulted in varying qualities of private educational providers catering to different economic sectors of the population. This is discussed further in later chapters.

The qualitative school classroom experience which is important in contemporary assessment is particularly difficult to assess. For the general African public, however, schools are primarily viewed as providers of the qualifications needed to gain entry into higher education and white collar employment. Better classroom design taking into account contemporary theories of pedagogy, enabling the use of new technologies or allowing nonexamination forms of assessment plays little role in school choice for most African parents.

For elite Africans, this is not the case. Independent schools such as the Atlantic College in Lagos, Nigeria and the Aga Khan schools networks in

East and Southern Africa teach to the international educational qualifications standards (the International Baccalaureate, or IB), and also their school learning environments are designed to ensure that these institutions are equivalent to other top fee-paying schools across the world. The same is the case for elite status religious colleges such as Bishops' College, Cape Town, South Africa and St Gregory's College, Lagos, Nigeria.[54]

In contrast, the privately run schools that are provided in poorer areas are more basic affairs. These are often located in homes or informal locations, where classrooms are converted rooms and the national education syllabus is taught. The facilities and qualifications of teachers in these schools are difficult to regulate, although pupil numbers are often less than in equivalent state schools in poorer areas. Student attainment at these schools can therefore sometimes be better than in the state sector due to the reduced classroom sizes and the fee tariff. This helps explain their relative popularity for poorer parents who value student attainment above qualitative issues such as classroom design.

Technology and new virtual learning environments

One of the most significant contemporary changes in learning and teaching pedagogy in Africa has been the miniaturisation of computing technology. Whilst computers were a breakthrough in education worldwide, the cost and rate of obsolescence of the early computers meant that the space and design of 'computer' labs and classrooms in schools that could afford to have this provision severely restricted their use and adoption. For most African countries, the sheer outlay was too expensive to have this rolled out away from urban centres where businesses and well-off middle class parents were able to help finance their use.

Over the last five years, the development of tablets, smartphones and intermediate 'feature' phones has meant that much of the information which larger desktop computers were able to access is now readily available on these cheaper, personally owned effective mini-computers. This has two transformational features. First, it is 'democratising' information spread, taking away the need for the textbook or large piece of school/state owned equipment. Secondly, it allows learning to take place anywhere that the phone or tablet can be used. Furthermore, with sufficient fore-planning, pre-downloaded information can be accessed anywhere, without direct power or internet connectivity.

Prior to the rise of today's ubiquitous micro-computing hardware, a number of intermediate computing devices were trialled. The best known was the One Laptop Per Child (OLPC) Negroponte-sponsored laptop scheme.[55] The scheme focused on reciprocal donations by first world purchasers of laptops to subsidise the state acquisition and spread of stripped-down laptops for educational use in schools across the emerging world. The OLPC scheme managed to gain significant uptake in Africa in countries such as Nigeria, Ghana and

16 *School planning and design in Africa*

Kenya, but it never achieved the international or in Africa's case continental success or penetration that had been planned, and finally folded up in 2014, although offshoots of the project continue mainly in South America.[56]

It has been important to foreground this aspect of educational change in Africa, as later chapters in this book will return to examine technology's influence on school design. Arguably, this is likely to be the most significant aspect of change to global learning. This is likely to directly affect future learning spaces planning in Africa, as it will elsewhere in the world. The size and flexibility of use and access to information that smartphones and tablets give to educational material has already begun to significantly change learning styles amongst more affluent African school children, as Kindles, tablets and smartphones are used as reading devices and to access the internet at home as much as in the classroom. The move of such learning to the less affluent is likely to take place soon with the spread of mass open online learning courses, or 'MOOCs', and free access to online tuition may make the school classroom as the typical learning space obsolete for some.[57]

Conclusions

School design in Africa, as seen from the foregoing, has had longstanding historic roots and is currently undergoing a major transformation, as future technologies and pedagogic approaches to learning fundamentally re-order the classroom and school model that has remained largely unchanged from the late 19th century to date.

Possibly the centuries-old stasis in classroom design development and change reflects both the robustness of the historic 'Western' educational process on the one hand, and on the other, the reluctance of educational providers, at all levels; state, NGO and private, to significantly alter the recognised modes of learning and forms of teaching spaces for education in Africa. Unlike in Latin America, and to a lesser extent parts of Asia where radical changes in education often linked to changed political regimes, on the African continent education has remained a conservative process.

Most African school classrooms remain designed in keeping to the advisory norms of international institutions such as UNESCO and the World Bank. This is despite the fact that these standards were established more than half a century ago in the 1950s and 1960s. The traditional standardised spaces have also ensured traditional 'teacher and blackboard'-focused learning practices have persisted to the present day. This is in contrast to new teaching practices such as those used by the escuela nueva movement schools found in South America, in which school spaces can be created in a range of environments for communal learning. Also the limitations of the standard 1950s design-standard classrooms, in most African countries has resulted in these classroom environments finding it difficult to accommodate new pedagogies such as peer-to-peer learning and the communal learning spaces needed to embrace the use of microtechnologies such as the Raspberry Pi TM in learning computer coding.

School planning and design in Africa 17

The radically restructured new national education programme that evolved in post-apartheid South Africa provides the most developed example of contemporary evolution of the African classroom at national level. Its promotion of international approaches to the design of classrooms as 'learning spaces' where different kinds of group-based and student-centred learning can take place has become a standard approach in school and classroom design for the elite private schools becoming common across Africa.[58]

School design in the 21st century seems set to change radically as new technology – in particular, communications and small portable computing hardware including netbooks, smartphones and tablets – have the potential to disrupt learning inside and outside the traditional classroom. As will be discussed later, when contemporary school design case studies in Africa will be examined in Chapter 5 and returned to in the concluding Chapter 6, there is clear evidence that the ways and methods of learning have already transformed phenomenally in the last two decades. This has already had a significant effect on emerging school and education models across Africa, as the introduction of the OLPC programme for schools in countries with significantly new and upgraded school infrastructure such as South Africa demonstrated.

How do these newly transformed learning spaces relate to the local, sociocultural conditions in which they exist? What engagement do children, teachers and communities in villages and towns have with these new technologies as gadgets for learning, particularly in spaces and places that are different in design configuration to traditional classroom spaces? Whilst contemporary reports suggest that pupils, staff and communities find the new technologies and modes of learning popular, will e-learning and its innovative learning processes prove enduring or just another Western 'fad' for cultures in which a good education remains associated with traditional, tried and tested educational methods and infrastructure? These are issues that are yet to be explored in what is after all a rapidly transforming field of educational change and research.

In most schools across the African continent, school planning and design remains focused on achieving guidelines based on the historic post-WW2 1950s school planning standards. This stasis in school planning and design is now being seriously challenged. This is taking place by the new 21st century school design discourse just discussed. Despite its conceptual basis being international in its conception and Western in its initial focus, this new educational discourse has the potential to respond in a more flexible way to the different contextual backgrounds to school location and design across Africa's villages and towns.

This will be important because just as Africa's past pre-colonial learning systems were spatially and spiritually located in the communities which they served, today's contemporary learning systems can and should have the ability to adapt to differences in location and purpose, as these traditional learning spaces of the past did. Future learning spaces then as new pedagogic institutions could contribute to creating a new template for the indigenous customization of contemporary e-learning and online teaching learning

18 *School planning and design in Africa*

spaces in both urban and rural African contexts. The following chapters of this book seek to examine these themes in more detail.

Book chapters

This chapter has sought to give an introduction to *Learning Spaces in Africa*: it provided an introduction to the general themes related to school design in Africa; historical context, environmental, socio-cultural and economics considerations which thread through the course of the publication. Is has also explained that schools in Anglophone Africa – particularly in West and Southern Africa – are the main the focus of this text. It also provided a review of relevant references related to educational policy and history as it relates to international school design, particularly as it relates to Africa. Also explained is the use of case studies from history and contemporary times through which to understand the historic and new issues which have influenced and provided the contextual background to the design and delivery of schools in sub-Saharan Africa.

In Chapter 2, titled 'School design in Africa: the background', a contextual analysis of school design in Africa is explored. The chapter seeks to set the background and context to the development of school design in Africa by setting this within the context of a summarised account African education social history. Past education historians from the late 19th century to date have produced very detailed accounts of Africa's encounter with Western education. References to these sources have provided the sources for significant sections of this chapter. The main focus of the chapter then is to highlight how school building design and evolution which, although influenced by local-national education policies of the day, has often had other contextual factors which have been equally instrumental in determining school building design and building in Africa.

The chapter seeks to capture the influence of the Christian missions in creating the initial school classroom model that has persisted with limited adaptation to the present day. It does also recount the efforts and effects of various international policies on stimulating school building and the limited effect these had on enabling African countries to adequately design and build schools for their rapidly growing school-age populations.

The research findings presented whilst focusing on British West Africa and South Africa do also extend to brief examinations of school design policies and examples in countries such as the *Ujaama* schools policy in Tanzania, East Africa and the formation of an early international school in Swaziland in direct contrast to the apartheid education policies that were being codified and legalised at the same time (the 1970s) in neighbouring Southern Africa.

It gives a brief account of how these key factors – environment, socio-politics, and economics – have had significant influence on school design. This focuses mainly on the schools and education history of Anglophone West and Southern Africa. Drawing from research sources, it traces the involvement of Africans in education from the children of the elite coastal

School planning and design in Africa 19

traders to the mass education movements in the mid-20th century. Giving examples of schools from across Africa, but focusing specifically on West Africa, it contextualises and compares the evolution process which took place across key countries in sub-Saharan Africa. It concludes by predicting that the context and purpose of education and the classroom and schools in which it has taken place to the present day is under pressure to change to respond to new influences on education at policy, technological and cultural levels.

The chapter concludes by surmising that most of the physical and operational features of the historical case study schools presented remain the basis of current school design guidelines, with there being little change in school design since the guidelines first introduced in post-WW2 UNESCO and international funding reports in the 1950s.

Chapter 3, 'Historical school case studies', derives from the author's PhD research which produced a critical history of African secondary school design in Nigeria. It presents an expanded survey of school design history in Africa, focusing on a combination of primary and secondary schools. Its specific area of focus, however, is on the UNESCO-defined basic education school provision. This comprises pre-primary education to the completion of junior secondary education. This is generally a 10-year period in the various educational schemes and syllabuses that operate the countries in Anglophone Africa.

The chapter introduces the reader to a number of school case studies selected from different countries and regions in Africa. These are used to provide a broad representation of the historical background and range of schools designed in Africa. A number of notable schools have been designed and built on the continent for over a century. By tracing the histories of these schools, we are able to understand and follow the different eras of educational policy, the key actors and contexts in which these took place. Furthermore, the analysis also helps us makes sense of the contextual background to the school designs which have influenced the specifically unique nature of educational delivery and school design in each nation state studied. This also allows a regional comparison of school design.

The selection of the school case studies presented reflects the author's research coverage of Anglophone African schools, focusing on West and Southern Africa, with reference being made to salient case studies from other regions of Africa. The historical examples from West Africa (Hope Waddell College, Calabar, Nigeria) and Southern Africa (Lovedale College, Eastern Cape, South Africa) rely on both manuscript data and more recent historical information and the author's photographic research records.

More contemporary historical case studies such as the International Development Agency (IDA)-Federal Government Colleges (Nigeria), the Department of Education and Training 'DET' schools of South Africa and the Fry-Drew schools in Ghana and Nigeria are also discussed in this chapter. Whilst the religious missionary colleges are supported by historical missionary archive material, these more recent buildings paradoxically have fewer archived documents. Instead much of the material for schools of this era and

20   *School planning and design in Africa*

the later period of the 20th century rely on the author's doctoral and post-doctoral research on school design in Africa undertaken from the 1990s to the present day.

The final three case studies are from the 1970s, and show a range of schools from countries in eastern, southern and western parts of Africa. Their selection has been based on the author's post-doctoral and contemporary research on school design, and seeks to give a broad range of school design examples across sub-Saharan Africa.

Chapter 4, 'African schools in the 21st century: context and background', provides an overview of contemporary policies and issues that may influence the design and provision of contemporary schools in Africa. It draws on the author's research findings from being involved in the EdQual Project. As part of a University of Bristol-led research consortium researching educational quality in emerging countries, EdQual involved in researching how improvements could be made to educational quality in the emerging world.

The chapter explores further alternative methods of pedagogy such as digital learning and possibilities of developing peer-to-peer learning and virtual classrooms. It then goes on to consider how these new teaching practices may ultimately change the conceptualisation of the school classroom. This is likely to change its terminology to the 'learning space', and also its situatedness in traditional classroom design standards to a more fluid use of available space within different community contexts.

It cites a few international and African examples of unique contemporary architectural responses to school provision, including Adeyemi's Makoko Floating School, both discussed earlier in the contemporary school design chapter, and a student-led proposal for an 'off-grid' ICT classroom to be deployed in areas of no infrastructure provision in Africa. It also considers the effect of World Bank and UNESCO declarations and policies since WW2, and their culmination in the Millennium and more recent Sustainable Development Goals. It attempts to situate African school design in the context of these international educational goals.

Chapter 5, titled 'Contemporary Case Studies', provides 21st century examples of school design projects in Africa which show different approaches to school design which have been deployed by the designers of these schools in response to client or other agendas. Examples are taken from West Africa (Dwabor, coastal Ghana), central Africa (two sites in Rwanda) and South Africa (Khayelitsha township, Cape Town). These identified case studies are described with a critique which seeks to assess their success or lack thereof in providing a relevant and responsive classroom learning space environment for today's learning requirements. This is considered with particular regard to the UN SDGs which encourage African nations to ensure that access to education amongst poorer groups is increased. This is to improve Africa's global bottom rank in educational provision, and in turn help to improve its other education-linked international development indicators such as child and maternal health nutrition, and improved gender equity.

School planning and design in Africa 21

The chapter concludes by suggesting that whilst there have been some successes in responding to the design requirements of classrooms and schools for contemporary times, most education policies and the school designs which they promote remain rooted in notions of education in the postwar 1950s, or earlier still from missionary approaches. It does, however, suggest that policies such as the UN Sustainable Development Goals – which actively support wider access to learning, better ICT coverage and different approaches to learning – are likely to transform learning spaces design in the near future.

Chapter 6, 'Conclusions and Reflections', is the final chapter of the book and provides the reader with an examination of and reflection on the effects of the more than century-long development of school design across Africa. It seeks specifically to consider how the past design and provision challenges from African school history, such as large class sizes and the difficulty of providing schools in remote locations, remain critical to contemporary discussions about the need to develop appropriate and relevant design practices to respond to school provision and design challenges for African schools in the 21st century.

The chapter concludes by speculating that key global factors such as the ubiquity of mobile telephony, the continuing push to improve access to education now embedded in the UN Sustainable Development Goals, and the growing development of successful collaborative partnerships with local communities and various organisations at national and international levels, will lead to a changed educational infrastructure landscape. These learning spaces of the future, if successful, should be beneficial and provide a fundamentally changed sustainable model of educational infrastructure design and provision for Africa.

Read in conjunction with the concluding 'Afterword', Chapter 6 seeks to provide the reader with a summarised version of the key findings of the book in terms of where school design is in the second decade of the 21st century and how key issues such as technology and push towards international cultural change are most likely to change learnings space design and also relate to historical social infrastructure provision schemes of the past.

Learning Spaces in Africa: Critical Histories, 21st Century Challenges and Change can be read in a linear fashion or as a set of discrete chapters. It does follow a chronological format, however, with the historical case study schools described in Chapter 3, giving a contextual basis and lens through which to view Chapter 5 which describes contemporary school design case studies. All chapters also have photographic illustrations which are gratefully acknowledged. A significant number of these are from the architects involved in the design of the schools examined. This is not only for the schools in the case study chapters, but for other school descriptions elsewhere in the book. With its focus on both the architectural and educational issues it offers itself to a wide audience of academics and practitioners who have an interest in Africa's educational past and the contemporary educational building issues which the continent faces.

22 *School planning and design in Africa*

Notes

1 Western education in this text is defined as a system which has a defined childhood entry period and traditionally had a primary or elementary phase, followed by a usually selective secondary grammar school phase, and finally a tertiary phase which is not covered in this text. See UNESCO (2008) *Inclusive Dimensions of the Right to Education*. Paris: UNESCO, *Introduction item 3* for the operational definition of basic education. This educational system in Anglophone Africa was identical in content and delivery to the UK, only transposed to Africa's tropical and sub-tropical conditions.

2 The first records of schooling in West Africa, for example, are documented as being related to the attempts of Christian priests to educate mixed children in slave fort schools; there are also records of slave traders in southwestern Nigeria asking for schools to be set up for their offspring to learn the rudiments of accounting etc. to enable them work more successfully in family trading activities, See Ajayi, J. F. A. (1965) *Christian Missions in Nigeria 1841–1891: The Making of a New Elite*. Evanston, IL: Northwestern University Press; and Davidson, B. (1977) *A History of West Africa 1000–1800*. London: Longman.

3 See Fafunwa, B. (1974) Chapter 1. In *History of Education in Nigeria*. London: Allen and Unwin, pp. 15–49.

4 For fattening room references see MacCormack, C. (1982) Ritual Fattening and Female Fertility. In T. Vaskilampi and C. MacCormack (eds.), *Folk Medicine and Health Culture: Role of Folk Medicine in Modern Health Care*. Conference Proceedings of the Nordic Research Symposium, 27–28 August, Department of Community Health, University of Kuopio, Kuopio, Finland, Brink, P. J. (1993) Studying African Women's Secret Societies: The Fattening Room of the Annang. In C. Renzetti and R. Lee (eds.), *Researching Sensitive Topics*. Newbury Park, CA: Sage. For traditional societies see Fafunwa reference 2, and Fyle, M. (1999) *Introduction to the History of African Civilisation. Volume 1: Pre-colonial Africa*. Lanham, MD: University Press of America.

5 See the following references: Ajibade, B., Ekpe, E. and Bassey, T. (2012, May) More than Fabric Motifs: Changed Meaning of the Nsibidi on the Efik Ukara Cloth. *Mediterranean Journal of Social Sciences*, 2(2), pp. 297–303. www.mcser.org/images/stories/2_journal/mjss_may_2012/babson_ajibade_ester_ekpe.pdf, Kalu, O. (1980). *Writing in Pre-colonial Africa: A Case Study of Nsibidi in African Cultural Development*. Ed. O. U. Kalu. Enugu: Fourth Dimension Publishers; Carlson, A. (2003) *Nsibidi, Gender, and Literacy: The Art of the Bakor-Ejagham, Cross River State*. PhD Thesis, Indiana University; and Isichei, E. A. (1997). *A History of African Societies to 1870*. Cambridge: Cambridge University Press, p. 357. ISBN 0-521-45599-5.

6 Term used to describe the North African countries occupying the land mass to north of the Sahara and bordering the Mediterranean Sea.

7 These comprise regions and countries located to the south of the Sahara Desert, such as Mali, Chad and parts of northern Bukina Faso, Ghana and Nigeria, which had all formed part of the historic Islamic Kanem Bornu Empire.

8 Comprising coastal parts of Kenya, Tanzania, Somalia and Mozambique.

9 See Graham, S. (1966) *Government Mission Education in Northern Nigeria, With Special Reference to the Work of Hans Vischer*. Ibadan: Ibadan University Press, and more recent links: Africa Insight http://westafricainsight.org/articles/view/126 and Archnet http://archnet.org/collections/385/publications/1340. Both accessed 10 January 2015.

10 In Nigeria, however, the rise of the militant Islam factions such as 'Boko Haram' in northeastern Nigeria which oppose all forms of Western education has resulted in the collapse of such arrangements.

School planning and design in Africa 23

11 This has explored by a number of anthropologists such as Herskovits, M. J. (1959) Continuity and Change. In M. J. Herskovits and W. Bascom (eds.), *African Cultures*. Chicago, IL: Chicago University Press.

12 Lovedale Missionary Institution (1904) *Report for Lovedale Missionary Institution 1903*. Alice, Eastern Cape, South Africa: Lovedale Press, and Waddell, H. M. (1863) *Twenty Nine Years in the West Indies and Central Africa: A Review of Missionary Work and Adventure*. London: T. Nelson and Sons.

13 See Strayer, R. W. (1973) The Making of Mission Schools in Kenya. *Comparative Education Review*, 17(3), pp. 313–330 in Taylor, W. H. (1996) *Mission to Educate: A History of the Educational Work of the Scottish Presbyterian Mission in East Nigeria 1846–1960*. London: Brill.

14 Uduku, O. (2000) The Colonial Face of Educational Space. In L. Lokko (ed.), *White Papers Black Marks*. London: Athlone Press, pp. 44–65.

15 Achebe, C. (1958) *Things Fall Apart*. London: Heinemann, also see Waddell (note 8), also full text of 1882 The Church Missionary Intelligencer, open access url, https://archive.org/stream/1882TheChurchMissionaryIntelligen cer/1882_The_Church_Missionary_Intelligencer#page/n1/mode/2up.

16 William Cooper's catalogue, https://archive.org/stream/IllustratedCatalogue OfGoodsManufacturedAndSuppliedByW.c.SperLtd/IllustratedComplete_djvu. txt, gives a clear description of what prefabricated buildings his company can 'ship' to the colonies, India and South Africa.

17 Ibid., p. 217.

18 The New College Archive collection at the University of Edinburgh, for example, has a number of images of Schools near to Calabar, southeastern Nigeria, where the missionaries Mary Slessor and H. M. Waddell and had both worked. (Reference codes: GB 0237 Edinburgh University Library Gen. 766/6 and GB 0237 Edinburgh University New College Library MSS CALA and MSS BOX 52.5.1–6, respectively).

19 See Dmchowski, Z. R. (1990) *Introduction to Traditional Nigerian Architecture. Volume 1: Northern Nigeria*. London: Ethnographica and also Schwerdtfeger, F. W. (1982) *Traditional Housing in Nigerian Cities: A Comparative Study of Houses in Zaria, Ibadan and Marrakech*. London: Wiley.

20 For a full description of the system in the then Colony of Nigeria, see Fafunwa (1974) and Unwin and Ayandele, E. A. (1966) *The Missionary Impact on Modern Nigeria 1842–1914: A Political and Social Analysis*. London: Longman Green and Co.

21 For a contemporary architectural perspective on some of these buildings Jackson, I. and Holland, J. (2014) *The Architecture of Maxwell Fry and Jane Drew*. London: Routledge, provides a good text to consult. There are also various publications on individual schools.

22 F. 1827 by the CMS Church at Mount Aureol in Freetown. Its original school building is now designated a UNESCO World Heritage Site. See Paracka, D. J. (2002) *The Athens of West Africa*. PhD Thesis, Georgia State University, USA.

23 See, for example, Community High School Old Umuahia, in Uduku (2002) The Socio-Economic Basis of a Diaspora Community, Igbo bu'ike. *Review of African Political Economy*, 29(92), pp. 301–311.

24 See Uduku (2000).

25 Historic texts include Ayandele (1966); Davidson (1977); Ajayi (1965), more recent texts include Le Roux, H. (2004) The Post-colonial Architecture of Ghana and Nigeria. *Architectural History*, 47, pp. 361–392, and Uduku, O. (2005) Architecture scolaire et éducation: en Afrique anglophone. *XIXe–XXe siècles de l'éducation*, no. 102, mai 2004 (parution: mars 2005).

24 School planning and design in Africa

26 Phelps-Stokes Reports (1925, 1927). For the 1925 and 1927 Phelps Stokes Reports see, Lewis, L. J. (ed.) (1962) *Phelps-Stokes Reports on Education in Africa*. London: Oxford University Press.

27 National Archives Kew, DO 167/3, Ashby Commission Report on Higher Education in Nigeria, 1960/61. See also Shaplin, J. T. (1961, May) Ashby Commission Report on Higher Education in Nigeria. *Higher Education Quarterly*, 15(3), pp. 229–237.

28 Paracka (2002).

29 Fry and Drew designed Ibadan, Kumasi was designed by Cubitt and Scott, whilst the British architectural practice Design Group designed the Fourah Bay College Extension, *West African Builder and Architect* (1963) Vol. 3, no. 1, pp. 8–12. The University of Ghana, at Legon, was designed by the more established British architect, Austin St. Barbe Harrison, who had worked in Malta before this commission. See Jackson and Holland (2014).

30 Uduku, O. (2010) *Tropical Ivory Towers: A Critical Evaluation of Design Symbolism and Practical Aspirations of the West African University Campuses in Their Fifth Decade*. Docomomo, 11th International Conference, Mexico City, 12 pp.

31 See Kallaway, P. (ed.) (2002) *The History of Education Under Apartheid 1948– 1994: The Doors of Learning and Culture Shall Be Opened*. New York, NY: Peter Lang.

32 See Le Roux (2004).

33 National Archives Kew, UNESCO Design Guidelines, Paris UNESCO 1966–88; Overseas Building Notes, BRE, London, 50–73 1950–73 (Preceded by Colonial Building Notes 1–50, and Anteceded by Tropical Building Notes). Also see Fry, M. and Drew, J. (1948) *Village Housing in the Tropics*. London: Lund Humphries.

34 The Liverpool School, for example, owed its foundation to a major grant from Lord Leverhulme, who had extensive trade interests in West Africa and therefore an interest in the health and well being of his workers and factors in this tropical region.

35 AA School archives 1966.

36 National Archives Kew, Colonial Building Notes (1900–1950); also see note 33.

37 See, for example, Colonial Building Note 57, Schools in the West Indies.

38 Skapski, A. (1962) *The Development of Technical Education and Its Relation to the Education System in Western Nigeria*. A Report Commissioned by the Government of Western Nigeria, and Goldway, M. (1962) *Report on Vocational Education in Eastern Nigeria*. Lagos: Ministry of Education. This was followed by Skapski, A. (1966) *Report of the Comparative Technical Education Seminar Abroad and Recommendation for a National Plan of Vocational and Technical Education in the Republic of Nigeria*. Lagos: Federal Ministry of Education.

39 See Dore, R. (1997) *The Diploma Disease*. London: Institute of Education.

40 Harvard Graduate School of Education, and USAID (1966) *Harvard/AID Project Progress Report and Work Plan*. Comprehensive High School, Aiyetoro, Western Nigeria, 31st March 1966, and Alafe-Aluko, M. O. (1973) *The Historical Development of the Comprehensive High School Aiyetoro, (f. 1963) Nigeria*. PhD Thesis, Washington University, Graduate School of Education, For Comprehensive Secondary School Port Harcourt (f. 1961) see US Congressional Serial Set, issue 12554, p. 495.

41 See A. Akyeampong, 4. Ghana (149–216), Mwira, 6. Kenya (227–304), and S. Weeks, Botswana (93–146), in Lauglo, J. and Maclean, R. (2005) *Vocationalisation of Secondary Education Revisited*. UNESCO UNEVOC Book Series. New York, NY: Springer.

School planning and design in Africa 25

42 Uduku, O. (1994b) *Schools in Africa: Perspectives on a Viable Physical Ideal.* Centre for African Studies Cape Town Seminar Semester 2, 1994, African Studies Centre, Robinson College. Cambridge: University of Cambridge.

43 See Kallaway (2002) and note 42.

44 See, for example, Bray, M. (1986) *New Resources for Education, Community Management and Financing of Schools in Less Developed Countries.* London: Commonwealth Secretariat.

45 See Uduku, O. (2015) Spaces for 21st Century Learning. In *Routledge Handbook on International Learning and Development.* London: Routledge, pp. 196–209 in contrast to Bray, M. and Lillis, K. (1988) *Community Funding of Education: Issues and Policy Implications in Less Developed Countries.* London: Commonwealth Secretariat/Pergamon Press; and Onsomu, E. N. et al. (2004) *Community Schools in Kenya: Case Study on Community Participation in Funding and Managing Schools.* http://unesdoc.unesco.org/images/0013/001362/136278e.pdf, who give a wider Africa overview.

46 See World Bank – IBRD Archive Papers Online, www.worldbank.org/en/about/archives/history. Accessed August 2017.

47 Uduku, O. (2008a) *Bolgatanga Library, Adaptive Modernism in Ghana, 40 Years On.* Presented at the Refereed Proceedings of the 10th Docomomo Conference, 13–20 September, Rotterdam, The Netherlands, 'The Challenge of Change' (ed. D. Van Heuvel), T-U Delft.

48 For Bolgatanga see ibid., and Bond, M. (1968, March) A Library for Bolgatanga. *Architectural Forum*, CXXV111, pp. 66–69.

49 As agreed at the Millennium Development Summit 2000, and enacted via the Millennium Development Goals to be achieved by 2015.

50 World Bank (1988) *Education in Africa Report.* Washington, DC: World Bank.

51 United Nations (2000) *Millennium Development Goals* www.un.org/millenniumgoals/ Accessed May 2017.

52 *The Economist* (2015a, August) Learning Unleashed, Low Cost Private Schools. (Print Edition briefing). www.economist.com/news/briefing/21660063-where-governments-are-failing-provide-youngsters-decent-education-private-sector. Accessed April 2018.

53 Ibid.

54 See School Prospectuses and URLs, Aga Khan Academy, Mombasa; Loyola Jesuit College, Abuja); and Bishops Diocesan College, Cape Town; and note 52 above.

55 OLPC website, http://one.laptop.org/. Accessed December 2017.

56 Only Uruguay was able to most successfully utilise the OLPC scheme, called Project Ceibal in recognition of its main local funder, as a basis for mass literacy and computer centred education for its schools. See Laborde, G. (2017) Congratulations to Uruguay on the 10th Anniversary of its National OLPC Program, Plan Ceibal! Feature: Uruguay Marks 10 Years of Bridging Digital Divide. *One Laptop Per Child.* http://blog.laptop.org/2017/05/15/congratulations-to-uruguay-on-the-10th-anniversary-of-its-national-olpc-program-plan-ceibal-feature-uruguay-marks-10-years-of-bridging-digital-divide/#.WlUaYFSFj2Q.

57 In Chapter 6, this will be revisited, as the case studies of the Asian 'hole in the wall' and Eritrean self-learning case studies will demonstrate.

58 These include, for example, the historic and new 'International Schools' found across Africa, and the Aga Khan schools network in East Africa.

2　School design in Africa
The background

Introduction

This chapter focuses on the key issues that influence school planning and design in sub-Saharan Africa. These include: climate, religion, post-colonial nationalist development policies, socio-economic needs and the opportunity costs of education in relation to local economic realities. A detailed analysis is undertaken of each of these issues and their influence on the development of school planning and design programmes in Africa. This chapter examines specifically the effects of these issues on post-colonial Anglophone countries which is the main focus of this book.

African Schools have had a long, historical established presence in towns and villages across the continent, however the factors that have influenced their design and development have been unique. Those that have had the most influence on schools provision, design and planning can broadly be examined under the following themes:

- environmental
- socio-political
- economic

There are other issues which have had an influence on African school design and planning that could be examined; however' the three factors identified here are considered the most critical for the purposes of this volume, as evidenced by earlier findings from research work undertaken into the history of school design in Africa.[1] These three factors are relevant to schools across Africa, in Lusophone and Francophone states, and not solely the Anglophone countries which are the book's main focus. The school examples discussed in this chapter attempt to reflect the universality of these themes in African schools across the continent and further afield in emerging countries throughout the world.

Environment

Strictly speaking, education or learning can take place in any environment where classrooms or teaching – learning spaces – can be placed. However, to achieve the optimal environment for learning, aside from good teachers

School design in Africa

and adequate textbooks and learning materials, the characteristics of the classroom are equally important.

The climatological factors affecting the built environment of schools are of specific relevance to all classrooms. Africa's continental mass has nearly the entire range of sub-tundra climate types.[2] The continent's geography also means much of its land mass is in the tropical zone, and therefore the majority of built spaces have to respond to the environmental comfort needs of warm to hot climate through appropriate passive, or non-mechanically assisted, building design.

Historically, vernacular buildings were designed with climate responsiveness incorporated in to their form.[3] Contemporary tropical buildings, including classrooms designed for affluent schools, often incorporate mechanical cooling devices ranging from electric fans to air conditioning systems to provide environmental comfort. This is both expensive due to the energy costs involved with running mechanical systems such as air conditioning, and often difficult to maintain as power cuts for long periods regularly occur across Africa.[4]

School design history

Christian missionaries were responsible for building the first significant number of schools in Africa. This was because their proselytisation involved not only church building, but also the setting up of schools and health care facilities to improve the livelihoods of their converts and residents in the communities in which they were based (see figure 2.1). The missionary builders involved in

Lagos Female Institution, c. 1845

Figure 2.1 Etching of Early Girls' School in Lagos
In Echeruo M. Victorian Lagos

28   School design in Africa

constructing this infrastructure, particularly the school buildings, soon evolved standard classroom designs which complemented the earlier mission church designs. The formwork for these buildings was designed to be prefabricated so they could be easily shipped out to missions across the world.[5]

These became design primers for school construction across the main regions of mission comprising Africa and Asia, and also the Caribbean archipelago. There are historic missionary diaries which give details of the siting, construction and organisational design of their mission classrooms.[6] Initially, the first classrooms were placed on the ground floor or as part of the missionary domestic residence. With time, the school became a separate building, integral to the mission 'compound', often simply called 'the mission'.[7] By the late 19th century, indigenous church communities and missions became established in Africa. This led to the establishment of building workshops and the training of indigenous builders, carpenters and joiners who were able to use local materials to build the next generation of missionary schools.

Environmental design of schools

The most intense period during which Western education was spread across Africa, through the efforts of both missionary and colonial parties, was from the early to mid-20th century. Developing the design of school buildings to meet with adequate construction and thermal comfort standards thus became an early focus for British colonial environmental design research bodies, who developed school design guidelines, discussed later in the chapter, for use in the colonies, particularly in the tropics including Africa.

A key reason for this was because in that era, schooling involved rote based teaching and was entirely classroom based in delivery. School learning focused on the acquisition of skills often referred to as the 'three Rs': reading, writing and arithmetic. Furthermore, schooling was introduced as a regular Monday–Friday activity, which was not affected by other cultural practices such as traditional festivals or other activities which children might be engaged in such as subsistence farming.

This was in contrast to the experiential traditional learning systems for female and male initiation ceremonies discussed in Chapter 1 in which the cultural schooling or learning involved an engagement with activities within the community and outside the specific initiation 'houses'. Western education was located in the classroom. It was therefore difficult to adapt existing traditional built forms to respond to the specific functional requirements of the Western educational classroom. The use of traditional shelter and space in the tropics responds to a lifestyle in which rooms and other indoor spaces are used predominantly for storage and sleeping. Most traditional daytime activities did, and still do, take place outdoors. Missionary school design had preceded the development of government school design standards.

Schools such as St Gregory's College Lagos (f. 1928) (see figure 2.2) show the height of missionary design. The historic original buildings were built

Figure 2.2 St Gregory's College Lagos, Nigeria
Author's own image

on elevated footings featured large wooden louvred windows and ventilated hipped roofs to allow for cross-ventilation below, through and above the main spaces. The orientation of most large windowed classrooms at right angles to the prevailing southeast trade winds also allows for maximum airflow across the room, and thus optimal thermal comfort for students. The generous verandah allow for adequate shading to classroom walls, whilst the size of the windows ensured that there was adequate daylight for working without artificial lighting during the day. The school shows a combination of local and international materials use in construction. The tropical hardwood for the main structure would have been locally sourced; however, the cast iron veranda details suggest these were likely to have been imported from Glasgow.[8]

Government schools built in British colonies furthered this attention to environment. The coastal schools, such as Kings College, Lagos (f. 1909) and Achimota College, Ghana (f. 1924), demonstrate the attention to climate in orientation and design. The same is true of the colonial government-built colleges in northern parts of West Africa. These include Wusasa College (f. 1929) in Northern Nigeria (see figure 2.3), where the significant distance from the coast and lack of trained Western builders presumably contributed to the colonial government's decision to have the college constructed in local 'tubali' stabilised earth.

Figure 2.3 Wusasa College, Nigeria
Author's own image

Colonial school design guidelines which determined school building across the colonies were based on British classroom requirements, and on a British school timetable. This meant that the design of the tropical school had to accommodate African pupils being in school from the morning to the hottest part of the day.[9] The 'standard' classroom design which evolved would have benefited from the guidance available from the aforementioned missionary design primers and also early colonial planning guidance which was based on early research studies from the schools of tropical medicine and hygiene in London and Liverpool.

By the end of WW2, with the development of research studies into human response to the tropical climate that had been initially focused on sailors involved in the merchant navy war effort, building science and environmental became a techno-scientific discipline in its own right. Thermal comfort was introduced as a concept which could be physically measured and quantified using equations related to temperature humidity and human response. Also, daylighting could be measured which meant that adequate light levels for tasks such as reading could now be recommended.

These new environmental science measurements had a direct effect on school design in the post-WW2 era and were incorporated into design guidance for schools housing and other social facilities being built in British colonies through to the post-independence era.[10] It is likely that African schools built in the postwar period benefited from design guidance which had been developed via the Colonial and then Overseas Building Service section of the Building Research Establishment, Garston, England.[11] The schools may also have had design advice from researchers working on the influence of tropical climate on buildings and comfort in laboratories attached to the London School of Tropical Hygiene and Medicine (LSTM), later in collaboration with the Architectural Association (AA) Tropical Studies Unit and eventually the AA Tropical School in London.[12]

Thus schools such as Barewa College (f. 1921), Zaria[13] and also the post-independence built 'Unity' School, Federal Government College, Sokoto,[14] (f. 1968) both located in northern Nigeria, had these new design guidelines incorporated in their design. The two schools demonstrate environmental design principles for optimum siting, thermal comfort and daylighting in the dry arid northern region of West Africa where they are located.

The schools are of concrete block construction with asbestos concrete roofing and their classrooms have been designed around courtyards to allow for the cooling effected by air movement into shaded internal courtyard spaces open to the elements. The school designs have been adapted from the typical vernacular architecture found in this climatic region.[15] Furthermore, classroom windows are set at high level to avoid direct glare which is essential for comfortable reading and studying conditions in this dry, arid region. The control of the windows also reduces the penetration of sandy 'harmattan' air during the dry season into these classrooms.

Environmental design principles for tropical schools also incorporated the adoption of landscape principles such as the positioning and utilisation of trees and other plants in respect to building orientation. These principles were developed as guidelines which encouraged architects and planners to incorporate selected vegetation, comprising both trees and plants in their planning with respect to building orientation and window positioning especially. Good landscaping and building position increased the possibilities for natural ventilation in warm climates, and used in combination with courtyard design elements in drier climates could improve night time cooling. Glare and overheating could also be reduced with judicious planting of specific plant species near school classrooms.[16]

Other educational facilities

Libraries and institutions with an extramural educational remit were also designed to take into account the new environmental design guidelines. The architects Max Fry and Jane Drew demonstrated early on in their West African career their commitment to tropical design for wider community and educational purposes than solely schools. Initially this was communicated in their 1940s design primer, Tropical Housing for the Tropics (1947).[17] Later on

32 School design in Africa

as they became involved in the national school design programmes in Ghana, the educational outreach remit spread to include libraries, technical colleges, colleges of arts science, and technology in anglophone West Africa. Arguably this culminated in the masterplan and design of key buildings for the University of Ibadan, Nigeria including the much acclaimed University Library.[18]

The American architect Max Bond's Bolgatanga library (1966) also provided a unique culture- and context-specific response in its design. The building successfully provided both the library and a space for other cultural-educational needs of this semi-rural community in this dry arid climatic region of Northern Ghana.[19] James Cubitt's Umuahia Regional Library (1964) (see figure 2.4) was in contrast designed as a response to its warm humid tropical location in southeastern Nigeria.

The library's location and orientation ensured that the resultant design ensured that all reading rooms had the maximum effect of natural cross-ventilation by the extensive use of floor-to-ceiling louvres positioned at adjacent walls in all public areas. Sustainability issues were also considered, as a sculpted water tank storage system was designed to ensure water could be stored for use by the library as a backup supply source to the unreliable pipe-borne water system in the town.[20]

Figure 2.4 Umuahia Regional Library, Nigeria
Author's own image

School design in Africa   33

School design guides: the Overseas Building Notes, UNESCO school design guides and school standards

The influence of the environment as a factor in school design in Africa can be seen then to have been an important consideration to school planners and builders. Guidelines and advice for school design had been codified since the missionary involvement in the design of churches and their associated 'missions' across Africa.

As discussed in Chapter 1, missionary schools – which formed the majority of schools in Africa until the 1950s – were largely designed and constructed by missionary staff with building skills with the help of local mission-taught converts who had acquired sufficient carpentry and construction skills to enable them work on missionary building projects. The initial schools that were established in the early 18th century were often built as 'ad hoc' structures to missionary residences where basic tuition, in addition to specific religious instruction in catechism, for example, took place.[21]

The regulation and inspection of these schools was initially the responsibility of the missions whose home countries provided much of the funding, personnel and initial infrastructure for these pioneer educational institutions. This continued up until the setting up of education inspectorates as part of the colonial administration established in the British protectorates in Nigeria, the Gold Coast, Kenya and also in the South African provinces.

The colonial education departments employed school inspectors whose job it was to ensure that not only appropriate standards of educational performance were met, but also that the school buildings were properly designed and maintained to colonial tropical school building standards, which was a condition of being eligible for grant aid. This was effectively a method by which the colonial government would support the running costs and development of non-government-established schools in colonies across the world through 'grants in aid', via the Colonial Development and Welfare Fund.[22]

The colonial office involved in funding the development of social infrastructure such as housing and schools in the tropics further worked with the colonial welfare office to develop a set of design guides. These were initially written as design notes, which superseded earlier publications such as Fry and Drew's aforementioned *Village Housing in the Tropics* (1948).

The colonial government's memos sent to the colonies on design were further developed into official building notes and guides as tropical building research became an established discipline located within the Government-run Building Research Establishment (BRE) in Garston, England.[23] These guides and notes influenced the development the United Nations Educational Social and Economic and Cultural Organisation's (UNESCO) international school design guides, as members of the schools research team at the BRE and the Architectural Association (AA) Tropical School collaborated with the UNESCO school planning team. The UNESCO guidelines were produced from the 1960s up until the early 1980s. These guidelines are now discussed.

34 School design in Africa

Colonial – Overseas Building Notes: By the postwar years, environmental science, aided by tropical research studies carried out during WW2 and onwards, improved design knowledge related to building in the tropics significantly.[24] The Colonial Office at the time was able to share this knowledge with its officers involved in the Public Works Departments in colonies across Africa and elsewhere through its publication of a series of building design guides called the Colonial Building Notes. As the colonies attained independence, the Colonial Building Notes were renamed the Overseas Building Notes but performed the same function.[25] A number of these publications did specifically suggest school building design guidelines, which formed the basis for both government schools and also as guidelines for missionary and non-government-run schools in Africa. This remained the case up until the development of national school guidelines, which were also influenced by the UNESCO school guidelines.[26]

UNESCO School Guidelines: At the end of WW2, the formation of UNESCO as a wing of the United Nations not only ensured the promotion of education and social development, but also through its education wing set up a school buildings programme with offices in Asia, Africa and headquarters in Paris.[27] The building research programmes had offices set up in each continent and were involved in both encouraging new research and funding new school design, and also setting continental-regional guidelines for school design. These offices had research work into various aspects of school design, from school siting to furniture design undertaken by a range of architects from the UK and the USA mainly, but also with a number of European architects from countries such as France, and in the case of Palumbo, from Italy.[28] The resulting UNESCO school design guidelines were used by international school design consultants such the UK's RMJM, which worked in association with the Nigerian firm Ekwueme and Associates on the National 'Model School building Programme' in post-independence Nigeria.[29] The guidelines used for these schools were eventually incorporated as international (UNESCO) standards into National School Design Standards across much of Africa, and are still form the basis for school design standards for schools in Anglophone Africa including Nigeria and Ghana.[30]

Other environmental design guides

In pre-1994 South Africa, the government-funded Council for Scientific and Industrial Research (CSIR) research organisation published its own guidelines which also referred to the UNESCO school design standards and provided design advice for environmental comfort, focusing on issues such as ventilation in schools. These guidelines, although based on empirical scientific research findings, also incorporated apartheid rhetoric to justify different thermal comfort standards for white and 'bantu' (black) schools in the 1960s.[31]

The CSIR's research informed the development of 'standards and norms' for all of South Africa's racially segregated schools. These remained in place until the dismantling of the apartheid national school building programme in the 1980s. From that decade onwards, the increased involvement of NGOs and corporate charities such as the Urban Foundation in the funding, design and provision of schools in cities such as Port Elizabeth ensured that the apartheid-influenced school design guidelines of the past were replaced by contemporary design thinking and ideas for schools. Since the full dismantling of national rule and move to democracy in 1994, South Africa has created a new education act which also incorporates a more contemporary set of school design standards and norms, whose implementation will be discussed in the next chapter.[32]

In the international arena in the 1970s and 1980s, the environmental design advice given in Koenigsberger et al.'s (1973) *Manual of Tropical Design* and in Baker's later (1987) *Passive and Low Energy Design for Tropical Island Climates* – whilst not specifically focused on school design – provided relevant criteria for design decisions for different tropical environments. Both books have had international popularity, particularly the *Manual of Tropical Design* which has been translated into a number of languages. This is likely to have been due to the links of the authors such as Otto Koenigsberger to tropical design via the AA school and his international consultancy work. A decade later Baker's book, a result of a project undertaken at the Commonwealth Secretariat on environmental design in the tropical island climates, and his subsequent work with the Martin Centre at the University of Cambridge, particularly with respect to lighting research, helped popularise his book and international work on passive energy approaches to design.[33]

Since the 1990s, a number of tropical design guides have also emerged in Australia and Southeast Asia. However, their focus has been on private domestic and commercial buildings and not on public institutional infrastructure such as schools.[34] There have, however, been a number of voluntary sector and aid organisations that have in effect promoted their international approach and guidelines to designing schools in rural areas of the tropics, and particularly Africa. These include the US-based architecture teams MASS design and UrbanLab, the Glasgow-based Orkidstudio and the reincarnation of the UK-based charity the International Technology Development Group (ITDG) as Practical Action.[35]

On the African continent, South Africa's post-apartheid schools, built from 1995 onwards, have benefited from the most comprehensive set of school regulations and guidelines that have been drawn up and come about as a result of the full reorganisation of its now nationally integrated education system. Spearheaded by the South African research body the CSIR, these guidelines provide a clear break with South Africa's segregated educational past.[36] The 1995 school design guidance takes into account pedagogy, costs, local involvement and environmental responses. The administrative make up of South Africa means that the country's different provinces are given the latitude to interpret and respond to the guidance in relation to their educational priorities.

36 School design in Africa

Figure 2.5 Vukani School, Khayelitsha, Western Cape, South Africa
Author's own image

This has led to the design of post-1994 schools in some administrative provinces such as in the Western Cape, having a lighter regulatory touch. In the Western Cape, architects such as Albertyn Wessels (see figure 2.5), Joe Noero, Groenwaald Preller, Wolf and associates, are given the freedom to interpret the school design conceptually keeping within the spatial and function guidelines as set out. This contrasts significantly from the past government's apartheid-determined school design standards that specified specific school and classroom designs for the different racially categorised schools across South Africa.[37] Contemporary South African schools designed by the aforementioned architects and others have been successful in projecting the differences and original approaches that have been developed by the creation of a direct working relationship with both the provincial educational departments and also importantly the communities in which the new schools are built.[38]

Economic and socio-political factors

In building construction terms, classrooms remain one of the most economical structures to design as they essentially comprise four walls, windows, a roof and a ceiling. This core design versatility has meant that the physical costs of school structures are not high. With the establishment of formal Western education via the missionary groups in Africa, the mission school was initially attached to the church or clergyman's quarters, prior to construction as a separate unit.

The costs of construction were usually affordable, as the basic build meant that local craftsmen were easily trained to carry this out and in rural areas local materials, such as mud block for walls and thatch for roofing, could be adapted for use in schools construction. Thus, compared to recurring the costs of employing school staff and tutors, the school and classroom were relatively inexpensive.

From the post-WW2 period in the late 1940s onwards, the use of concrete blocks and various forms of metal sheet roofing further reduced the time costs of construction and improved the permanency of schools as compared to traditional thatch and mud; schools made from 'modern' materials lasted longer as they required less maintenance and were easier to build with less skilled local labour.

In this period also, the construction of most basic primary schools was undertaken by colonial education departments, financed by the aforementioned Colonial Development and Welfare Fund. In the southern parts of Ghana and Nigeria in West Africa, schools were also being funded and built by enterprising local community groups, often in association with local missionary denominations. This was at a time that coincided with the reduction of direct missionary involvement with educational provision in this region.[39]

Thus in Eastern and Western Nigeria, for example, a number of communities were involved in building schools which were adopted by local missionary groups to become primary and, in some cases, secondary schools.[40] This meant that up until Nigeria's independence, community constructed schools which had been handed over to religious missions could then avail themselves of same grant-aid funding to enable the employment of the right quota of staff required to teach the schools, in exchange for being subjected to annual review by the colony's educational inspectorate.

Today, as the typical design of classrooms across Africa has remained essentially unchanged, the basic construction costs of most primary and secondary schools have remained relatively low at (62,200 Ksh/m^2).[41] However, in rural areas and informal settlements in cities, schools are often located in hard-to-reach locations, which makes their connection to basic infrastructure such as pipe-borne water, sanitation, power and reliable access roads difficult or impossible to achieve. This has the knock-on effect of increasing the real cost of school provision as the add on infrastructure costs significantly increase school provision costs in these areas.[42] Similarly, overcrowded informal settlements that have closer access to areas of economic activity in cities, despite having good service connections to electricity and water, have the problem of land acquisition for schools, because of prime urban land costs in Africa as elsewhere globally. This again has an effect on real school classroom costs in urban areas.

38 *School design in Africa*

Future school costs

The design of future African schools is likely to respond to the emerging international educational landscape. This global focus is moving more towards universal access of all learners to open online learning systems and on digital connectivity, rather than on building more of the traditional brick-and-mortar school classrooms. As the costs of technology fall and 'know how' becomes more open source, future school design costs are set to remain affordable as the traditional modes of learning are set aside for more fluid and less classroom dependent pedagogies. *Learning spaces*, as today's classrooms are now called, are being designed to be flexible places in which different modes of contemporary learning: peer-to-peer, online and collaborative learning events can take place.[43]

The 'opportunity costs' and other non-economic costs of school design

The opportunity costs, as opposed to the financial costs, of education and school design can be extremely high. In traditional African societies, the displacement of local knowledge systems and processes by the mission – including the church, the school house and other social infrastructure such as hospitals and agricultural demonstration farms – had lasting disrupting effects on all aspects of local life. Old traditions were changed forever as the receivers of 'book education' became more important than village elders, and the new Christian religion replaced traditional religion in communities across Africa.

Education and its main apparatus the school thus was a total societal disrupter in much of Africa. Societies and villages which did not embrace the school and its new ways of thought quickly lost their status and relevance in the new order. As Achebe's trilogy on Eastern Nigeria records, the ultimate cost of not doing this could have tragic consequences, with the eponymous hero Okafor paying the ultimate price for not being able to cope with his son running away to join the new missionary converts.[44]

As stated earlier, by the early 1950s governments, missions and enlightened communities in parts of East and West Africa were rapidly contributing to the building of schools as the need and benefits of a Western education for local children and youths was understood as being a critical resource for entry into the modern, capitalist world. In some West African communities, rivalries were rife over which home town associations were able to build local schools first in their villages.[45]

During this era, well publicised government backed universal education schemes, which involved the construction of numbers of primary schools across the southern part of Nigeria, were also in place.[46] The Gold Coast (later to become Ghana) also in this period (1951 and 1961) had its First and Second National School Buildings Programmes.[47]

The school buildings in these universal education programmes acquired political symbolism as they proved the commitment of the then colonial government to contributing to the educational welfare of its colonies.

In contrast at this same period in South Africa, the imposition of the race-based 'apartheid' education system in Nationalist South Africa, from 1948 onwards, arguably had the opposite effects.[48] The Nationalist government's 'apartheid' school building policy, involving different construction programmes for the country's differently identified racial groupings, was implemented to justify its 'separate but equal' education of all South African students.[49] The 1976 'Soweto' uprising, and the increase in civil resistance which subsequently followed, demonstrated the failure of this school policy socio-politically. Schools were often both the sites and targets for the violent protests which broke out in townships in opposition to the imposition of the 'apartheid' education policies as the Soweto and subsequent events demonstrated.

Global education policies

By the 1960s, when most of Africa had attained, or was in the process of attaining, self-rule, the International Development Agency (IDA) – a wing of the World Bank set up to provide direct funding aid and assistance for global development projects – was able to fund development assistance for the construction of schools across Africa in association with UNESCO. Aside from the financial assistance, via loans and technical know-how, the international political imperative has been to lift countries out of poverty by investing in more schools and school infrastructure, increasing teacher education, and overall improving enrollment, particularly at primary level education.[50]

Unfortunately, the global economic turmoil in the 1970s, culminating in the oil crisis, led to the collapse of many African state economies. Also, a spate of political coups d'etat had crushing effects on African countries. At the international level also, the fluid financial deals that had been available from the post-colonial era of the 1950s and 1960s dried up as World Bank lending was less favourable to African and other emerging nations than the former IDA loans and bilateral agreements with countries had been.

International moves led by UNESCO and other organisations towards attaining universal primary education for all globally also stalled by the 1970s. A series of international policies and conferences related to this had taken place since the 1960s, as discussed in Chapter 1. The main outcome of these conferences had been the call for universal enrolment in basic education across this world. To achieve this, the various conference declarations pushed for the increase in school enrolment of children and the eradication of illiteracy, especially amongst females and excluded groups.[51]

By the late 1970s, with funding for UNESCO being severely diminished with the pulling out of the organisation for political reasons by the USA, the World Bank became the main instigator and funder of these global policy programmes.[52]

40 School design in Africa

These policies, from the late 1970s onwards, worked in conjunction with the World Bank's education projects and reports. The 1980s reports supported a self-help 'sweat equity' approach to physical school building, with more investment being made in the funding of better teacher education and equipment for schools than for school building. This move towards de-linking state or institutional provision of schools and their infrastructure was further strengthened with the neo liberalist policies gaining popularity globally from the mid-1980s onwards. Private provision of education was supported, which resulted in a mixed economy of educational provision, with the state, formalised private providers such as churches and private groups, small and large, being able to set up and offer education.[53]

State education systems generally remain fee free. 'Free' also has to be qualified: books, equipment and school uniforms are often not free, and other costs including school building fund payments are not unusual, particularly for well-regarded high-status state schools in countries such as Nigeria and post-1994 South Africa.

Well-financed private schools in Africa do not disguise their upfront costs, and have become popular for Africa's growing middle classes since their introduction in the 1990s. Religious and third sector organisations, such as the Aga Khan Foundation and the Catholic Church, have also become education providers, or re-entered the education market in the case of religious groups particularly. Although many such organisations are able to offer some philanthropic scholarships for the poor and needy, most children in attendance are fee-paying.[54] There is often limited provision of scholarships for poorer academically able students, but in reality, few poor students have had the education preparation to pass the selective entrance exams for these elite schools.

Facilities at private schools can vary widely. Generally, as might be expected, the higher the fee paid, the better the facilities and teaching delivered to students. At the extreme end of the private spectrum are the schools run in residential homes in informal settlements across Africa. These schools are often cheaper in terms of actual fees or levies paid than local free government schools. However they can offer a more bespoke form of tuition to pupils, due to the relatively lower class sizes, and also a more quantifiable fee cost, than state schools which often levy other 'costs' on parents for school provision that some poorer parents cannot afford.[55] In some cases also, this form of basic private educational provision may have better outcomes in respect to academic pass rates than poorly supported state provision.[56]

Contemporary schools

African schools today bear a strong resemblance in their operation and design particularly to those built in the early 20th century. Unlike Latin America and some parts of Southeast Asia, school and classroom design have shown no radical changes in their provision for most students. Education

School design in Africa 41

programmes in continental Africa have not undergone the transformations of mass education programmes found elsewhere such as in Latin America or post-WW2 Eastern Europe.

In Tanzania, Nyerere's *Ujaama* Schools in the 1960s and 1970s attempted to challenge the inherited Western–Christian missionary-fashioned education system in Tanzania with their focus on mass 'education for self-reliance' through local learning and the promotion of the village school model. The *Ujaama* programme came to an end with the collapse of the Tanzanian economy in the 1980s and the country subsequently adopting World Bank reform measures and moving towards the prevailing African neoliberal Western education model. This has led to a mixed approach to educational provision, with private and state actors involved in the provision of education and with this the design of schools within a less regulatory environment.

Decades later in South Africa, the post-apartheid 1994 South African National Education Policy sought to fundamentally change and democratise the racially segregated education system that the National Party had put in place.[57] The country's education system is now non-racialized; however, arguably there is now instead an economic class divide to school provision and classroom design. The poor, who are predominantly black, have the worst access to good schooling and classrooms built since 1994 in townships and poorer areas are less likely to have benefited from new school design concepts focusing on child-centred learning and schools as community assets. Thus, despite progress made in some provinces such as Cape Town, most South African schools have not benefited from progressive 21st century school design. Furthermore, the national education curriculum has had limited transformation from the historic Western exam-based curriculums in place in the early 20th century. This has meant schools have remained designed to both symbolise and sustain the symbolism of the traditional historic school building and their classrooms, the elite schools in the country being good examples of how this remains perpetuated.

In West Africa similarly, the West African Examinations curriculum designed in the 1950s, despite having considerable African-sourced content, was modelled on the Cambridge Certificate examinations system, and focused on academic subjects required to be studied for university entrance examinations. Today's WAEC examination curriculum has more technical and vocational subjects, but the elite schools which students most want to attend retain the traditional curriculum. These schools are also designed and maintained to emulate the English public school and associated traditional classroom designs that they symbolise.

The nature of school design norms and standards have remained relatively unchanged across most of Africa. In Nigeria for example, the current school design standards owe their creation from the IDA-UNESCO school design programme and technical assistance era in the 1960s. Also in Ghana, the standards developed during the first and second national school building programmes in the 1950s, augmented further by schools guidelines used to develop school buildings in the new towns of Tema and Akosombo in the 1960s, form the basis of school design standards and norms in Ghana, and have also had little change. The post-Jomtien Conference 'Education for All' Declaration basic education programmes adopted across the world including Africa, despite increasing school and classroom building programmes, did not alter the design of these schools.

The new methods of delivering mass education via computer-based distance learning schemes, as found in India and some other parts of Southeast Asia, become popular at basic education level have also yet to take root in Africa.[58] The rapid changes in education engagement brought about over the past decade with the miniaturisation of computing and the ubiquity of online access, however, is likely to change this.[59]

One notable change that has taken place has been the introduction of school feeding programmes at kindergarten and early primary school levels in many countries. This has been as a direct result of UNESCO and national education policies in many African countries seeking to respond to the 1995 United Nations Millennium Development Goals (MDG) which focused not only on the need to have all children access a basic education, but also the need to improve maternal health and with it child welfare up to early (pre-school) years.[60] (See figure 2.6.) This is because it was proved by

Figure 2.6 School Feeding Programme, Kontonkoshie, Ghana
Author's own image

School design in Africa   43

evidence-based research that school feeding programmes are particularly effective in improving not only maternal and child health care, but also educational attainment for children.[61]

Future schools

African school classroom of the future will still be required to deliver the same fundamental educational experience for their users. Education and knowledge systems, however, are likely to depend less on traditional textbook study and teacher-directed learning, as interactive online systems make remote learning more possible for much of the continent. *Learning spaces*, as future classrooms are being called, will exist but may begin to inhabit non-traditional spaces, libraries and other communal places instead of dedicated classrooms. Also, as learning becomes less teacher-focused, and shifts towards peer-to-peer and remote learning formats, the design of the traditional classroom is set to become redundant.

This may take some time, considering the vastness of the African continent and the remote regions to which education has yet to make inroads since the last century's numerous international drives discussed in Chapter 1. However the proliferation of the Global System for Mobile Networks (GSM) which enable phones globally achieve instant interactive telephony means that e-learning in Africa may happen much faster as more students have access to smartphones. There are already a number of trial e-learning projects taking place across Africa, and information communications technology systems from the one laptop per child projects to new e-learning systems that already exist, but they form only a small although growing segment of Africa's school landscape. This leap from the historic classroom 'chalk and talk' setting to a more distributed learning approach will eventually happen. When it does it will represent a transformational step in classroom design and educational history in Africa.

Summary

This chapter has investigated the three key themes – environment, socio-economic issues and policies – which have had the most influence on school design and its development in Africa. It concludes that Africa – despite its schools having benefited from the actions of positive players and philanthropists from the early missionaries and benign colonial governments through to local community development unions and progressive international education policies, promoting and funding school building to enable universal access to basic education – remains the continent which has been least able to meet with the international targets of education enrolment set by the UN in its SDGs, which have now become MDGS.

The new Sustainable Development Goal target in relation to education does shift the goalposts for access to basic education targets in Africa, relying

44   School design in Africa

less on enrollment figures in schools and more on longer-term access to basic education by a wider range of the population than just school-age children. It remains, however, by no means certain that African states can deliver on this target in the SDG timeframe. This is particularly uncertain as the schools being built do not respond to the wider remit of basic education and lifelong learning in their continued use of the 1950s–1960s-developed traditional school design standards and norms.

As discussed, despite the continent's centuries-long engagement with Western education, the challenges remain that the first missionary pioneers encountered as they set up the first schools in the 19th century such as inaccessibility to rural areas and lack of basic infrastructure such as communications, sanitation, and power. Possibly the most critical challenge, as it was then, is local hostility to 'Western' education, remain the same, if not worse, in areas such as parts of northeastern Nigeria controlled by the Islamist group Boko Haram today.[62]

Further contemporary challenges now include access to new 'e-learning' technologies and also the teachers and administrative set up to engage with these potentially critical learning tools for the future. The design of future classrooms or learning spaces that allow for the successful engagement with these technologies might make a major difference in the future that might help overcome some, if not all, of the hindrances in educational delivery today.

For urban Africa, which is projected to increasingly be the birthplace of most of Africa's 21st century youth,[63] this is likely to make access to a good education considerably easy. How this will work out in parts of remote, rural Africa is less certain, despite many anecdotal case studies suggesting its potential.[64] There will be no doubt a reckoning and assessment of these as we move to the middle of the 21st century. What is clear is that as these technologies change learning globally, Africa will not be left out. The continent should – it is hoped – therefore gain from this new diffusion of educational practice, and the effect this will have on the design of traditional school infrastructure that has been synonymous with the African education narrative since the mid-19th century.

It may be that there will be more liberal, pragmatic education policies promoted by the international agencies such as UNESCO. These policies might allow for a more mixed approach to education infrastructure and delivery, via a variety of private and state providers.[65] For school infrastructure this might be a positive move, as research for this chapter has found that the national regulatory school design standards and norms guidelines, which are typical of most African state education systems, remain based on UNESCO and colonial design guidelines of the 1950s and 1960s.

These international guidelines might be seen to restrict the design and delivery of more child-student-centred classroom designs by non-traditional government school building providers. However, this might not be the case. The example cited of the adoption advisory guidelines for standards and

School design in Africa 45

norms adopted successfully by architects and designers involved in the design of post-1994 schools in the Western Cape Province in South Africa being a case in point.

Producing appropriate relaxed guidelines for designing spaces for digital learning is likely to prove equally challenging. This will be discussed in later chapters. It is, however, clear that few state schools have been able to benefit from classrooms that respond to the spatial needs of laptop-focused collaborative learning in the classroom.

Environmentally also, African school design has benefited from sustained historic research and development of demonstration school plans, taking into account the specific environmental factors related to building design in the tropics. African schools have already benefited from design guidelines which largely incorporated the research undertaken by UNESCO, the Architectural Association Tropical Design School and other early environmental design pioneers, whose work was incorporated in the UNESCO international school design guidelines.

Environmental conditions in schools can now be recorded using data loggers and sensor recordings, and used to successfully simulate and predict different environmental conditions in schools. This technology is already in use in the modelling of school classrooms internationally. These findings are already being incorporated into developing school design guidelines in in tropical regions including Australia and Singapore. These findings are also being incorporated by architects and designers in South African schools, and by the international design teams such as MASS Design, Orkidstudio and others involved in school building projects in Africa.

At a socio-political level also, both governments and the parental community are aware of the need to engage with education and the power of new technologies in future development. There remain communities which for cultural or religious reasons remain resistant to educational uptake on gender, religion or for other reasons, but the overwhelming majority are aware of the economic and social benefits of their offspring acquiring basic education.

There does, however, remain the need to incorporate the new design knowledge related to school provision in areas of e-learning to environmental sustainability with the historic themes related to community building and development which are central to the success of school buildings in Africa at urban and rural level. Currently e-learning and sustainability issues are viewed and considered separate from the objective of most Africa policymakers, whose focus remains the building more classrooms to the now historic traditional UNESCO guidelines regulation format. The community link to the school is often limited, except where explicitly encouraged as in the post-1994 South African school design guidelines.

It is hoped that a more negotiated approach to the target-driven global education standards and a better understanding of the need to engage communities in the school design process from inception to post-occupancy use

46 School design in Africa

will help with this. The new SDGs, therefore, have the challenge to 'nudge' the actors involved in school design, from policymakers to the local community into becoming part of the process.

Whatever the case, there is likely to be a change in future African school design and its provision, from this historical overview of relative stasis, and limited gradual transformation over time, to the rapid technological developments from the late 20th century to the present day. Optimistically, the globalising nature and spread of new media and digital technologies in learning should, if not allow Africa to 'leapfrog' its educational infrastructure to Western standards, at least significantly improve childhood learning environments across the continent.

Notes

1 This includes; Uduku, O. (1993b) *Factors Affecting School Design in Nigeria.* PhD Thesis, University of Cambridge; Uduku, O. (1994a) *Factors Affecting School Design in South Africa.* Report, Centre for African Studies, University of Cambridge; Uduku, O. (1993a) *Factors Affecting School Design in Ghana.* Report, Centre for African Studies, University of Cambridge; Uduku, O. (2008b) *Designing Schools as Development Hubs for Learning.* Final Report. Bristol: University of Bristol; and Uduku, O. (2015) Spaces for 21st Century Learning. In *Routledge Handbook on International Learning and Development.* London: Routledge, pp. 196–209.

2 For the purposes of this chapter, the koppen classification of climate is used, with tundra being the most northerly typology found at the poles and warm humid being the most 'tropical'. See Kottek, M., Grieser, J., Beck, C., Rudolf, B. and Rubel, F. (2006) World Map of the Koppen-Geiger Climate Classification Updated. *Meteorol. X*, 15, pp. 259–263.

3 Rapoport, A. (1969) *House Form and Culture.* London: Prentice Hall, Oliver, P. (1976) *Shelter in African.* London: Barrie and Jenkins, and Denyer, S. (1978) *African Traditional Architecture.* London: Heinemann have written major texts on vernacular architecture, which have identified the link between local buildings and climate.

4 School prospectuses in Nigeria such as Atlantic Hall School and the American International School, both in Lagos, for example, indicate that their classrooms have air conditioning. URLS Atlantic Hall, *FAQs*, www.atlantic-hall.net/faqs/ American International School of Lagos, *History Blog*, www.aislagos.org/about-aisl/aisls-history-50-years-of-the-american-international-school-lagos. Both accessed May 2017.

5 See Herbert, G. (1978) *Pioneers of Prefabrication: The British Contribution in the Nineteenth Century.* Baltimore, MD: Johns Hopkins University Press; and Thompson, N. (2014) *A Study of Early Corrugated Buildings in Scotland.* www. arct.cam.ac.uk/Downloads/ichs/vol-3-3097-3116-thompson.pdf.
  Coopers Catalogue, https://archive.org/stream/IllustratedCatalogueOfGoods ManufacturedAndSuppliedByW.c.SperLtd/IllustratedComplete_djvu.txt. Both accessed 2017.

6 See, for example, the diaries of Waddell, H. M. (1863) *The Diaries of H.M. Waddell and the Calabar Mission.* Edinburgh: National Library of Scotland Archives/ Centre for Special Collections University of Edinburgh; or for Lovedale Missionary Institution (1904) *Report for Lovedale Missionary Institution 1903.* Alice, Eastern Cape, South Africa: Lovedale Press.

School design in Africa   47

7 Uduku, O. (2000) The Colonial Face of Educational Space. In L. Lokko (ed.), *White Papers Black Marks*. London: Athlone Press, pp. 44–65.

8 In the case of Hope Waddell College, which is located near Calabar, this is circumstantially likely as there is documentation that King Eyamba Bassey had an iron house imported from Scotland in the same era. see note 5, and also Fafunwa, B. (1974) *History of Education in Nigeria*. London: Allen and Unwin.

9 The timetable for Hope Waddell College Calabar in can be seen in Aye, E. (1986) *Hope Waddell Training Institution Life and Work: 1894–1978*. Edinburgh: National Library of Scotland.

10 The use of environmental science also informed the development of school design guidelines developed by the newly formed postwar UNESCO school building research units that collaborated with the Architectural Association Tropical School Design Course for the tropics to develop tropical school building design guidelines and prototypes used in Ghana, for example. Thus, the AA Committee minutes in 1963 record J. Owuso Addo as having gained a certificate in the Educational Building Course. The school design guidelines developed at such courses still form the basis for school design standards and guidelines in Ghana and Nigeria.

11 For a sample of these reports see National Archives Kew, UNESCO Design Guidelines, Paris. UNESCO 1966–88; Overseas Building Notes, BRE, London, 50–73, 1950–73, and *West Africa Builder and Architect* Vol. 2, no. 4, pp. 77–79. Factors Governing School Building Programmes Harris and White, West African Building Research Institute Accra.

12 The AA Committee Minutes from 1960–1966 note the activities of the tropical studies unit, culminating in the formation of the Tropical School linked to the Kwame Nkrumah University of Science and Technology (KNUST) in Ghana.

13 Built to house Katsina College, which moved from the city of Katsina to the teaching centre of Zaria in 1949. See Hubbard, J. P. (2000) *Education Under Colonial Rule: A History of Kastina College, 1921–1942*. Latham, NY: University Press of America.

14 Uduku (2015).

15 See Dmchowski, Z. R. (1990) *Introduction to Traditional Nigerian Architecture. Volume 1: Northern Nigeria*. London: Ethnographica, Denyer (1978), and Schwerdtfeger, F. W. (1982) *Traditional Housing in Nigerian Cities: A Comparative Study of Houses in Zaria, Ibadan and Marrakech*. London: Wiley.

16 See Fry, M. and Drew, J. (1964) *Tropical Architecture in the Warm Humid Zone*. London: Architectural Press.

17 Fry, M. and Drew, J. (1948) *Village Housing in the Tropics*. London: Lund Humphries, See also Uduku, O. (2014) *Village Housing in the Tropics*, with Special Reference to West Africa: Jane Drew, Maxwell Fry, and Harry L. Ford Humphries, 1947 134 pages, and *Fry, Drew, Knight, Creamer: Architecture*: Stephen Hitchins Lund Humphries, 1978 160 pages. *Journal of Architectural Education*, 68(2), pp. 265–266, and Drew, J. and Fry, M., with introduction by I. Jackson (2014) *Village Housing in the Tropics* (reprint). London: Routledge.

18 See Jackson, I. and Holland, J. (2014) *The Architecture of Maxwell Fry and Jane Drew*. London: Routledge; and Uduku, O. (2010) *Tropical Ivory Towers: A Critical Evaluation of Design Symbolism and Practical Aspirations of the West African University Campuses in Their Fifth Decade*. Docomomo, 11th International Conference, Mexico City, 12 pp.

19 Uduku, O. (2006, December) Modernist Architecture and 'the Tropical' in West Africa: The Tropical Architecture Movement in West Africa. *Habitat International*, 30(3), pp. 396–411; Bond, M. (1968, March) A Library for Bolgatanga.

48　*School design in Africa*

    Architectural Forum, CXXV111, pp. 66–69; and Le Roux, H. (2003, September) The Networks of Tropical Architecture. *Journal of Architecture*, 8, pp. 337–354.
20　Uduku (2008b).
21　See Waddell (1863).
22　Both mission and government schools were entitled to varying forms of government aid towards the cost of teacher employment and school running costs.
23　The first Colonial Building Notes were published in the early 20th century.
24　These were primarily focused on improving military and naval performance in the tropics, where some theatres of war were situated (such as Libya and Singapore) or where troops had to travel through (e.g. Burma, Egypt and the West Indies).
25　Overseas Building Notes, BRE, London, 50–73, 1950–73, various, and Le Roux, H. (2004) The Post-colonial Architecture of Ghana and Nigeria. *Architectural History*, 47, pp. 361–392.
26　For example UNESCO consultants were involved in developing the design for model demonstration schools in Nigeria in the 1960s, Uduku, O. (2016) The UNESCO-IDA School Building Programme in Africa: The Nigeria 'Unity' Schools, Chapter 14. In J. Willis and K. Darien-Smith (eds.), *Designing Schools, Space, Place and Pedagogy*. London: Taylor and Francis, pp. 175–187.
27　UNESCO, *History*, www.unesco.org/new/en/unesco/about-us/who-we-are/history/. Accessed May 2017.
28　See De Raedt, K. (2014) Between True Believers' and Operational Experts: UNESCO Architects and School Building in Post Colonial Africa. *Journal of Architecture*, 19(1), pp. 19–42.
29　See Uduku (2016) in note 26.
30　See Uduku (1993b) and Uduku (2008b).
31　Van Straaten, J. F., Richards, S. J. and Lotz, F. J. (1967). *Ventilation and Thermal Considerations in School Building Design*. Pretoria: CSIR.
32　See Uduku, O. (1994b) *Schools in Africa: Perspectives on a Viable Physical Ideal*. Centre for African Studies Cape Town Seminar Semester 2, 1994, African Studies Centre, Robinson College. Cambridge: University of Cambridge. Today South Africa's CSIR continues its research into educational design and environmental conditions, but the guidelines for school design are covered via National Norms and Standards, which acknowledge the need to respond to local environmental conditions.
33　Baker, N. (1987) *Passive and Low Energy Building Design for Tropical Island Climates*. London: Commonwealth Secretariat. Koenigsberger, O. H. et al. (1973) *Manual of Tropical Building and Housing*. London: Thames and Hudson. Much of Koenigsberger's text emanated from research undertaken at the AA school of Tropical design and relevant UCL research into lighting, ventilation, etc., that sometimes overlapped with work undertaken by the BRE which published the Overseas Building Notes.
34　See, for example, www.cairns.qld.gov.au/__data/assets/pdf_file/0003/45642/BuildingDesign.pdf and www.bca.gov.sg/Sustain/sustain.html for Australia and Singapore, respectively. For Practical Action see: Stone, H. (2009) Schools Buildings in Developing Countries. *Practical Action, Technical Brief*. https://practicalaction.org//docs/technical_information_service/school_buildings_in_developing_countires.pdf.
35　For Practical Action, see note 34; MASS Design Material, https://massdesigngroup.org/ and Orkidstudio, https://orkidstudio.org/. Both accessed May 2017.
36　Uduku (1994a) and South African Government (2009) *Department of Education Notice, No. of 2009 The National Minimum Uniform Norms and Standards for School Infrastructure*.

School design in Africa 49

37 Uduku (1994b), and see Kallaway, P. (ed.) (2002) *The History of Education Under Apartheid 1948–1994: The Doors of Learning and Culture Shall Be Opened*. New York, NY: Peter Lang.
38 Uduku (2008b); South African Government (2009).
39 Fafunwa (1974).
40 See, for example, Uduku (1993b); Fafunwa (1974); Ayandele, E. A. (1966) *The Missionary Impact on Modern Nigeria 1842–1914: A Political and Social Analysis*. London: Longman Green and Co.; and Ajayi, J. F. A. (1965) *Christian Missions in Nigeria 1841–1891: The Making of a New Elite*. Evanston, IL: Northwestern University Press.
41 Turner and Townsend (2017) *International Construction Market Survey*. www.turnerandtownsend.com/media/1518/international-construction-market-survey-2016.pdf. Accessed May 2017.
42 In Nigeria most of the historic schools that were initially located in the CBD area of Lagos Island moved to the suburbs as increased land costs in central Lagos during the 1970s during the 'oil-era', meant that school sites were acquired by business concerns. See, for example, Baptist Academy Lagos in Uduku, O. (2003a). Educational Design and Modernism in West Africa. *Docomomo Journal* (28 March), pp. 76–82.
43 Uduku (2015).
44 Achebe, C. (2010) *The African Trilogy*. London: Everyman.
45 See Uduku, O. (2002) The Socio-Economic Basis of a Diaspora Community, Igbo bu'ike. *Review of African Political Economy*, 29(92), pp. 301–311.
46 See Ayandele (1966) for a description of Eastern and Western Nigeria education schemes of the era.
47 See Le Roux (2003, September); and also for Ghana, see Jackson and Holland (2014) Chapter 4. pp. 162–175, Missionaries and Modern Schools in Ghana.
48 Kallaway, P. (ed.) (2002) *The History of Education Under Apartheid 1948–1994: The Doors of Learning and Culture Shall Be Opened*. New York, NY: Peter Lang.
49 South African Government, The Bantu Education Act No. 47 of 1953 (later renamed the Bantu Act 1953).
50 The World Bank (2017) *History Page*. www.worldbank.org/en/about/history. Accessed in May 2017.
51 See Chapter 1.
52 Usually these policies were drawn up in collaboration with UNESCO, but the balance of policy and financial power had shifted to the World Bank by the 1980s.
53 See Psacharopoulos, G. (2006, May) World Bank Policy on Education: A Personal Account. *International Journal of Education Development*, pp. 329–338, and Theyuenk, S. (2009) *School Construction Strategies for Universal Primary Education in Africa: Should Communities Be Empowered to Build their Schools?* Washington, DC: World Bank.
54 Website information accessed for the Aga Khan School, Mombasa, Kenya, www. agakhanacademies.org/mombasa/financial-assistance and Atlantic Hall School, Nigeria, http://atlantic-hall.net/admissions-aids/scholarships/. Both accessed May 2017. The Aga Khan schools can provide some financial assistance to Kenyan nationals, but this depends on circumstances and available funding; Atlantic Hall has one full fee scholarship for the top performing student in the entrance examination.
55 As stated earlier, state provision is supposed to be free, but other costs related to textbooks and sometimes uniforms, etc., are often levied as being additional to free tuition; if fees are not paid in the state system, students are often excluded from school. In the private schools in informal settlements, there is often more

50 School design in Africa

negotiation about fees and a willingness of entrepreneurs to accept payments by instalment if required.

56 See *The Economist* (2015b, August) The $ a week School. www.economist. com/printedition/2015-08-01. Accessed April 2018; but for a contrasting view see UNESCO (2015b) *Rethinking Education for a Global Common Good*. http:// unesdoc.unesco.org/images/0023/002325/232555e.pdf. Accessed December 2017.

57 For *Ujaama* education, see Nyerere, J. (1968) Education for Self Reliance. In *Freedom and Socialism: A Selection From Writings & Speeches, 1965–1967*. Dar es Salaam: Oxford University Press and also Molony, T. (2015) *Nyerere, the Early Years*. London: James Currey. For South Africa see Kallaway (2002).

58 The education philosophers such as Freire, P. (1970) *Pedagogy of the Oppressed*. London: Penguin, and Psacharopoulos, G., Rojas, C. and Velez, E. (1993). Achievement Evaluation of Colombia's Escuela Nueva: Is Multigrade the Answer? *Comparative Education Review*, 37(3), pp. 263–276 had little influence on educational policies or design in Africa, compared to their adoption in Latin America (in countries such as Colombia and Ecuador) and parts of Asia, in particular India.

59 This is discussed further in Chapter 6.

60 See United Nations (2000). MDGs and relationship to maternal child care and improved education. In the new Sustainable Development Goals this has been changed to Goal 4, 'ensuring quality and inclusive education for all and promoting lifelong learning'. See UNDP (2015b) *Sustainable Development Goals*. www. undp.org/content/undp/en/home/sustainable-development-goals. html. Accessed June 2017.

61 See Uduku, O. (2011) School Building Design for Feeding Programmes and Community Outreach: Insights From Ghana and South Africa. *International Journal of Educational Development International Journal of Education Development*, 31, pp. 59–66.

62 See Hentz, J. J. and Solomon, H. (2017) *Understanding Boko Haram: Terrorism and Insurgency in Africa*. Abingdon, Oxon; New York, NY: Routledge, Smith, M. G. (2015) *Boko Haram: Inside Nigeria's Unholy War*. London: I. B. Tauris, and Raufu, A. (2014) *Sects and Social Disorder*. London: James Currey.

63 See African Development Bank (ADB) (2017) *Africa's Urban Population Projection Statistics*, www.afdb.org/fileadmin/uploads/afdb/Documents/Publications/ Tracking_Africa%E2%80%99s_Progress_in_Figures.pdf. Chapter 1. Accessed August 2017; and United Nations (2017) *Population 2050 Projections*, www. un.org/sustainabledevelopment/blog/2017/06/world-population-projected-to-reach-9-8-billion-in-2050-and-11-2-billion-in-2100-says-un/. Accessed August 2017.

64 See Mitra, S. (2006) *The Hole in the Wall*. New York. www.hole-in-the-wall.com/ abouthiwel.html. Accessed June 2017; and Talbot, D. (2012) Given Tablets But No Teachers, Ethiopian Children Teach Themselves. *MIT Technology Review*. www. technologyreview.com/news/506466/given-tablets-but-no-teachersethiopian-children-teach-themselves/. Accessed May, 2017. See also UNESCO (2015a) *The Investment Case for Education and Equity*, p. 49. www.unicef.org/publica tions/files/Investment_Case_for_Education_and_Equity_FINAL.pdf. Accessed June 2017.

65 Arguably this is already the case and is backed by monetary bodies such as the World Bank, as is seen by the mixed educational economy in countries such as Nigeria, Ghana and Kenya. However, smaller countries and more historically socialist countries have had less deregulation of school provision.

3   Historical school case studies

Introduction

There have been a number of school buildings that provide a symbolic record of Africa's educational history. This varied built legacy shows the different ways by which the main actors involved in schools provision and educational policy enactment engaged with educational provision, specifically school design on the continent. In this chapter, a selection of case studies are presented representing the historical span of schools designed in Africa for over more than a century.

The selection of the school case studies presented reflects the author's research coverage of Anglophone African schools focusing on West and Southern Africa, with reference being made to salient case studies from other regions of Africa. The chapter is split into two sections, the historical and the contemporary school design case studies.

The historical case studies discussed from West Africa (Hope Waddell College [f. 1894], Calabar, Nigeria) and Southern Africa (Lovedale College [f. 1824], Eastern Cape, South Africa) rely on both manuscript data, more recent historical information and the author's photographic research records. More contemporary historical case studies such as the IDA-Federal Government Colleges in Nigeria, the 'DET' (Department of Education and Training) schools in South Africa and the Fry-Drew schools designed in Ghana and Nigeria are also discussed in this chapter. The missionary college case study schools discussed are supported by historical missionary archive material.

It is paradoxical, however, that the more recent school buildings discussed have the least information or archival information. Instead, much of the material for schools of this era and the later period of the 20th century relies on doctoral and post-doctoral research undertaken from the 1990s to the present day on school design in Africa.[1] These final three case study schools are from the 1990s, and show a range of schools from countries in eastern, southern, and western parts of Africa.[2] Their selection has been based on the author's post-doctoral and contemporary research on school design, and seeks to give a broad range of school design examples across sub-Saharan Africa.

52 Historical school case studies

Early school design case studies: missionary schools in Africa

The missionary involvement and input into school design on the African continent cannot be underestimated.[3] From the early days of mission and evangelisation in the mid-19th century until the era of self-rule from the 1950s, missions across Africa were responsible for providing the majority of schools at primary and secondary levels. In some parts of West and East Africa, this was supplemented by the establishing of a government school system that provided basic primary schools and an elite network of secondary schools, the latter which were focused on educating future national elites to European educational qualification levels to allow them gain admission into usually overseas training for the professions including law, engineering, medicine and entry into the colonial civil service.[4]

The older missionary schools were characterised by a few key features: the centrality of the church or chapel to the planned layout; the preferred campus system, where pupils and teachers were expected to live on campus throughout the school year; and the focus on the traditional 'three R's in education.[5]

By contrast, the colonial government colleges, which were established from the late 19th to the early 20th century across most colonially governed regions in Africa, were secular, non-denominational entities. In the case of these schools such as Achimota College (f. 1924) in Ghana or Kings College Lagos (f. 1909) in Nigeria, the central feature of the government college architecture often focused on the clock tower or other non-denominational feature related to the administrative buildings within the school campus layout. As with their missionary counterparts, the top schools were also campus-based, with students compelled to be boarders. However, as most government schools were in established towns or cities, which was often not the case with missionary schools, government-employed teachers did not all have to be housed on college campuses.

The government colleges also were more likely to have a range of subjects that spanned further than the 'three Rs'. This might often include technical and vocational subject classes. This was particularly the case in the subject teaching at second-tier government schools in which colonial educational policy sought to develop local education and expertise in vocational skills.[6] In southern African countries, such as Zimbabwe (then called Rhodesia) and South Africa, this distinction in subject teaching in schools was undertaken within a racialised perspective. This meant that 'coloured' (mixed race) educational institutions historically had vocational and technical subject streams, whilst 'black' institutions had more limited educational choice and the 'white' system focused on the traditional academic subjects in the sciences and the arts.[7]

The case study schools presented here include the missionary school Hope Waddell College, Calabar in Eastern Nigeria, founded by the Presbyterian Mission in 1895, and the aforementioned Kings College Lagos in

Western Nigeria, established by the colonial government of the then Lagos Protectorate.

Hope Waddell College, Calabar

Founded by the Scottish Presbyterian Mission in southeastern Nigeria, as a teaching college attached to the Presbyterian church in Calabar, it became the city's most prestigious school by the 1950s. The Nigerian military government nationalised the school in 1970, which ended its missionary links until the 1990s, when religious bodies and private institutions were allowed to take on the running of historic and new institutions.[8]

School layout and design

The school is laid out as a campus on a ridge overlooking the city of Calabar. The main classrooms are designed as wood framed elevated structures, with lightweight internal wooden wall partitions between classrooms and to the exterior surrounding veranda. Walls are punctuated by large wood frame windows, or shutters. The classrooms have suspended wooden floors, built onto the elevated wooden foundation piles. The ceilings also are made of wooden panels which are secured below the corrugated iron roofing sheets. Some of the ceiling panels have been replaced by fibre concrete-asbestos roofing. The external 'veranda' or balcony, which serves as the main form of circulation, encircles the entire classroom building area. The roof overhangs also provide full shading to the veranda.

CLASSROOM LAYOUT

Classrooms have been designed and remain in use in the 'traditional' classroom format. Desks and chairs are individual, and are arranged to face a front area where the teacher 'teaches' with a blackboard as the main teaching aid. Ancillary blocks include science labs, a technical workshop and the admin and library block (see figure 3.1).

ENVIRONMENTAL CONSIDERATIONS

The lightweight structure and large areas of wooden and glazed slatted windows makes these traditional classrooms easy to ventilate. There is also no thermal heat gain due to the low thermal capacity of the materials used in the construction of the classrooms. Furthermore, the airflow through and across the elevated classroom stilt foundations ensures that underfloor airflow provides further cooling to the classrooms. Also, the large windows ensure that all classrooms have adequate daylighting, this would have been crucial before the introduction of regular power supply in Calabar in the early 20th century.

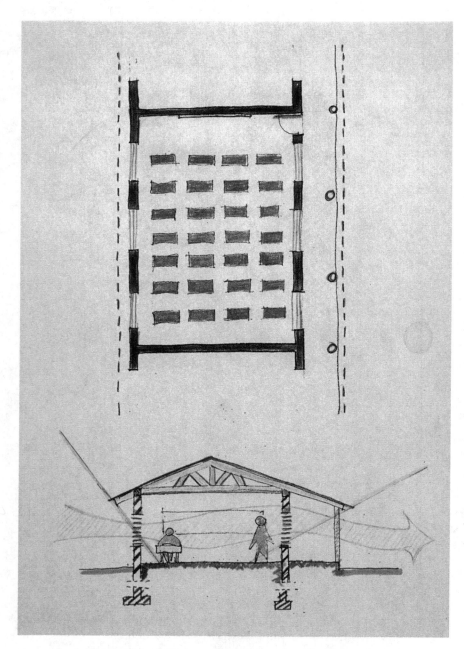

Figure 3.1 Typical School Plan
Author's drawing

CONTEMPORARY ISSUES

Between the 1970s–1980s, there was considerable state government under-funding of former missionary schools such as Hope Waddell College, as education priorities focused on delivering universal primary education to all Nigerians and the funding of secondary education stalled.[9] From the 1990s to the present, there has been an increase in school building funding from the state and private sources including the Presbyterian Church with tacit approval from national to international levels.

This has been as a direct result of the stronger neoliberal economic climate fostered by the World Bank and other funders of international education policy, from the mid-1980s, as set out in their Education In Africa Report.[10] This has encouraged governments in the emerging world to share and in some cases reduce educational provision including school building to institutions such as churches which have had historic links to communities, private enterprises, third sector organisations and charities that have more recently developed local community links.

The regulatory role that governments are expected to take on in order to ensure the standard of this newly devolved educational landscape, however, has had varied results. This is because that in today's climate, schools have to meet the higher standards of the new breed of private and third-sector institutions in educational attainment and also built infrastructure provision.

Lovedale College, Eastern Cape, South Africa

Established by the Presbyterian Mission in the Eastern Cape Province, South Africa, the College evolved from the missionary station of the same name founded by the Presbyterian missionaries in the mid-18th century and named Lovedale after a prominent missionary forebear, the Reverend Love. The college initially commenced as a missionary school attached to the other missionary buildings and infrastructure built on the initial mission 'compound'. The original school buildings were built using local materials and thatch. In later years and with further missionary investment, the school blocks were eventually built with local bricks. This led to the creation of the Lovedale campus with the mission church at its centre (see figure 3.2) and classrooms spread across the site.[11]

School layout and design

In keeping with the grant-aid school requirements of the Cape Colony at the time, schools were designed to the traditional classroom block style. Rows of three to four classrooms were designed to have veranda access, with windows and opening on adjacent sides to allow for airflow. Initial building materials were thatch, wattle and daub, but with the setting up of a brick factory and teaching of building skills, classrooms were built of more durable brick with operable wooden windows. As with other schools elsewhere in the British colonies, Lovedale had annual inspections by the

Figure 3.2 Lovedale College, Eastern Cape, South Africa
Courtesy: William Martinsen, South Africa

Historical school case studies   57

Cape Education Department which assessed the school building and also academic performance. Lovedale and other missionary colleges had part funding from the government, as well as missionary funding for buildings teachers and infrastructure until the stoppage of funding for education to non-white schools by the Nationalist government in South Africa in 1955.

CONTEMPORARY ISSUES

When closed by the nationalist regime in South Africa, Lovedale College became a teacher training institution for the 'bantu' reserve of Ciskei. Since the advent of democratic rule in 1994 of South Africa, all South African schools are now multi-racial in intake. Lovedale Mission now operates from three campuses and has become a technical and vocational college for Ciskei, which is part of the Transkei region of the Eastern Cape. The historic Lovedale College building has become part of the University of Fort Hare.[12]

Kings College, Lagos

Founded in 1907 by the Education Department in the then Lagos Protectorate, Kings College became the premier colonial government-run school in Nigeria. Situated near what had been the central business district area of Lagos and close to both the protectorate's administrative buildings and the government residential area, it has retained its prime position on Lagos Island to the present day. A number of historic missionary colleges predate Kings College's founding, such as CMS (Anglican) Grammar School (f. 1859) and St Gregory's (Catholic) College (f. 1928); most have now moved location from Lagos Island to new campuses on the mainland.[13]

School layout and design

Kings College is located on approximately one acre of prime land in central Lagos. Its original buildings are single-storey elevated classroom blocks with veranda access (see figure 3.3). In building materials and layout, they are similar to the Hope Waddell case study classrooms. The original Kings College classrooms were designed as elevated lightweight wooden classroom blocks. Walls and floors are of wooden construction, whilst large wood framed casement windows on opposite sides of the classroom spaces allow for adequate cross-ventilation. Lightweight wooden ceiling panels are overhead, and classrooms have been fitted with ceiling fans. The roofing material for all the school blocks was historically of fibre-concrete asbestos roofing.

Further classroom and accommodation block additions to the school estate were built in the 1950s. They were constructed using concrete beam and post construction with breeze-blocks used for infill walls. Windows remained generously designed into the newer classroom blocks ensuring that adequate daylighting in classrooms was achieved.

Figure 3.3 Kings College, Lagos, Nigeria
Author's own image

CONTEMPORARY ISSUES

The colonial government's investment and funding of Kings College is likely to have contributed to Kings College's continued maintenance of its premier academic status and retention of its land and premises at its prime location on Lagos Island. Few of its contemporaneously established schools such as those mentioned previously have managed to retain their central Lagos sites, most having moved away from the Lagos Island business district to the Lagos mainland. This is in part due to its colonial history and also to its well-heeled alumnae who are some of the most prominent citizens of Nigeria. Thus, despite the high land value of the mini campus, there is no real temptation for college administrators to 'take the money' and relocate the school elsewhere, as its location and buildings are symbolic of the status and power of arguably the country's top government school.

Post-WW2 school building design

This design of schools in keeping with colonial and missionary styles continued until well into the post-WW2 era as British colonial rule continued across its former colonies up until the granting of self-rule for most African dependencies from the late 1950s through until the end of the 1960s.

From the late 1950s, however, in West Africa a new era of investment in education began. Presumably with the foreknowledge that the end of

Historical school case studies 59

colonial rule in this part of Africa was imminent and the clamour for higher education expressed by indigenous elites, the colonial governments commissioned a number of reports on higher education provision in Africa.[14] This led to the establishment of affiliated Higher Colleges in Lagos and Ibadan, Accra and Sierra Leone. At primary and secondary levels, the political and local pressure for education resulted in free universal education programmes in Eastern and Western Nigeria, with schools being built by a number of 'Home Town Development Unions'.

In contrast in the Gold Coast (now Ghana) the retiring Colonial Government established two national school building programmes, which both built new government schools, at primary and secondary technical level, but also funded the improvement and extension of existing schools.[15] Unlike the self-help infrastructure construction pursued in the Nigerian free education programmes, the Gold Coast building programmes were nationally funded.

This enabled Gold Coast Colonial Welfare Development funds for education to be used for the new government schools built and upgrading of existing school infrastructure.[16] Thus some new government schools were built to the designs of architects in the colonial Public Works Department. Also British architects such as Maxwell Fry and Jane Drew, James Cubitt and others were involved in the expansion of existing school facilities and also the design of new schools, such as Prempeh College, Kumasi and Technical Secondary School Takoradi.

Adisadel College extension, Cape Coast, Ghana

The first case study from this period is from Cape Coast in the then Gold Coast, and now Ghana.[17] Historically, Cape Coast was the first administrative capital of the Gold Coast, and also the first location of most of the 'mission' establishments in that region of West Africa. Adisadel College has its origins from the founding of the CMS (Anglican) mission in the then Gold Coast. The mission had an historical school and church in Cape Coast. With funding received from the Second National School Buildings Programme, it had its existing secondary school classroom facilities further expanded and developed by the British architects Maxwell Fry and Jane Drew.

School layout and design

Adisadel College was historically laid out as a missionary compound, with the chapel at its apex and classrooms and accommodation for teachers, who were often also priests, on site (see figure 3.4). The original classroom blocks were built close to the residential quarters for both staff and students. Fry and Drew's plan integrated the new classroom blocks to the existing infrastructure to form a new set of buildings, arranged on either side of the vista to the chapel.

With tropical design principles being fully pursued, the classroom blocks are oriented to attain natural cross-ventilation and optimum daylighting. Building materials used include concrete blocks and the use of brise soleil

60 *Historical school case studies*

Figure 3.4 Adisadel College, Cape Coast, Ghana
Author's own image

screens to form part of the balcony access for the one-storey classrooms and within the stairwells. Ceiling materials were originally of asbsestos concrete roofing and adsorbent ceiling panels. These have since been replaced.

CONTEMPORARY ISSUES

Adisadel College remains one of Ghana's top secondary schools. This has meant that it has been able to attract significant funding since the 2000s from its wealthy alumnae. It has therefore undergone further redevelopment since the Fry and Drew additions; however, the integration of the school campus that they achieved and also the distinctiveness of their now historic building additions remain visible in the current school campus design layout.[18]

Federal Government College, Sokoto, Nigeria

The Nigerian Unity Schools were planned in the early 1960s by the Nigerian government, with funding received from the International Development Agency (IDA), a wing of the International Bank for Reconstruction and Development (IBRD), a precursor to the World Bank.[19]

The post-independence Nigerian government, having had a significant level of past support with the development of educational facilities in the colonial

Historical school case studies   61

era, brokered a deal with the IDA for the funding of the development of a number of demonstration schools later to become called Unity Colleges, which were to showcase the new education pedagogy. This new approach to education had been discussed at the UN/UNESCO-sponsored African education summit held in 2000 at the World Education Forum in Dakar.[20]

Conceived of between 1964–1965, the schools were to be designed and overseen by the Nigerian firm Alex Ekwueme and Associates with the involvement of UNESCO- commissioned school design consultants.[21] The British architectural consultants Robert Matthew Johnson and Marshall Associates (RMJM) acted as advisers and consultants to the project.[22]

For sub-Saharan Africa, this was an early case of collaboration between indigenous architects and international counterparts. Alex Ekwueme, founding member of the firm, had like other architects of his generation been trained in the UK, and would therefore have had exposure to the 'tropical' architecture training taking place not only at the Architectural Association but at schools such as Liverpool and Manchester, which as port cities with global links had schools of architecture with a significant enrolment of international students.[23]

With the funding and design team in place, the first school was to be built in the town of Okposi in the Eastern Region of Nigeria in 1966. This unfortunately coincided with Nigeria's descent into the three-year Biafra-Nigerian civil war, with the Delta region where the school was to be located being particularly involved in the hostilities. Thus, despite the foundations and initial building work having commenced prior to the civil war, the initial school project was mothballed and the first school was built in a different part of the Delta region in the town of Warri and opened in 1970.[24]

In 1966, when the Unity Schools programme had initially been planned to be inaugurated, the country of Nigeria had been politically devolved into twelve autonomously governed States as a result of the coup d'etat that preceded the civil war. With this twelve-state setup, a unity school was planned to be built each of the twelve states. Also included as 'honorary' demonstration Unity Schools were the two top former colonial government schools, Kings and Queens Colleges, Lagos.[25]

The initial Unity Schools were designed to be co-educational secondary boarding schools. By the early 1970s, however, each of the twelve states also had a single-sex girls boarding school built in addition to the already established co-educational boarding schools. The schools also came to be called Federal Government Colleges and Federal Government Girls' Colleges, or "Unity" schools. This could be viewed as a politically symbolic move of the postwar federal military government to use its centralised educational funds directly for the development and running of these institutions across post-civil war Nigeria, as a demonstration of the country's post-civil war 'unity' in education.[26]

There were originally 24 Unity Schools that were planned and built, which including the two honorary Lagos schools made a total of 26. All schools were designed to run the full complement of secondary education classes;

62 Historical school case studies

from Form 1–5, usually with three streams for each year, and including a lower and upper sixth form stream. Entrance to the school was by a national examination that selected students on merit and on state representation.

All new schools were designed on government-acquired land. However, a few schools were built on temporary sites, which in some cases eventually became permanent. The schools were designed as single-storey, ground floor only, groups of classrooms, arranged around small courtyards. There was also a larger "assembly hall" building, and further single-storey administration areas including staff rooms, the library and book store. Further single-storey wings comprised science, technical drawing and fine arts and domestic science classrooms.

Prime consideration was taken to accommodate orientation for maximum cross-ventilation to occur. Also, classrooms had significant window openings on adjacent walls to allow airflow across the room, and also to ensure there was sufficient luminance for the 2% daylight factor to be achieved. Their similarity in layout and design to the earlier Fry and Drew-inspired Ghanaian schools, designed two decades earlier, can clearly be seen.

The classrooms themselves remained designed primarily for traditional teaching to take place – teacher in front and students in serried ranks facing the teacher. Science laboratory blocks were equipped with storerooms for chemicals and equipment and offices for teachers, to the UNESCO education specifications. Other ancillary administrative functions including staff rooms, the bursars and head teachers' office were designed and provided for, as was the library block, which being pre-personal computing, solely accommodated both textbooks and borrowable books and reading space for students, who as boarders could use the library for homework in the evenings.

The boarding house buildings were also generally single-storey buildings with ablution facilities built east-west, as opposed to the boarding blocks, which again were laid out to allow for maximum natural ventilation. The design and placement of fenestration, in this case, worked with the standard metal frame bunk bed accommodation for junior students. Sixth form students were allowed single beds. The architects, Ekwueme and Associates[27], retained the contract to design and run the contracts for the construction of all the original 24 Unity Schools across Nigeria, the plan layout and design for all schools remained essentially the same, with some adaptations for site location.

School layout and design

Federal Government College, Sokoto, was the second Unity School to be inaugurated, in 1968. Being located in the northern Nigerian climatic zone characterised by high temperatures and low humidity for much of the year, classrooms were designed around courtyards to allow for shade and cooling. This design layout also helps to protect from the 'Harmattan' winds from the Sahara Desert (see figure 3.5).

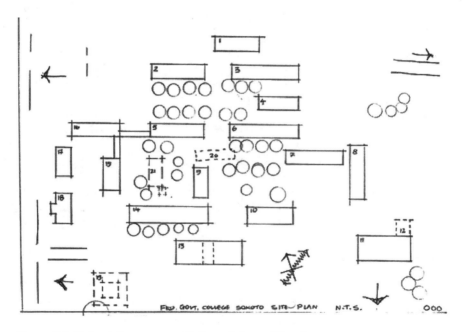

Figure 3.5 Federal Government College, Sokoto, Nigeria
Author's own image

64 Historical school case studies

In terms of construction, Federal Government College, Sokoto, like other Unity Schools, was designed and built to conventional standards. This resulted in the main classrooms being designed as single-storey three-classroom structures.

The classrooms also have operable windows on one wall and on the adjacent high clerestory windows and windows with limited operable areas. This was to enable classrooms to deal with high levels of glare in the semi desert climate but also comply with the 2% daylight factor recommendation required for reading and performing other classroom tasks using natural daylight.

CONTEMPORARY ISSUES

With the collapse of the Nigerian economy from the mid-1980s onwards, and also the wholesale revision of the educational curriculum and the introduction of a neoliberal approach to education, a number of privately funded schools were established from this period onwards whose aims and objectives, though regulated by the Federal Ministry of Education, are explicit to their target fee-paying students and whose selection criteria are school determined. As a contrast, the Unity Schools remain in existence but are poorly funded by the federal government, and consequently are no longer the schools of choice for the middle classes.

The mid-20th century post-independence period, from the late 1950s through to the early 1970s, proved the busiest decades in relation to the design and production of schools built to UNESCO design advice and tropical modernist architectural design. Amongst the schools which were significant during this period in Nigeria included Godwin and Hopwood's Baptist Academy, Lagos, c. 1967.[28] This was designed for the Baptist Church, which moved out of central Lagos to the mainland in the early 1960s and had the new Baptist Academy designed in its place.

The Ansar Ud Deen Primary school in Lagos was also designed in this period by the Architect's Co-Partnership (ACP), to a strict budget and with innovative 'flap' windows. Fry and Drew's schools built as part of the Second National School Building Programme in Ghana, including Prempeh College, Kumasi; Mawuli School Ho; and Cubitt's Technical School, Takoradi are also significant examples of educational architecture of the period.

Post 1960s – 20th century school design across Africa

The majority of African countries rapidly built and expanded their existing education infrastructure with the promotion of national expanded education policies, supported by UNESCO and the IBRD-World Bank loans during

Historical school case studies 65

the 1960s post-independence era until the global economic downturn at the aftermath of oil crises in the 1970s.

A few small, well-resourced countries, such as Botswana and Gabon, were most able to build a significant and extensive primary and secondary school network during this period.[29] Even larger, more diverse and poorer countries were at least able to build a significant set of basic schools and classrooms for children in an era of significant international investment and support for development through both bilateral loans and international aid via agencies such as UNESCO via the IBRD. Other philanthropic organisations, such as the Aga Khan foundation in East Africa, were amongst large philanthropic agencies and organisations who helped fund school building.[30]

In the 1960s, even in war-torn Congo during the 'Katanga emergency' and subsequent governance crises, the UN mandate brought into govern the country also had a school building programme, led by the Italian architect and education consultant Eugene Palumbo.[31] In Nigeria, despite being the theatre of a bloody civil war, the country's finances from its oil boom ensured that the universal primary education plan resulted in a significant increase in primary schools and classrooms built across the country to support the policy.[32] In French West Africa, education and schools remained closely linked to the French education system, and school design consultants funded both by UNESCO and Franco-European aid were involved in designing and building a number of prototype educational buildings across countries such as Mali, Senegal and Cameroon.[33]

Two other unique school planning and building systems emerged during this period. The first was the Tanzanian *Ujaama* development philosophy-inspired school movement. Promoted by Tanzania's first president Julius Nyerere, communities in rural and urban areas were encouraged to build and maintain schools using self-help or *Ujaama* principles.[34] There had also been the help of Scandinavian architects in the design of model schools in newly planned towns such as Kibaha by the architects Christoffersen and Hyalbye.[35] This policy continued until the collapse of the Tanzanian economy in the 1980s as commodity prices bankrupted the country and support for developing country members of the non-aligned movement waned with the end of the cold war and with it the funding the country had received from Eastern Europe.

The second was the emergence of the separate education system put in place by the post-WW2 Nationalist government in South Africa. The Bantu Education act of 1952 essentially ended the government assistance and funding for the construction of new schools for South Africa's African population by missionaries and other non-government charities and institutions. This was two decades prior to the 'apartheid' – or separate but equal – education legislation enacted in 1976, which sought to put in place a different curriculum for African schools which was to be taught in Afrikaans.[36]

From the 1950s onwards, the South African government constructed schools of generic plans and with different facilities for its designated racial groups. The 'African' schools called the Department of Education and Training (DET) schools were characterised in design by single-banked classroom blocks with administration units, and limited ancillary teaching classrooms for science, technology or vocational subjects.[37] These school blocks were built to South Africa's Building Research Institute's (CSIR) design standards,[38] which in turn sought to comply with UNESCO and other international organisation standards for classroom design, as evidenced by the building notes and guidance published at the time. South African architectural firms such as Stauch Vorster were involved in the design and development of these schools.[39]

Different design layouts and standards were issued by the South African Nationalist government at provincial level for schools designed for the country's different designated racial groups. By the final enactment of the full 'apartheid' education policy in 1976, which promulgated Afrikaans language-only teaching schools, African townships had become fortified with high fencing and barbed wire as they became sites of demonstration and defiance by the black population and sympathisers in townships across South Africa who protested against this and other nationalist segregationist education policies (see figure 3.6).[40]

Figure 3.6 Typical 'DET' School, Langa, South Africa
Author's own image

The private school landscape

In the immediate postwar era, organisations such as UNESCO, aid agencies and various bilateral aid donor countries articulated the global support across developed nations to promote the expansion of school provision and educational attainment across the 'third' world. This was achieved by support for the implementation of universal school building standards, and creation of education policies to ensure that the global goal; as 'education for all' would be achieved by the 1970s.[41] Early postwar educational aid had focused on the funding of new nation-states' expansion of their existing school infrastructure and teaching programmes. This resulted in the funding of teacher training programmes and also the creation of the UNESCO school building division with branches in Asia, Latin America and Africa, which advised on regional school design and classroom standards.[42]

By the late 1970s, however, it became clear that the goal of universal free basic education would not be met. The effects of the global oil crisis and slump in commodity prices adversely affected most African states. This is because the majority of African states are dependent on commodities such as copper, bauxite and aluminium, or agricultural products such as cocoa, tea or coffee, as their prime sources of income. The projected incomes from these commodities were often used to negotiate loans in the 1960s and early 1970s. This meant that with the collapse of these commodity prices, and the overall decline in economies across the world with the oil price hike and the global economic crisis which ensued, African countries often had no choice but to default on their loans.

As loan repayments were re-negotiated with the help of the World Bank and other international institutions, African and other defaulting countries had to commit to 'structural adjustment policies', which curtailed investment in social infrastructure including schools. This tied in with the 1980s neoliberal view on economic policy, as advocated by institutions such as the IMF, which also demanded less spending on social infrastructure and a new 'sweat equity' model in which school building was devolved to local communities with government investment being focused on teacher education and curriculum development. The right to a free education was also reframed to expect community and parental contribution to school costs or fees.[43]

Despite there being a small cohort of private schools, prior to this neoliberal change from the late 1970s onwards, the effective deregulation of the 'free' school provision model to a 'paid for' model, albeit with minimal public contribution to fees, can be traced to this era.

During the early 1960s, Africa's post-independence era, a number of early elite private educational institutions were established. The Ibadan International School (see figure 3.7) for example was founded as an institution for the children of expatriate and Nigerian academic staff associated with the newly founded University of Ibadan and the University College Hospital in the same city.[44]

Figure 3.7 International School, Ibadan, Nigeria
Author's own image

The school was designed by the British architectural firm Design Group and followed the principles of tropical design in its classroom orientation and use of modern materials which best responded to the tropical climate.[45] Significant to its design was the open air refectory that demonstrated that it was possible to conduct social activities such as dining, which required shelter in a transitional pavilion style 'indoor-outdoor' space which did not require full enclosure (and therefore mechanical cooling), something more typical of such communal spaces in the tropical warm humid climate of Ibadan.

In East Africa, the Aga Khan Development Network (AKDN) has also been involved in supporting education through its schools for more than four decades. The first Aga Khan School in Africa was founded c. 1905 in Zanzibar (now part of Tanzania). Kenya's first school was founded in Mombasa, the Aga Khan Academy, in 1918, whilst a Nairobi school was opened in 1970. There are also schools in Uganda initially founded in the early 1930s[46] Funded by the Aga Khan foundation, these schools combine fee-paying access to better-off families, with philanthropy to allow poorer students access to an international education. The school design and infrastructure of these schools distinguished them from the public government schools that dominated education provision in East Africa. Despite not overtly proselytising the Shi'a religious identity of the foundation, all Aga Khan schools are characterised by well-designed campus layouts which focus on the educational community the schools seek to promote (see figure 3.8).[47]

Historical school case studies 69

Figure 3.8 Aga Khan Academy, Mombasa, Kenya
Courtesy Aga Khan Development Network

Finally, in the late 19th century in what had been British-ruled Southern Africa, a small number of elite schools that operated to traditional English public school standards, and had been founded to educate the sons of the African settler elites. Differing from the premier government and missionary colleges established in the same era in West and East Africa, these Southern African colleges were more closely modelled on English public schools.[48] Often these Southern African colleges were initially set up to train the offspring of missionaries and clergy in Southern Africa. These schools and colleges were generally located in designated white residential areas; thus as the segregation and stratification of Southern African society occurred, the schools soon became open to the white elite families with less connection to the clergy. The segregated location of the schools and the socio-political situation in Southern Africa meant these schools were rarely open to non-white students.

Examples include Diocesan College, Cape Town; St John's College, Johannesburg; and Michaelhouse, Pietermaritzburg, all of which are Anglican-founded colleges. Also Waterford College, Mbabane, Swaziland founded in 1963 by Michael Stern (1922–2002) and Kenya's Hillcrest School, founded in 1963.[49] The Anglican-founded colleges in particular are characterised by their collegiate campus layout often directly translated from the architecture

70   Historical school case studies

of the 19th century English public school fused with the Oxbridge 'quad'. All the private schools mentioned have residential boarding amenities, and have a focus on traditional 'academic subjects'. Many of the older Anglican-founded colleges have links to Oxbridge and other top UK universities, which remains the destination of many of their most academically able students.[50]

A century of school planning and design . . .

Africa's schools have had an historic legacy, lasting more than a century. In former British colonies particularly, the similarities of schools – in physical layout, planning design and in taught curriculum to the 'home' or British education system – have been very close, and remain so. Classroom design in particular remains closely aligned to classroom design standards as set out as 'norms' by missionary and colonial government school providers in former British colonies in the years prior to WW2. After the war, these standards were consolidated further by the UNESCO school building programme guidelines. These guidelines combined consultancy advice from the British Overseas Building Research stations, and also American school design research guidelines, both organisations benefiting from increases in tropical research on account of army and navy residence during WW2 in the tropics.[51]

As this period coincided with the most significant investment global spending and funding of schools at primary and secondary levels, a significant proportion of African primary and secondary schools were built to these standards. The relative quality of construction has meant these classrooms and schools have set the standard for school design in much of Africa.

Since the mood changed in the 1970s from one of optimistic funding to a time of austerity with the collapse of commodity prices and limited international lending or funding of post-1970s schools, it is unsurprising that the quality and design of Africa's school infrastructure has not improved significantly since this period. Nigeria's mass Universal Primary Education project exemplifies this as the poor funding and planning of the exercise resulted in badly constructed buildings with few facilities that barely responded to the schooling needs of the communities in which they were located.[52] In East Africa also, Nyerere's *Ujaama* schools failed to survive the collapse of the Tanzanian economy by the early 1980s.[53]

Paradoxically, South Africa's education system possibly proved the most robust in school design and delivery over this period as the Nationalist Party's separate education policies ensured that funds were invested into the construction of 'model' schools for each of the separate school systems. The adoption of 'scientific' methods to prove these schools' appropriateness for their environment, and in some cases dubious cultural contexts,[54] demonstrates how school construction can be achieved for politicised moral purposes for a discredited apartheid education system.

Similarly, the growing number of private school systems in Africa did, by virtue of the expansion of neoliberal economic policies, begun to take a central place in education policy and design. Whilst the exclusive elite schools remain accessible only to an international affluent group of families from Africa and elsewhere, various other forms of private schools are both helping contribute to the reconsideration of educational design provision in Africa (such as the Aga Khan academies), and also do give access via scholarships to poorer Africans. This has become an ever-growing phenomenon in contemporary school design and planning discussed in Chapter 4.

At the other end of the spectrum, however, are the small private schools run from residential houses in formal and informal areas which offer lower class sizes and often more resources than the overcrowded government schools, where they are in existence. These private schools cater for a poorer segment of Africans, mainly in urban areas who can effectively choose between these two forms of school provision, particularly at nursery to junior secondary (age 14 or 8th–10th grade) education.[55]

At senior secondary school level, few of these 'private' schools exist. Reasons for their absence at this level is that there is more regulation of the senior secondary school sector at national government level. This means that higher standards of infrastructure (school and classroom) design and provision, better staff qualifications and more scrutiny of national test results are undertaken. Also, as the development statistics show that few African children go on to post-basic or junior secondary school education. Thus, there is less incentive by non-specialist private entrepreneurs to set up small private senior secondary schools for which there is more investment required for a much more limited pupil demand for.

Conclusions

School design history in Africa has had a varied and regionally different cultural history across the continent. There have been, however, clear commonalities that point to similar threads and themes in the spread and development of schools. These threads are closely related to the historical missionary- and government-initiated origins of Western education in Africa. The socio-economic and political events of colonial and world history have also had a significant role in shaping African education, both in terms of its content and delivery, and also the infrastructure of education. The mid-19th century basic origins of the missionary classrooms had, by the end of the 20th century, transformed to the full education campus designs of the Aga Khan schools in East Africa and various government-funded school schemes designed to varying standards across the continent.

School policy and provision has turned full circle as private and missionary organisations that were fundamental to establishing Western education systems in Africa, as elsewhere outside of Europe, have now returned to this role. Furthermore, few of today's governments in the emerging world have

72   Historical school case studies

the financial resources, political strength or will to deliver the quality or level of education that the continent requires. Multinational organisations, which had originally supported mainly government education policies have since the later decades of the 20th century, worked in collaboration with various private and other non-governmental organisations (NGOs) to help achieve the recently promoted Sustainable Development Goals, of which access to basic education remains prominent on the list.[56]

There has been a limited response in African school and classroom design in particular to the change in the norms and standards set out since the mid-20th century as the policy focus changed from school design in the 1960s to teacher training, education policy and metrics from the 1970s. School design standards in particular remained determined by the World Bank-supported UNESCO school building programme standards that had involved international teams of experts determining and documenting school standards across the globe.[57] Arguably also for much of Africa, access to basic, first-level education required only the most fundamental standards of classroom school equipment. Thus, the debates around child-centred learning that were aired and implemented in demonstration classrooms at teacher training colleges rarely transformed traditional classroom layouts in poorer urban and rural settings.[58]

South Africa's new post-apartheid education system and associated schools as have emerged from the late 1990s have been one of few exceptions to the traditional school design approach discussed. The combined challenges of new technology, materials and learning methods, however, are now significantly changing 21st century schools, which is the subject of Chapter 4. It is clear also that there is a growing divide between the well-resourced private school sector and a struggling state school sector in the delivery of schools or learning spaces – the infrastructure in which this 21st century learning takes place.

The contemporary African school case studies presented in Chapter 5 enable an examination of how South African and other schools have been able to respond to challenges of change in education provision. This is happening at national level, where schools and learning spaces are being built by African states and with the help of international NGOs in areas with lacking educational infrastructure. The strategy remains to increase the construction and subsequent operation of schools in African countries that are yet to achieve the UN Sustainable Development Goal 4, which calls for universal access to education within the next decade. Added to this are the contributions of the private education entrepreneurs, who, as discussed earlier in this chapter, operate in Africa different levels; from the house conversion schools to the well-resourced educational campus institutions such as the Aga Khan academies. Furthermore, the re-emergence of religious-affiliation educational establishments in countries such as Nigeria have also contributed to the new African education landscape. Chapter 6 considers what the next directions

Historical school case studies 73

might be for school design in Africa to respond to the contemporary issues and policy targets of present-day international education bodies. To do this successfully it will be important to take into account this nearly 200-year historical engagement with Western education on the continent and learn these lessons from case studies of past school design which this chapter has sought to present.

Notes

1 See Uduku, O. (1993b) *Factors Affecting School Design in Nigeria.* PhD Thesis, University of Cambridge; Uduku, O. (1993a) *Factors Affecting School Design in Ghana.* Report, Centre for African Studies, University of Cambridge; Uduku, O. (1994a) *Factors Affecting School Design in South Africa.* Report, Centre for African Studies, University of Cambridge.
2 Ibid.
3 For a comprehensive view of this from the Anglophone West African perspective, the following authors are important: Fafunwa, B. (1974) *History of Education in Nigeria.* London: Allen and Unwin, Ayandele, E. A. (1966) *The Missionary Impact on Modern Nigeria 1842–1914: A Political and Social Analysis.* London: Longman Green and Co., Adesina, S. and Ogunsaju S. (eds.) (1984) *Secondary Education in Nigeria.* Ile-Ife: University of Ife Press, and Igwe, S. O. (1986) *Education in Eastern Nigeria 1847–1975.* London: Evans.
4 See Ochiagha, T. (2015) *Achebe and Friends at Umuahia.* London: James Currey, Introduction; Uduku (1993b); and Fafunwa (1974).
5 Uduku, O. (2000) The Colonial Face of Educational Space. In L. Lokko (ed.), *White Papers Black Marks.* London: Athlone Press, pp. 44–65.
6 See Note 4.
7 Uduku, O. (1994b) *Schools in Africa: Perspectives on a Viable Physical Ideal.* Centre for African Studies Cape Town Seminar Semester 2, 1994, African Studies Centre, Robinson College. Cambridge: University of Cambridge. Kallaway, P. (1996) Policy Challenges for Education in the New South Africa: The Case for School Feeding in the Context of Social and Economic Reconstruction. *Transformation*, 31, pp. 1–24; and Christopher, A. J. (1986) *Atlas of Apartheid.* London: Routledge.
8 See Uduku (1993b), and Igwe (1986).
9 Hope Waddell College had also closed down during the 1966–1970 Nigerian-Biafran civil war, and re-opened as a government-funded college, with Presbyterian links cut until the 1990s.
10 World Bank (1988) *Education in Africa Report.* Washington, DC: World Bank.
11 Lovedale Missionary Institution (1904) *Report for Lovedale Missionary Institution 1903.* Alice, Eastern Cape, South Africa: Lovedale Press.
12 Williams, D. (2001) *A History of the University College of Fort Hare South Africa: The 1950s the Waiting Years.* Ontario: The Edwin Mellen Press.
13 Uduku (1993b).
14 For West Africa, this was the Asquith Commission (1945) which initially suggested one university college for West Africa, at Ibadan; this was challenged and the Elliot Commission sanctioned the establishment of the University of Ghana, and later on Kumasi. In East Africa, this was the 1937 commissioned De la Warr report. For more see Hussey, E. R. J. (1945) Higher Education in West Africa. *Journal of African Affairs*, 44(177), pp. 165–170; and Ashby, E. (1965) A Contribution to the Dialogue on African Universities. *Higher Education Quarterly*, 20(1), pp. 70–89, a contribution to the Dialogue on African Universities.

74 Historical school case studies

15 For references to Ghana's School Building Programmes, see Jackson, I. and Holland, J. (2014) *The Architecture of Maxwell Fry and Jane Drew*. London: Routledge; and also Le Roux, H. (2004) The Post-colonial Architecture of Ghana and Nigeria. *Architectural History*, 47, pp. 361–392.

16 Note 15, and for Nigeria see Ayandele (1966); and Fafunwa (1974), and the British National Archives Files on Colonial Welfare Development funding related to Education funding in West Africa.

17 Uduku (1993a).

18 Uduku, O. (2016) The UNESCO-IDA School Building Programme in Africa: The Nigeria 'Unity' Schools, Chapter 14. In J. Willis and K. Darien-Smith (eds.), *Designing Schools, Space, Place and Pedagogy*. London: Taylor and Francis, pp. 175–187.

19 Sewell, J. P. (1975) Regeneration? Chapter 5. In *UNESCO and World Politics*. Princeton, NJ: Princeton University Press, pp. 199–278. http://unesdoc.unesco.org/images/0012/001211/121117e.pdf.

20 See http://unesdoc.unesco.org/images/0012/001211/121117e.pdf. Accessed August 2017.

21 UNESCO was one of the initial UN bodies that were set up in the late 1940s. A key part of its remit has been to deliver basic education globally as part of the initial UN declaration. Thus, UNESCO was involved directly in promoting, supporting and funding mass education worldwide.

22 See Canmore [Scottish] National Record of the Historic Environment Archive collection. Reference no. 561 357/2. Category All other, Robert Matthew Johnson-Marshall and Partners Collection c. 1965–1986. http://canmore.org.uk/collection/1178029. Accessed April 2018; Glendinning, M. (2008) *Modern Architect: The Life and Times of Robert Matthew*. London: RIBA, Chapter 11, p. 366.

23 Local West African architects from Ghana and Nigeria in particular gained early entry into regional architectural practice, supported by the national governments of the time. Educational infrastructure proved an early area of collaboration for a number of these actors.

24 See Uduku (2016) and Uduku (1993b).

25 Ibid., see also Adekunle J. (2002) Nationalism Ethnicity and National Integration: An Analysis of Political History, in A. Oyebade (ed.), *The Transformation of Nigeria, Essays in Honour of Toyin Falola*. Trenton, NJ: Africa World Press, pp. 426–429.

26 See Forsyth, F. (1969) *The Biafra Story*. London: Harmondsworth Penguin; Achebe, C. (2012) *There Was a Country*. London: Penguin; and Falola, T. and Ezekwem, O. (eds.) (2016) *Writing the Nigeria-Biafra Civil War*. London: James Currey.

27 The founder Alex Ekwueme (1929–2017), went on to become vice president of Nigeria between 1979 and 1983.

28 Front cover of book shows Baptist Academy, Lagos (Godwin and Hopwood, c. 1967).

29 See UNDP Report (2016) *Country Profiles for Botswana*. http://hdr.undp.org/en/countries/profiles/BWA; and Gabon http://hdr.undp.org/en/countries/profiles/GAB respectively. Both Accessed August 2017.

30 See Aga Khan foundation website Education Overview, www.akdn.org/our-agencies/aga-khan-foundation/education/education-overview. Accessed August, 2017.

31 De Raedt, K. and Lagae, J. (2014) Building for L'Authencite, Architect Eugene Palumbo in Mobuto's Congo. *Journal of Architectural Education*, 68(2), pp. 178–189.

32 De Raedt, K. (2014) Between True Believers' and Operational Experts: UNESCO Architects and School Building in Post Colonial Africa. *Journal of Architecture*, 19(1), pp. 19–42.

Historical school case studies 75

33 De Raedt, K. (2013) Shifting Conditions, Frameworks and Approaches: The Work of KPDV in Postcolonial Africa. *ABE Journal*, 4. http://journals.openedition.org/abe/566?lang=en.
34 *Forms of Freedom: African Independence and Nordic Models*, Exhibition on Scandinavian architecture and aid in East Africa, National Museum Nairobi, in collaboration with the National Museum of Art Oslo, November 2016–January 2017.
35 Ibid.
36 Kallaway, P. (ed.) (2002) *The History of Education Under Apartheid 1948–1994: The Doors of Learning and Culture Shall Be Opened*. New York, NY: Peter Lang, and Uduku (1994a).
37 Ibid.
38 Uduku (1994b).
39 Ibid.; and Uduku, O. and Criticos, C. (eds.) (1994) *Learning Spaces in Africa Conference*. Durban: University of KwaZulu Natal.
40 See Kallaway (2002) and Uduku (1994a).
41 National Archives Kew, UNESCO (1961) Conference for African States on the Development of Education in Africa Addis Ababa Leading to the Outline of a Plan for African Educational Development or *Addis Ababa Declaration*.
42 For the late 1960s through to the 1970s, see National Archives Kew, UNESCO had regional school building research offices in Bangkok, Dakar and Beirut (see www.unesco.org/education/pdf/BAT0029.PDF. Accessed August 2017).
43 Psacharopoulos, G. and Woodhall, H. (1986) *Education for Development: An Analysis of Investment Choices*. New York: Oxford University Press (for the World Bank).
44 See *West Africa Builder and Architect* (1963) Vol. 5, no. 6, pp. 108–112. International School, Ibadan (Design Group) Phase 1.
45 Ibid.; Uduku, O. and Le Roux, H. (2003) *The AA in Africa Exhibition*. Exhibition, 17 January–14th February, The Architectural Association, London; Uduku, O. (2003b) Video Recorded interview with Michael Grice. London: Architectural Association.
46 Aga Khan Foundation, Schools Information. www.agakhanacademies.org/sites/default/files/AKA%20Mombasa%20brochure%202014.pdf. Accessed May 2017.
47 Ibid.
48 For the South African private-public school system see Randall, P. (1982) *Little England on the Veld: The English Private School System in South Africa*. Johannesburg, South Africa: Ravan Press.
49 See also: Hawthorne, P. (1993) *Historic Schools of South Africa*. Cape Town, South Africa: Pachyderm; Waterford Khambala webpage for History, www.waterford.sz/about/history.php; *The Guardian* (2002) Michael Stern Obituary. www.theguardian.com/news/2002/aug/01/guardianobituaries.highereducation; and also Hillcrest School, www.hillcrest.ac.ke/hillcrest-history/. All accessed in August 2017.
50 For example, David Potter, the Prince Edward College, Harare alumnus, founded the UK Technology firm Psion, whilst the Bishop's College Alumnus Mark Shuttleworth, a successful technology entrepreneur, was one of the first private individuals to travel to space.
51 See National Archives Kew, UNESCO Design guidelines, Paris, UNESCO 1966–88; Overseas Building Notes, BRE, London, 50–73, 1950–73 .
52 Uduku (1993b).
53 See Molony, T. (2015) *Nyerere, the Early Years*. London: James Currey.
54 See, for example, Van Straaten, J. F., Richards, S. J. and Lotz, F. J. (1967). *Ventilation and Thermal Considerations in School Building Design*. Pretoria: CSIR for principles of ventilation for schools in South Africa.

76 Historical school case studies

55 See also the *The Economist* (2017a, January 28) Could do better: Bridge International Academies Gets High Marks for Ambition but Its Business Model Is Still Unproven. www.economist.com/news/business/21715695-its-biggest-challenge-may-well-be-financial-bridge-international-academies-gets-high-marks. Accessed April 2018.
56 For example, the UK research council's Global Challenges Research Fund (GCRF) launched in 2016, the British Council-DFID funded Newton fund (launched 2014) and other research-aid related schemes.
57 See Glendinning (2008), and De Raedt (2014).
58 For example, see Bray, M. (1986) *New Resources for Education, Community Management and Financing of Schools in Less Developed Countries*. London: Commonwealth Secretariat.

4 African schools in the 21st century
Context and background

This chapter describes both the strategic issues that currently face African school design and planning, and also the contextual background to this. It draws on research findings on school design from the *Schools as Hubs for Development* project that was jointly funded by the University of Bristol, and the Department for International Development (DFID) as part of the EdQual Education Quality in Schools Project (EdQual 2008).[1] *Schools as Hubs for Development* had as its key aim the examination of the link of classroom and school design to improving school quality. Research findings from schools visited in the two African countries, Ghana and South Africa, surveyed for the project are referred to in the course of the chapter.

The political context and socio-cultural and economic issues which can influence school design policies and practice are also considered. The discussion and analysis which concludes the chapter is framed around three key themes:

- contemporary education policies;
- the incorporation of the United Nation's new Sustainable Development Goals, as a development of the original Millennium Development Goals; and
- the practical, physical and technical design issues that influence the creation of successful contemporary learning spaces.

Within the *contemporary education policies* theme discussion, the chapter analyses current education policies at both national and international level. It questions what effects the international communiqués and national targets have on school planning programmes. This is considered in relation to the success, or otherwise, of schools and associated educational infrastructure such as libraries and nursery classes being built at the local level. It also attempts a critical evaluation of international educational funding and aid programmes. It examines specifically their success in supporting local school planning and building programmes and the development of indigenous learning space uses and design.

The chapter also considers the role of the post millennium *Sustainable Development Goals* (SDGs) as a theme. In 2015 the United Nations (UN)

78 *African schools in the 21st century*

launched the SDGs as a continuation of the development objectives from the earlier Millennium Development Goals (MDGs). The MDGs had been initiated almost two decades earlier by the UN.[2] Both the MDGs and SDGS have had at their core the setup of global development targets in areas such as education, health and housing, for all nations to achieve.

They have been adopted following on from the MDGs (1995–2015), to SDGs (2015–2030) globally by all countries and international bodies. The earlier MDGs had achieved success in some areas, but key development goals such as universal access to basic education, and improved access by the poorest societies to sanitation and pipe-borne water, failed to be met within the 2015 MDG timeframe. The millennium SDGs can thus be seen as the UN's attempt to recalibrate the earlier SDGs to encourage the global achievement of not just the earlier development targets but also a broadening of the targets and an acknowledgement of the need to consider the sustainability issues which underpin these broader targets to be achieved by 2025.

This section particularly focuses its examination building sustainability covering the current focus on building sustainability at a physical construction design and energy level in response to the post-Rio climate protocols up to the 2014 Copenhagen meeting.[3] Also this section will examine how schools can operate within a sustainable local community or neighbourhood framework. It investigates the introduction of the school as a central structure within the contemporary community hub to be a transformative *learning space* and its role within a holistic, cyclic sustainable development context. It references relevant school design examples in existence in Africa and internationally.

The final theme that the chapter explores is the *practical-physical* and also *conceptual* design development of *Learning Spaces Design* at classroom level. Here consideration is given to how disruptions to traditional forms of learning, such as the introduction of digital learning – and with it the adoption of electronic learning devices via laptop computers, e-books and digital tablets – are influencing both the classroom spaces in which learning takes place. Also, the section critically considers how the engagement of African schools with the e-learning process has begun to show the potential to transform historical teacher-based learning pedagogies to peer-to-peer, dispersed learning networks. This theme is explored and developed further in Chapter 6, the final chapter, where the direction and development of future themes and concepts for learning in Africa and the associated *Learning Spaces* in which these might take place are examined.

Policy themes for schools

The planning policies and design of African schools have had a long and documented history. Most education policy has evolved from late 19th–20th century early missionary policies and philanthropic reports such as the early 20th century Phelps-Stokes Reports, which reported on the state of African education in West, Southern and East Africa prior to WW2.[4] These were followed by the reports of The United Nations Educational, Scientific and

African schools in the 21st century 79

Cultural Organisation (UNESCO), the International Bank for Reconstruction and Development (IBRD), the Organisation for Economic Cooperation and Development (OECD) and other third-sector organisations.[5] As these reports were being published at the end of WW2, their key aspiration and objectives were to ensure that mass literacy and education would be achievable across the world before the turn of the 21st century.

During this same time period, newly independent nations in Africa and elsewhere were also engaged in publicising their development programmes in which mass education and literacy programmes featured prominently. For these new nations, education was a development priority. The expansion of education to all citizens through the building of more primary and secondary schools and increased access to tertiary education was key to creating an educated electorate, which had been a key manifesto pledge that the fledgling democratic parties who gained power at independence were anxious to achieve.[6]

The central goal of these reports and later policies was to ensure that there was the expansion and improvement of education, particularly at basic primary to secondary level, for all citizens. This underpinned the large-scale school building programmes throughout the world in the postwar era from the late 1940s onwards. Education was seen as a way in which the world could ensure the next generation would be equipped for employment in the postwar world and also learn the importance of global histories to avoid the turmoil of the past world wars. Thus, the basic need for education is enshrined in the text of the founding United Nations Charter, and its associate organisation UNESCO was given mandate to deliver this.[7]

This positive postwar global consensus on educational goals and progress, however, changed after the global economic downturn caused by the oil crisis in the 1970s. The ambitious plans to have education available to all have remained unmet in much of the emerging world to the present day. Education policy in the West has largely succeeded in legally ensuring free access to basic education to all minors.[8] In the emerging world, great progress has been made to achieve free access to basic education in parts of Asia and Latin America. African countries, however, remain the least equipped or able to meet the past and current UN SDG educational targets of delivering basic education as a human right to all citizens.[9] There are also issues related to the quality of education being provided in African schools relating to areas such as pupil performance, curriculum relevance and teacher qualification, for example, which are beyond the scope of this book.[10]

Current educational policy varies from country to country in Africa. The change in economic policy from the non-governmental organisations (NGOs) aid and finance –organisations such as the World Bank, UNESCO, and country-backed aid organisations such as the UK's Department for Aid and International Development (DFID, formerly the Overseas Development Agency or ODA), to a neoliberal economic funding model from the 1980s onwards – has inevitably influenced educational development and growth in Africa's different countries. Earlier funded education programmes in Africa

80   *African schools in the 21st century*

focused on aid agencies supporting the construction of schools and classrooms to respond to the need for more educational infrastructure as well as increased teachers and equipment for schools.

The later NGO-supported neoliberal programmes from the 1980s focused on teacher training but switched from fully funded school building projects to 'sweat equity' schemes in which communities were encouraged to self-build classrooms and schools which were then promised governmental aid with teacher provisioning and materials. Often these schemes were unsuccessful, either because the communities were too poor and did not have the skills or wherewithal to build the new schools, or when schools were built the support, either with teaching staff or equipment, as had been promised was not forthcoming.[11]

International education policy, usually developed by UNESCO and allied organisations, such as the Commonwealth Council for Education, has from the late 1970s onwards focused on the funding of support areas in education which has involved areas such as teacher training, and the production of vocational education materials.[12]

The funding given to these areas of educational development reflected the change of policy focus from school buildings provision to other areas of education support from the late 1970s onwards. This allocation of policy funds to other areas education development also, however, resulted in the withdrawal of funding for the development and promotion of new approaches to school buildings design. At UNESCO, the effect of this funding priority switch resulted in the UNESCO school building research offices that had been established in Africa, Asia and Latin America in the 1960s being closed by the early 1980s.[13]

The World Bank, which became the major funder of educational development from the 1980s onwards, had policies that promoted a 'sweat equity' approach to schools provision. This focused on encouraging predominantly rural communities to build classrooms which would then be provided with government-funded teachers to teach and run such schools.[14] The effect this had on education and school design in Africa had limited success. Few very poor communities could afford the costs of building schools or local classrooms. Furthermore, most African national governments to this day find it difficult to send trained teachers to teach and run schools in remote rural or poor urban areas due to the lack of adequately built infrastructure such as school classrooms and ancillary facilities such as accommodation for teachers sent to these rural areas.[15]

There are regional variations in educational policy specifically as they relate to school design in Africa. West Africa has by and large continued its development of education policy as relates to school design in keeping with the legacy it inherited in the late 1950s. This had largely been developed by the Architectural Association (AA) Tropical School architects Maxwell Fry and Jane Drew, who were involved in the design of schools in the First and Second National School building programmes in the then Gold Coast (see figures 4.1 and 4.2).

Figure 4.1 Mawuli School, Ghana
Author's own image

Figure 4.2 Mawuli School, Ghana
Author's own image

82 African schools in the 21st century

Also their AA trained associates, including John Godwin and Gillian Hopwood,[16] and the Architects Co-Partnership (ACP) team comprising Leo De Syllas et al., who were all involved in designing schools in Ghana and Nigeria. James Cubitt and Kenneth Scott, were also part of the AA-trained group of architects involved in school design and also like Fry and Drew in university and college layout planning and design in both countries.[17] Most of West Africa's contemporary school design standards derive from this period. These were adopted by the UNESCO mission which advised on subsequent school design programmes, including the Unity Schools built in Nigeria from 1966 through the late 1970s.[18]

In East Africa, the Nyerere-inspired *Ujaama* schools were rural in focus and owed more to the socialist ideology of Tanzania's first prime minister, who had hoped to promote basic education across Tanzania with schools and teachers working primarily in rural areas in locally constructed schools.[19] Aside from the Tanzanian *Ujaama* schools model, however, East Africa benefited from a number of Scandinavian aid projects which extended to areas including school design. An interesting example of this programme was a set of school building projects in Zambia built and funded by the Scandinavian aid agency, 'Noraid' (see figure 4.3). The actual designs are likely to have

Figure 4.3 Noraid School Zambia Image from Forms of Freedom Exhibition, Kenya, 2016

Author's own image

African schools in the 21st century 83

been adapted from a school design scheme by the AA-trained Pat Wakely who had developed a set of school designs for Ghana in the 1960s which bear remarkable similarity to the designs produced for the Zambian schools project (see figure 4.4).[20]

The designs for these suggest a link to Pat Wakely's school building designs of the 1960s.

The collapse of commodity prices for major cash crops like coffee and the effects of the global world oil crises precipitated the collapse of many emerging economies in the 1970s. In Tanzania, these events hastened the demise of this idealistic socialist education model, which had not been nationally popular. By the early 1980s the *Ujaama* school experiment had ended, and the nation's education system required external funding to deliver basic education to all its citizens. Tanzania requested and received World Bank funding for infrastructure development including schools as part of a negotiated structural development plan. From this period onwards, schools in Tanzania have been funded and run in keeping with these World Bank education policy financial cost models which have been integrated into the national education policy.

Elsewhere in East Africa, particularly in Uganda and Kenya, greater similarities existed with West Africa's educational policies and its inherited school design framework. As with Nigeria and Ghana, much of Anglophone East

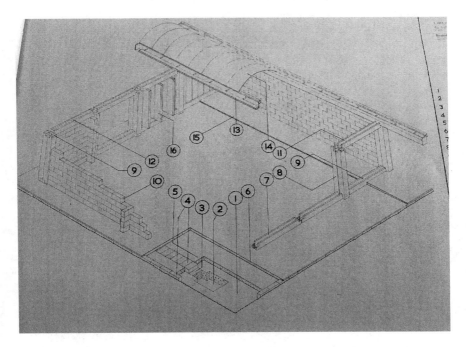

Figure 4.4 School Tema Ghana School Design Project, Pat Wakely

84   *African schools in the 21st century*

Africa had inherited a pre-independence group of schools which had been designed to missionary and colonial government standards. Post-independence educational policies, except in the case of the Tanzania *Ujaama* school policy, as discussed, largely also worked with the policies in place. However, unlike in West Africa, the transition from expatriate to indigenous architect led practices in East Africa was slower. This might have helped ensure that the status quo in relation to school design remained in place. This meant that schools designed by expatriate architects to pre-independence Colonial Welfare Department design standards remained in place for longer. This is in contrast to the involvement of indigenous architects such as the Nigerian Alex Ekwueme (1932–2017) and Ghanaian John Owuso Addo (b. 1927) in educational design schemes in West Africa from the 1960s.[21]

Education policy in Lusophone Africa lies without the remit of this book; however, a brief analysis of policy and school planning in these countries reveals that both had much closer ties to its former colonial ruler, Portugal, up until the 1970s when both Angola and Mozambique achieved self-rule. Independence for both countries, however, had been preceded and anteceded by periods of armed struggle. The design of schools and access to an education for indigenous Africans in these nations was significantly stifled by the lack of Portuguese investment in social infrastructure in its colonies.[22] Furthermore, as with Southern Africa, the long-term interests of the settler populations in Angola and Mozambique were not in support of improving the educational lot of indigenous Angolans or Mozambicans. This meant that there was limited investment in mass school building programmes in the region, and concurrently limited basic education only available for 'assimilated' Africans up until the self-rule or independence era of both nations which took place in the 1970s.[23]

Education in Francophone African countries is also not covered in detail in this text. An analysis, however, suggests that in former French African colonies, there was significant investment in primary and secondary level education; however, the colonial education system in place was closely aligned to educational policy and provision in mainland France. Two different school streams were in place, an elite stream for students expected to continue to Western formal education in France, from upper high school onwards, and a traditional stream for those who were expected to attain a basic education only. The few post-secondary institutions which were established prior to national self-rule in the 1960s were predominantly missionary founded and run (as in the case of seminaries and convents) and closely aligned, as in the case of schools with 'mother' churches and similar founding institutions in mainland France.

Senegal, in Francophone West Africa, was also the location of the regional UNESCO building research office. At its height in the 1960s and 1970s, UNESCO funded and ran school building research offices in various regions of the world in including Asia (Bangkok), Latin America (Mexico) and in Senegal. The objective of these offices was to demonstrate and new school

African schools in the 21st century   85

building techniques and work with local education planners and architects to design and deliver appropriate schools for the environmental and physical context in which these schools were located.[24]

In Southern Africa, the deleterious effects of the Nationalist government's attainment of power in South Africa in 1948 and the various polices which initially affected the funding of 'native' education, culminating in the 1976 'separate but equal' apartheid education policy, had a significant effect on school design policy, as entire planning and design standards for schools became both segregated in spatial location terms, and also in classroom design standards and provision.[25] Whilst the specific 'apartheid' education policy was a South African creation, similar de facto policies for design of separate segregated school facilities for different racial groups had been in existence in pre-independence Zimbabwe (Rhodesia), Mozambique, Angola and other South African Nationalist government sympathiser states, such as Namibia, up until each country's transition to majority rule from the 1970s to the 1990s.[26]

In contrast to these Southern African states' segregated educational planning policies of the 1970s, there were at the same time non-racial school design projects being undertaken by NGO-supported architects in parts of independent Southern African states such as Lesotho and Swaziland. This included, for example, the architect and academic Iain Low's school design and construction project in Lesotho in the 1980s.[27] This period also saw the construction of one of the first private NGO-funded institutions in Africa, the United World College (UWC) movement's Waterford College (f. 1963) in Mbabane, Swaziland.[28]

Despite Africa's improvement in economic development from the 2000s, contemporary education policies in most African countries remain inextricably linked to the World Bank, the IMF and other major financial institution lending policies. These institutions by and large remain primarily focused on neoliberal economic development models in which private schooling and local ability to 'pay' an amount towards education and by association school provision is expected. This often excludes the poorest in society, who do not have the resources to participate in an education market. This in turn means many very low income communities are excluded from educational aid as they do not fit with the criteria expected of today's aid recipients.

For school design policy and strategy this has encouraged the increased development of the 'free market' or private or running of African schools at primary and secondary level.[29] Elite-level independent schools in Africa are designed and run in the same way as their equivalent status schools are in Western countries. The fees for such schools are equivalent or only slightly lower in currency exchange rate terms to those paid in the West. Furthermore, there is the option for students to be taught within an international curriculum and sit examinations to gain entry to Oxbridge, the Ivy League colleges in the USA and other high-status international tertiary institutions.

86 *African schools in the 21st century*

At the lower income level, however, particularly in poorer urban areas, there has also been the development of 'free market' privately run schools. These are much more basic in scale, and often operate from converted private residential homes.[30] This form of private school caters to a considerably less affluent audience. This is the other side of the neoliberalisation coin. These schools, aimed at a poorer African clientele, are often slightly more expensive than state schools to attend as they charge a tuition fee, which state schools do not. These private schools can, in some circumstances, provide a successful educational outcome for some of their students, because their class numbers are significantly lower state school class sizes.[31] The objective for such schools is to provide a nursery to junior secondary education; normally two years nursery, six years primary and three years junior secondary. Their successful students would be expected to pass admissions examinations to prestigious state or privately run higher secondary school institutions. The proportion of pupils from this low-cost private education sector who complete their education is unsurprisingly significantly higher than in the state sector.

A key difference with these small private schools, their expensive private counterparts and state schools are the official regulations that schools are expected to comply with in order to pass inspection. These inspections are carried out by government-employed education inspectors, who have to certify that schools as being fit for purpose in terms of teaching quality, built environment and management. For state-owned and the more expensive private schools, this is rigorously enforced. These regulations are more difficult to enforce in the smaller low-cost private school sector, and this is done less rigorously as many are not purpose-built schools but home conversions. It is not uncommon for some low-cost private schools in very poor areas to operate under the radar without certification, as enforcement is often lax or non-existent.

In West and East Africa, this form of deregulation of educational provision has become widespread. The small private schools for the poor are becoming as successful as the elite schools in gaining enrollments. There are reasons for this. First, there is a large and growing poor population whose children are being enrolled into these cheap private institutions. The main reason for this is that the national 'state' education sector remains poorly financed and overcrowded, which means that, as discussed, a few private schools can deliver better individual results than the state sector, despite limited regulation and poor facilities. This is becoming a dilemma for educationists as the low-cost private education model suggests that the long-held principle of free, non-fee-paying education for all is being challenged by these low-fee, less regulated private alternatives, which have had backing from organisations such as the World Bank and new liberal economists.[32]

In South Africa, the devolution of school management design and planning to provincial level has resulted in different school design approaches

African schools in the 21st century 87

in different provinces. In the Western Cape, the devolution of school design to private architects has resulted in the improved design of state schools for some pupils. The Vukani School case study in Cape Town discussed in Chapter 5 provides evidence of this.[33]

Generally, South African provinces have had more autonomy to provide schools through engagement with local architects as well as the use of 'in-house' architecture teams. With the collapse of the apartheid state in the 1990s, all education departments, up to eleven in some provinces, were merged. The budget for education thus became unitary but the demand was much higher as previously excluded disadvantaged schools in townships and 'homelands' were now included in the provincial budgets. Effectively, however, as schools in formerly 'white' neighbourhoods were granted 'model C' status and encouraged to diversify their intake and enrol more disadvantaged students, they were also allowed to raise funding for school development via parent association levies, etc.

Other schools in the system however have had to rely more heavily on limited government funding and occasional commercial funding. A number of commentators such as Neville Alexander, who set up the Project for the Study of Alternative Education in South Africa (PRAESA) in Cape Town have suggested a complete overhaul of the continuing segregated, now by economics and less so by race) state school system. The PRAESA published book, *Taking South African Education Out of the Ghetto* (Smit and Hennesey, 1995), described in detail a strategy for this to take place.[34]

In West Africa, policies to enable Islamic education become integrated into state education and the continued segregation of schools have also made some inroads into increasing educational access for children who are difficult to reach for religious and cultural reasons.[35] Thus, for example, in Northern Nigeria Islamic 'madrasa' schools often are able to run in the afternoons, after the formal (primary) education teaching periods. These madrasa schools however are attached to local mosques or sometimes take place in the homes of local Muslim clerics or 'imams', and so are separate from the formal national education system which takes place in government-built schools.

Furthermore, there have been instances where programmes have been set up to encourage female education by enabling schools make provision for young married women to return to complete their education after having had early marriages and sometimes their first children.[36] There had also been programmes initiated with some success that provided peripatetic education for nomadic groups in northern Nigeria such as the Fulani.[37]

These gains in educational access have however been limited, as wider scale universal access to basic education remains poorly supported in many parts of Africa where cultural practices and the interpretation of Islamic gender norms discourage female access to education. This has become particularly true since the ascendance of Islamic militant groups in areas such as

88 *African schools in the 21st century*

northeastern Nigeria. The 'Boko Haram' threats in the region have necessitated the design of 'security-proof' schools and boarding house accommodation to protect scholars, especially girls from being kidnapped or prevented from acquiring a 'Western education'.[38]

Wider access and use of new technologies

The key contemporary policy issue, however, that most influences school design development in Africa is the availability of adequate legislation for wider and better access to education for all students. This necessitates a commitment and investment in the design and development of schools and classroom infrastructure, and also methods of teaching appropriate to 21st century school pupils in Africa. Whilst most countries in Africa and across the world have signed up for past UNESCO declarations and the more recent Millennium and Sustainable Development Goals which call for this, the actual implementation of this goal varies at country and local level. As discussed, here certain countries and localities have for various cultural, religious and historic reasons have not made significant improvements in school provision and pupil enrolment targets despite national commitments to universal education.

In line with UNESCO's most recent education manifesto, promoting a humanist approach to future learning,[39] there also needs to be a commitment to improving accessibility to educational spaces. This is important for all in the community so that classrooms can become development hubs for community learning. This would entail the school building being a community-used facility, and being used until late in the evenings for adult classes and not only for children's education within the school day. This is particularly important in poor and remote communities, where there needs to be a national commitment to ensure sustained national investment in education for all, ensuring 'no one is left behind' in contemporary challenging socio-political and economic scenarios.

Millennium and Sustainable Development Goals

Since the conclusion of the fifteen-year period of Millennium Development Goals (MDGs) that had been aimed at ensuring access to free basic education to all children, a new set of Sustainable Development Goals have been established. Seventeen in number, the emphasis remains on attempting to achieve the goals not reached by the original MDGS, and to incorporate today's contemporary relationship to sustainability, equity and the need to deal with an ever urbanising world.[40]

Of the Seventeen SDGs, Goal 4 – to "ensure inclusive and equitable quality education and promote lifelong learning opportunities for all" – has the most explicit link to the support for educational development, and thus by extension school design. The Organization for Economic Development (OECD) views these goals as they relate to the delivery of an *international education* standard through the lens of 'global competence', this being shaped by three principles: equity, cohesion and sustainability.

- Equity: The increased inequality of income and opportunities, along with the fact that poor children receive poor education, puts the issue of equity and inclusive growth high on the global agenda. The digital economy is hollowing out jobs consisting of routine tasks and radically altering the nature of employment. For many, this is liberating and exciting. It is a great moment to be a twenty-something entrepreneur with a disruptive internet business model. But for others, it means the end of a livelihood.
- Cohesion: In all parts of the world, we are seeing unprecedented movements of people, with the most dramatic flows coming from countries mired in poverty and war. How can receiving countries integrate diverse groups of people and avoid rising extremism and fundamentalism?
- Sustainability: Delivering on the UN Sustainable Development Goals is a priority in the international community. Development that meets the needs of the present, without compromising the ability of future generations to meet their own needs, is more relevant than ever before, in the face of environmental degradation, climate change, overconsumption and population growth.[41]

The MDGs/SDGs place the same emphasis on the need to have better design and provision of and access to schools, with the added requirement from the SDGs to consider the sustainability of the development, planning designing and building of these educational spaces. These new learning spaces in turn have to work within both the highly urbanised spaces in city areas and also under-resourced environments in rural areas in which much of the world's poor children and youth now live. Conceptually, the SDGs seem to suggest that the world needs more cohesive spaces – as expressed by the OECD, and places in which integration can occur successfully. Implicitly, it seems that well designed future schools, classrooms or learning spaces are well placed to be these spaces.

The SDGs, thus despite being only launched in 2015, are set to frame our assessment and engagement with development. This is because levels of impact and sustainability now form the critical discourse to development projects. Schools, their design and development are part of the 'Cinderella' social infrastructure; also including housing, primary health care facilities, halls, libraries and other community spaces, which are going to be crucial in providing the cohesive spaces or 'hubs' for development that the SDGs call for.

90 *African schools in the 21st century*

The Adoption of New Technologies

The other key contemporary issue which African schools have yet to fully deal with is the inclusion of digital, formerly desktop computers into schools. Whilst the library block was a well-known feature in some schools, its usurping or dislocation by digital technologies and learning has been more difficult to accommodate. This remains a major disruptor as whilst African schools struggle to create computer areas, digital technology has moved to the utilisation of the hand-held smartphone 'app' or reading device for which the space required in the past for desktop computers is now obsolete. Classrooms need to be designed to incorporate these and future digital and physical technologies if they are to incorporate future methods of learning. The future learning space models which incorporate forms of digital learning are what the final chapter will examine.

Contemporary learning spaces design: practical and conceptual design concerns

Despite more than 150 years of educational provision across most of sub-Saharan Africa, the contemporary school classroom remains close in design conception and use to its Victorian predecessor.[42] Learning concepts, methods and theories have changed and begun to influence national curriculums and educational content. In general, however, school design remains wedded to the past, which harks to the symbolism of Western education as it was delivered via the missions and colonial government to an initial elite group of indigenous citizens.[43]

Practical issues that affect school design

Contemporary Africa is perhaps more affected than other emerging regions in other continents by long-term legacies of man-made and natural disasters and a slow developmental uplift of its rural populations. It is not the intention of this chapter to delve into the structural causes of this; however, two key aspects associated with these legacies – migration and restricted infrastructure development in rural areas – are explored. This is because these are identifiable issues that significantly affected improved school provision and educational coverage for some of Africa's most vulnerable learners.

Forced migration and internally displaced persons

School building programmes – and, in turn, access to education – have also been affected by local instability due to incessant wars, other forms of civil insurrection and natural disasters such as famines, landslides and flooding.

African schools in the 21st century 91

This is the case across diverse African regions in countries such as Sierra Leone, Sudan and Somalia. These events have led to large-scale shifts of population, who have become Internally Displaced Persons (IDPs). Whilst the international media is aware of the plight of migrants attempting to leave Africa for the West, the majority of IDPs remain in Africa as aggregate refugee populations. Settlement camps for refugees and IDPs are often created via international policies via agencies such as the United Nations High Commission for Refugees (UNHCR) and Habitat (the Housing sub-department of the United Nations). They often have to work alongside the countries on whose land the camps are set up. Thus, the Dadaab camp in Northern Kenya was set up in consultation with local chiefs in the area.

Many IDPs, however, are less fortunate than those who are accommodated in the UNHCR resettlement camps. They instead have to move to areas which have little or no infrastructural support, such as shelter, schools and health care facilities, for example. In many cases, the spaces that such migrants move to have little or no funding to ensure that schools are built to provide for the educational needs of the large number of children and young adults whose educational futures will have been severely affected as families and children are caught up in the long term, and sometimes permanent displacement from their homes. This is partly due to the transitional nature of these spaces, and also the limited funding and aid available.[44]

Poor and rural areas

There also remains the fundamental problem of limited school provision in very poor and rural parts of Africa. Here the geographical remoteness of communities far from the basic electricity and telecommunications infrastructure networks in Africa makes the provision of schools most difficult to deliver. National education policies from the 1950s to date have attempted to encourage investment in school provision in the remote communities. Often the remoteness means that even when schools are provided, retaining teaching and administrative staff is difficult to achieve. In the long term, such communities are likely to be served via remote online educational networks discussed in Chapter 5.

Conceptual design concerns

The stasis in educational design and school provision has perhaps been most challenged by and also received its most innovative responses in the new post-apartheid school projects being built across most provinces in South Africa. This represents a clear break with the past extreme level of educational segregation and limits to educational provision in the pre-1993 apartheid racial education policy. In poor township areas, a number

92   *African schools in the 21st century*

of provincial governments, notably in the Western Cape, have delivered ambitious school building programmes, most left to the design sensibilities of local South African architects, who with a ballpark budget sum and the South African government's classroom "standards and norms" document have been given free rein to reinterpret the contemporary post-1996 South African school and its relationship to its local community and farther afield.[45] The results of these projects have been noteworthy and a few will be discussed in Chapter 5, which presents contemporary African school design case studies.

Elsewhere in sub-Saharan Africa, this engagement with contemporary education has been less systematically examined, particularly within the state education sector. Private schools have successfully created their exclusive and successful interpretations of contemporary learning spaces, but these classroom design innovations are only fully enjoyed by the children of Africa's new and old elites who can afford the fees for these mainly private institutions.

Arguably the most successful adaptation to the historic school design template in countries as diverse as Ghana and South Africa are those that have been made to accommodate pre-primary education and also the introduction of primary school feeding programmes to take place within the school premises. Whilst this had already been introduced by South African schools from the late 1990s, further support for this to take place in schools across was championed by the United Nations and World Bank. This is because there was evidence-based research to show the benefits of these measures to improve educational access and nutritional needs amongst poorer African populations[46]

The more enterprising schools in both South Africa and Ghana have incorporated local community into the running of their school feeding programmes, both as kitchen staff and providers of the local vegetable produce often grown on 'school land' with the surplus absorbed by local families. This version of the development hub, though not strictly design focused, responds to the goals set out by the OECD sustainability initiative.[47]

The introduction of contemporary, if not necessarily new, concepts of teaching including peer-to-peer learning and child-centred learning have again remained largely absent in publicly funded schools in Africa. All South African state-run primary schools have incorporated child-sized furniture and classroom layouts for the pre-school and early primary years intake. Teachers in these schools also do have teaching sessions which involve school children working in circular whole-class and small teaching groups. Elsewhere, state education in Africa remains traditional in delivery with the focus on the teacher as the only knowledge provider and the students absorbing the information received, with an expectation that end-of-year written examinations will prove that this knowledge has been successfully digested and thus learnt.

African schools in the 21st century   93

Summary

This chapter has shown that school design in Africa has been particularly affected by a number of key issues. Those which have been discussed in detail – in the areas of policy, strategic issues and educational concepts – are considered to be the most strategic to the improvement of educational design and school delivery across Africa.

The typical definition of school design comprises practical space planning, creative design endeavour responding to ergonomic needs and an appropriate response to the space standards and environmental context of the school's location. In the African context, however, this definition covers only the physical design aspect of school and classroom design and delivery.

From this chapter, we can see that the contextual framework in which schools are built and learning takes place has a significant grounding in socio-cultural, economic and phenomenological issues which are specific to local and national concerns. In African and other countries in the emerging world, these are critical issues which have to be addressed in direct connection with the physical requirements of contemporary school design. In order for governments and other agencies to successfully build the volume of schools and classrooms needed to achieve universal and free access to education for all African children, these strategic issues need to be considered and dealt with. Thus far, this 'inter-contextual' approach is rarely used in school design planning and delivery across Africa.

The failure to do this has been a drawback which has hindered the achievement of the 2015 Millennium Development Goal, calling for universal access to free primary education in Africa as the regions and children who are hardest to reach are represented in the strategic areas which this chapter has highlighted.

International education policies have played a critical role in both the framing of and the directing of national discourses and approaches to school design in the majority of countries across the world.

Thus, the UNESCO-UNDP initiative in social policy issues such as education have support and consensus from both neoliberal and socialist countries in their implementation. Most are signed up to aiming to achieve the Sustainable Development Goal (SDG) targets, that have now superseded the Millennium Development Goals (MDG) targets discussed earlier in this chapter. Another international assessment criteria which has international involvement and participation in is the OECD's Programme for International Student Assessment (PISA) assessment score system in which the attainment of school children in different countries is measured against their counterparts across the globe. Traditionally, African state schools have performed poorly, which again may be an indication that even where there has been significant investment in school provision and education, the quality of this education could be significantly improved if the contextual features discussed in this chapter were taken into account.[48]

94   *African schools in the 21st century*

African countries, similar to those from other emerging regions, have their education policies linked very closely to international education policy themes. This is first because most are signed-up members of the UN and other international agencies, and therefore implicitly in agreement with these themes. Also, and importantly, as recipients of education loans at international and bilateral level, most African countries are 'contractually' expected to have education policies in place that aligned to the international education policy themes which their donors dictate.

The sustainability of school design programmes, including effectively contemporary school design issues, are local-national issues, as policy frameworks rarely drill down to the management of specific design projects. National reports are often generic and rarely involve detailed case studies. The contemporary critique in relation to school design and provision is that aside from census data on the quantities built and 'educational effectiveness', which again is measured via quantitative statistics related to school enrolment dropout and pass rates, the evaluation of the effectiveness of the designed school learning environment or space has had less attention, particularly in the emerging world.

Also needed is for state-funded education systems in Africa to commence a fundamental examination of the conceptual basis for education, learning and teaching in the African classroom. Educational success in the 21st century will not depend solely on new classroom and school provision, but also on the quality and kind of education and learning that African schools are able to provide to their 21st century students. Child-centred learning and new modes of teaching are likely to feature high in this reconceptualistion and reorganisation of African education at the primary and secondary levels.

Notes

1 Uduku, O. (2008b) *Designing Schools as Development Hubs for Learning.* Final Report. Bristol: University of Bristol.
2 United Nations (2000) *Millennium Development Goals.* www.un.org/millenniumgoals/. Accessed May 2018, and UNDP (2015b) *Sustainable Development Goals.* www.undp.org/content/undp/en/home/sustainable-development-goals.html. Accessed June 2017.
3 IPCC (2014) www.ipcc.ch/. Accessed May 2017.
4 See Lewis, L. J. (ed.) (1962) *Phelps-Stokes Reports on Education in Africa.* London: Oxford University Press and his description of the Phelps-Stokes 1929 and 1927 reports on schools in Africa and associated policies.
5 See UNESCO (n.d.b) *History.* www.unesco.org/new/en/unesco/about-us/who-we-are/history/. Accessed May 2017; UNHCR Blog. www.unhcr.org/uk/protection/operations/5149ba349/unhcr-education-strategy-2012-2016.html?query=ICT%20education. Accessed August 2017; and World Bank – IBRD Archive Papers Online. www.worldbank.org/en/about/archives/ history. Accessed August 2017.
6 For example, Nigeria had a ten-year development plan which featured an entire section on facilitating Universal Primary Education (UPE) and committing a percentage of spending to technical education.
7 UN Article 26.1 begins: "Everyone has the right to education." www.un.org/en/universal-declaration-human-rights/. Accessed May 2017.

African schools in the 21st century   95

8 See UNESCO (n.d.b); UNESCO (2015b) *Rethinking Education for a Global Common Good*. http://unesdoc. unesco.org/images/0023/002325/232555e.pdf. Accessed December 2017; UNDP (2017) *World Development Report*. Washington, DC: World Bank.

9 Ibid.

10 A good report on quality issues in schools in the emerging world for example can be gained from the summary findings of the University of Bristol's EdQual Project, www.edqual.org/research.html.

11 See, for example, Uduku, O. (1993b) *Factors Affecting School Design in Nigeria*. PhD Thesis, University of Cambridge. Ch. P. Case Study, Evangel High School, Old Umuahia.

12 Psacharopoulos, G. and Woodhall, H. (1986) *Education for Development: An Analysis of Investment Choices*. New York: Oxford University Press (for the World Bank).

13 The USA withdrew funding to UNESCO for political reasons in the 1980s, which greatly reduced its effectiveness in funding education policies. This happened again in October 2017 under the Trump administration see Foreign Policy (2017) *US to Pull Out of UNESCO Again*. http://foreignpolicy.com/2017/10/11/u-s-to-pull-out-of-unesco-again/. Accessed December 2017.

14 Uduku, O. (1993a) *Factors Affecting School Design in Ghana*. Report, Centre for African Studies, University of Cambridge; and World Bank (1988) *Education in Africa Report*. Washington, DC: World Bank.

15 Uduku (1993a).

16 They had originally been part of the Architects Co-Partnership (ACP) team, but soon set up their own practice, Godwin and Hopwood, in the late 1950s.

17 All architects mentioned were involved in school design in Africa and had AA links. Fry and Drew went on to masterplan Ibadan University, whilst Cubitt and Scott did the same for the University of Science and Technology Kumasi.

18 UNESCO were consultants on the Nigerian Unity Schools (Uduku 2016).

19 Mwira, K. (1990, August) Kenya's Harambee Secondary School Movement: The Contradictions of Public Policy. *Comparative Education Review*, 34(3), pp. 350–368. See also Space Group (2014) Forms of Freedom: African Independence and Nordic Models. The 14th International Architecture Biennale, The Nordic Pavilion, Venice, 7th June–23rd November 2014.

20 See Pat Wakely School designs (1966) AA archives.

21 The GIA and NIA were founded in 1960, whilst the Kenyan and Tanzanian equivalents were established in 1967 and 1982, respectively.

22 The Catholic Church was the main religious organisation which did, however, fund and run schools, hospitals and churches in Lusophone Africa; however, educational provision was limited and determined by colonial policies.

23 See Cross, M. (2011) *An Unfulfilled Promise: Transforming Education in Mozambique*. Addis Ababa, Ethiopia: Organisation for Social Science Research in Eastern and Southern Africa; and Birmingham, D. (2016) *A Short History of Modern Angola*. Oxford: Oxford University Press.

24 UNESCO had regional school building research offices in Bangkok, Dakar, and Beirut. See UNESCO (n.d.a) *Architecture for Education*. www.unesco.org/education/pdf/BAT0029.PDF. Accessed August 2017.

25 See Uduku, O. (1994a) *Factors Affecting School Design in South Africa*. Report, Centre for African Studies, University of Cambridge, and Kallaway, P. (ed.) (2002) *The History of Education Under Apartheid 1948–1994: The Doors of Learning and Culture Shall Be Opened*. New York, NY: Peter Lang.

26 History of education in Rhodesia.

27 Low, I. (2010) Space and Transformation: Reflection on the New WCED Schools Programme. In E. Pieterse (ed.), *Countercurrents, Experiments in Sustainability in the Cape Town Region*. Johannesburg: Jacarana, pp. 202–215.

96 African schools in the 21st century

28 Waterford is an international school fostering world unity which was adopted in 1981 by the United World Colleges (UWC) movement. Its alumnae include the Mandela daughters.

29 There have been private universities in West Africa since the 1990s.

30 *The Economist* (2017b) Emerging Markets Should Welcome Low Cost Schools. www.economist.com/news/leaders/21715665-east-african-crackdown-bridge-international-academies-hopelessly-misguided-emerging. Accessed April 2018.

31 Ibid.

32 See, for example, *The Economist* (2015a) Learning Unleashed, Low Cost Private Schools, (Print Edition briefing). www.economist.com/news/briefing/21660063-where-governments-are-failing-provide-youngsters-decent-education-private-sector. Accessed April 2018, and *The Economist* (2017b) This needs to be contrasted with the latest UNESCO mini-manifesto, UNESCO (2015b) *Rethinking Education for a Global Common Good.* http://unesdoc.unesco.org/images/0023/002325/232555e.pdf. Accessed December 2017.

33 See Chapter 5, p. 108, and also Uduku (2008b).

34 Smit, W. and Hennessy, K. (1995) *Taking South African Education out of the Ghetto. An Urban-Planning Perspective.* Cape Town: UCT Press Buchu Books.

35 Ahmed, I. (2013) Northern Nigeria Launches Massive Literacy Campaign. *Voice of America.* www.voanews.com/a/northern-nigeria-launches-massive-literacy-campaign-for-400000/1812906.html.

36 See, for example, this mass literacy programme launched in 2013: www.voanews.com/a/northern-nigeria-launches-massive-literacy-campaign-for-400000/1812906.html. Accessed 15 December 2017.

37 Aderinoye, R. A. (2007) Expanding Access to Adult Basic Education in Nigeria: The Intervention of Open Distance Learning. *Adult Education in Nigeria*, 14, pp. 216–226.

38 See Hentz, J. J. and Solomon, H. (2017) *Understanding Boko Haram: Terrorism and Insurgency in Africa.* Abingdon, Oxon; New York, NY: Routledge; and Smith, M. G. (2015) *Boko Haram: Inside Nigeria's Unholy War.* London: I. B. Tauris.

39 See UNESCO (2015b) *Rethinking Education for a Global Common Good.* http://unesdoc.unesco.org/images/0023/002325/232555e.pdf. Accessed December 2017.

40 United Nations (2000); and UNDP (2015b).

41 Today, all three principles are at risk. But the OECD sees global competence as the centrepiece of a broader vision for 21st century education international education goals, www.bbc.co.uk/news/business-36343602.

42 Echeruo, M. J. C. (1977) *Victorian Lagos: Aspects of Nineteenth Century Lagos Live.* London: Macmillan; and Fafunwa, B. (1974) *History of Education in Nigeria.* London: Allen and Unwin.

43 Ayandele, E. A. (1966) *The Missionary Impact on Modern Nigeria 1842–1914: A Political and Social Analysis.* London: Longman Green and Co.

44 UNHCR Blog. www.unhcr.org/uk/protection/operations/5149ba349/unhcr-education-strategy-2012-2016.html?query=ICT%20education. Accessed August 2017.

45 South African Government (2009) *Department of Education Notice, No. of 2009 The National Minimum Uniform Norms and Standards for School Infrastructure.*

46 Uduku, O. (2011) School Building Design for Feeding Programmes and Community Outreach: Insights From Ghana and South Africa. *International Journal of Educational Development*, 31, pp. 59–66.

47 See note 8.

48 With possibly the exception of the remains of the Cuba socialist education model.

5 Contemporary school design case studies

Whilst the majority of Africa's schools have seen little or no transformation in design standards from the last century, a small but growing number of school buildings that have been built in the last few decades demonstrate the potential that exists to radically transform classroom spaces and, by association, education in Africa through a different approach to school design. These new schools reflect responses to education policy from local to global levels. Some schools demonstrate the potential of design to incorporate new ways to use local building materials in construction. Others have successfully been designed to adopt new communication and learning technologies into classrooms. Finally, and importantly, some school projects presented here have also been involved in designing classrooms or learning spaces that engage with new pedagogies, focusing on child-centred learning and also the enabling of some schools to have community learner groups access and shared use of classrooms and other learning spaces at planned times.

This chapter seeks to present commentary and analysis of a number of recently designed schools that show how contemporary approaches to design and new pedagogies can and have initiated a transformation in school design in Africa. The schools presented here as case studies for discussion have been selected from a number of different sources using different criteria. A number of these have been completed in the late 20th century, from 1996 onwards. These have been selected because they provide interesting exemplars of different approaches to school design within the constraints of a specific African context. A few schools have been selected from schools visited during past research into school design as part of the EdQual DFID project *Designing Schools as Development Hubs in Africa*, conducted between 2006 and 2008.[1] The last case study school was completed in 2016 and provides a good case study analysis of current contemporary approaches to school design.

Aside from the time span covered, from the late 20th century to the present day, the reviewed schools are diverse in location, building finance and ownership. It is hoped, therefore, that the case studies presented provide a selective but representative set of buildings which show the wide variations in school design that now exist in Africa's contemporary neoliberal school

98 Contemporary school design case studies

landscape. The locations of the case studies range from Ghana and Sierra Leone in West Africa, Kenya in East Africa, Rwanda in Central Africa and South Africa.

In this chapter the case studies are presented regionally, because African school design has regional as well as linguistic-colonial characteristics. The case study schools discussed here are all from sub-Saharan Anglophone Africa, further research is planned to integrate Francophone and Lusophone school case studies in the future.

West Africa school case studies

Despite having had significant capital investment in school buildings in the 1950s and 1960s, much of Anglophone West Africa's schools have suffered from under-investment and under-development since the 1970s. The education landscape in West Africa is varied. There is now a private market in educational provision from kindergarten to tertiary education level in Ghana and Nigeria. Sierra Leone, and also Liberia, have also only recently over the past decade emerged from long civil wars. A major effect of this period of civil strife in both countries was the destruction of the formal education framework in each nation.[2] The Gambia, West Africa's smallest nation-state, has a primary and secondary education network which also has a mix of state and private provision. The country had no tertiary education provision until the 2000s; prior to this, Gambians went or were sponsored to go elsewhere in West Africa or farther afield for higher education provision. Since the 2000s, this has changed significantly.[3] For the West Africa region in this text, representative case study schools in Ghana and Sierra Leone are discussed. Both case studies contextually fit within the timeframe in which contemporary case studies are being examined in this chapter. The case studies also provide examples of state- and privately funded and managed schools.

The Dwabor kindergarten and primary schools project, Ghana

This is a kindergarten school design which has resulted from an innovate charity-corporate partnership between the Sabre Charitable Trust and Arup International Development.[4] The project originated from Sabre's desire to develop an optimal design for kindergarten schools in rural communities along Ghana's southwestern coastline (see figure 5.1). Sabre and Arup have been working in partnership for nearly a decade to develop, test, optimise and scale the school design concept as quality addition to the public education system in Ghana, in close collaboration and consultation with the local community. Its design principles have stayed true to the low-energy sustainable design ideals of tropical architecture but have also formed a focus for community engagement and input into a number of other schools and educational initiatives linked to the Safe Sustainable Kindergarten School Project.

Figure 5.1 Dwabor School, Cape Coast, Ghana
Courtesy D. Bond and Sabre Charitable Trust

Technical details

The prototype design, built in the community of Dwabor, used local materials including bamboo strips as cladding and wooden operable windows to allow full natural daylighting into the classrooms during the teaching day. All buildings were oriented on an east-west axis to allow for maximum cross-ventilation and minimum direct glare from the sun. The metal roofs which help with rainwater collection have underside coconut husk lining to deaden the noise during the rainy season. Blocks used stabilised locally sourced earth, and where concrete was required, this was supplemented with pozzolan stabilised coconut kernel, emphasising again local sourcing. As Southern Ghana is within an area of seismological risk, the classrooms were also built in modular form to reduce the risk of significant earthquake damage.

Curriculum support

Alongside its school construction programme, Sabre works with the Ghana Education Service on teacher training, both for new teachers studying at training college and practising teachers already in the field. The Sabre trust works in collaboration with the Ministry of Education to aid and support the new 'active and play-based' learning programme for kindergarten education

100 *Contemporary school design case studies*

being promoted in Ghana. The Dwabor school design was the prototype and since its completion an additional eleven schools have been built across the coastal districts of the Central and Western Regions. Sabre is increasingly using the schools as District Model Schools, which provide a catalyst for increased value on kindergarten education and pave the way for the introduction of district-wide teacher training, providing a focal point and showcase for active, play-based learning in child-friendly and safe facilities.

Community links

As most materials used for the building of the classroom were locally sourced, this enabled the construction team – supported by technical assistance from Arup's specialist International Development team and the wider Arup Engineering Group – to work with members of the local community to build the school and in so doing help with the transfer of sustainable building skills and the use of materials such as pozzolan stabilised concrete, stabilised earth blocks and the use of coconut fibre as an acoustic damper to roofing.

Interviewing Dominic Bond, Sabre's Managing Director, confirmed that the architectural and engineering input into the school design was informed by and responsive to community consultation and a review of the shortcomings of traditional school construction projects in Ghana. In Sabre's case, the input of the engineers and designers from Arup was critical to the success of the Sabre School model.[5] Local communities have also been instrumental with the ongoing development and success of Sabre's education projects. This is demonstrated by all schools built by Sabre-Arup being incorporated into the Ghana education system. Sabre's technology for school construction and teacher training is now under active consideration by the Ministry of Education for replication at a national scale – achieving the founding vision on the project, and potentially benefiting many thousands more children that Sabre can reach directly.

Article 25 prototype primary school for rural communities, Sierra Leone

Sierra Leone has recently emerged from the horrors of a brutal eleven-year civil war, from 1991–2002, in which students and children were enlisted as soldiers and suffered first-hand from the trauma of war. The pre-civil war school system thus has had to be rehabilitated and developed to serve the needs of Sierra Leonean children.

Despite significant international investment in the reconstruction of the capital city Freetown, one of the main theatres of the civil war, there was little rehabilitation or investment in the remains of the war-ravaged school infrastructure left at the end of the war. One of the initial moves to upgrade and design new schools in Freetown was made by the British architectural

Figure 5.2 Kailahun School, Prototype Design Sierra Leone
Article 25

practice Foster and Partners, which in 2009 was involved in the pro-bono design of a new school near Sierra Leone. The firm teamed up with the engineering firm Buro Happold and under the umbrella of the British NGO Article 25 to work further on the project from 2009–2014. This multi-disciplinary team then further went on to develop a prototype school and clinic design for use in rural communities in eastern Sierra Leone. The first prototype was built for the Kailahun community (see figure 5.2). The project's performance and success was further re-evaluated in 2014. The school structure remains in use in Kailahun, and today is also used as a computer training classroom for the community.

Technical details

Similar to the Sabre Trust's Dwabor Kindergarten Project, the Kailahun community school project prototype was designed to use local materials and planned to make the most use of local environmental conditions such as daylighting and cross-ventilation potential in relation to the orientation and design of the building to allow this.

A team of engineers and architects, from Buro and Happold and Foster and Partners, worked on developing prototype school plans with some local

102 *Contemporary school design case studies*

consultation. Locally sourced materials such as bamboo battens, wooden window frames and stabilised earth were chosen to be used for school construction. The design prototype as conceived by the team was planned to involve the community, particularly local craftsmen, in the construction of the school. It also demonstrated the possibilities of the application of good planning and environmental principles to school design in remote rural locations.

Curriculum support

In terms of curriculum support in the case of the Kailahun community school, the integration of the school into the wider education curriculum of Sierra Leone was less clear. As a war-torn country, the education system and its curriculum remained in development in 2014 when the prototype was designed. Article 25, the charity involved with Foster and Partners and Buro Happold in planning Kailahun School, said at the time "it is hoped this design will also provide a cost-effective prototype for replication across Sierra Leone".[6] (article 25, 2014)

Community links

The design for the Kailahun school prototype was worked on collaboratively by a British team of engineers and architects. Visits to the site in Sierra Leone had been undertaken early on in the process by members of the Foster and Partners team, but ultimately this remained a prototype design project which was built in one location only, Kailahun, but not replicated. The potential for extended local community links, although high, could not be fully explored in practical terms.

Southern Africa school case studies

The two South African schools presented here represent a case study from the mid-1990s post-apartheid period, and a more recent school completed near the end of the first decade of the 21st century. In this period, the educational landscape in post-apartheid South Africa changed significantly. The initial hope that education funding in the new nation would be more democratically spread and inclusive in coverage was unfortunately unattained. As part of the DFID-University of Bristol EdQual Project, the Dalweide school was revisited a decade after it had first been reviewed. Both schools reviewed are state-funded, and both also have been designed by independent architects who have worked with the South African schools standards and norms related to space standards and siting but have been able to design each school to their interpretations of the educational needs of the children and local township communities in which the schools were built.

Dalweide Primary school, Paarl, Western Cape, South Africa[7]

Dalweide Primary school is located in the rural Paarl agricultural region of the Western Cape. It was built in 1996 as a new school after South Africa's attainment to self-rule in 1994. It was designed by the architects Albertyn Wessels, using the novel school design funding formula set up by the Western Cape Province whereby architects were expected to design schools to their own brief, but were constrained to the Province's fixed project costs apportioned to each school in relation to design, construction and project management. The design was subsequently rebuilt for the Vukani Primary school in Khayelitsha, Cape Town in 1998. Both schools were visited as case studies during the DFID Edqual project.[8]

Technical and design specifications

The school challenges the traditional rational design norms of South African schools. It is conceived as a series of forms that frame the Boland Mountain Range in the background, and the school's wall colours are bright and eye-catching. The classrooms are arranged around a covered area, which serves as the hall, following the Western Cape design guidelines to enable schools to have meeting halls or fora between classroom blocks. Classrooms are rectilinear, some with storage and some without. Windows are shaped in keeping with the non-rectilinear form of the school with the introduction of circular windows in some areas.

The main structure is constructed of traditional brick infill construction with steel girder frames for the central hall area, and concrete beam and post construction for other walls. School finishes are basic. The original finish to the hall area was screed, but with the efforts of the principal in fundraising it has now been floored in wood. Classrooms, however, have screed floors and the WCs are also screeded with limited tiling to the walls.

Curriculum support

South Africa's then relatively new Education Curriculum had been implemented in all schools built in the post-1994 period.[9] Discussions with the staff at Dalweide School produced the following response to the efficacy of the curriculum: the staff felt that the new curriculum demanded a different teaching approach, which meant that classrooms had to be better able to respond to experiential requirements. With the large classroom sizes and administration requirements, teachers felt overstressed. They also explained that many children came in with social problems. It was felt that the school needed to better designed to allow staff to work more as social workers to support children better. The free primary school feeding programme, and child-friendly

104 *Contemporary school design case studies*

furniture for pre-school and kindergarten classes, were recorded as a success. The staff, however, felt that other school interventions such as a uniform exchange for indigent children could take place within the school premises if the community had more access to the school during non-teaching periods. More flexible classroom design to allow for the large class sizes and more creative learning classes such as group learning were also called for.

Community links

Designed and planned as a purpose-built primary school for a small rural community, this original design has worked well as an addition to the community. The school taught evening technology classes, had an under-resourced library and was awaiting the arrival of computers. The community used the school hall for after school meetings and was involved in after-school computing lessons. The principal had raised funds by encouraging donations from local businesses and parent association fundraising to buy a bus for the school and it was already involved in sports development activities in the region.

He was hoping to raise further funds for playground facilities for the children. There is the chance for the further development of after school educational opportunities for the community using the school facilities. The school did have some playing grounds, but no farm. It was the beneficiary of two feeding schemes, one which was provincial government-funded and one which was NGO-funded.[10]

During the visit, there was no adult learning Adult Education Basic Education and Training (ABET) programme at the school, either. The hall was hired out to the community for family functions and also to religious groups for church activities. Also, chairs are hired out to individual homes nearby. The hall was also frequently used for fundraising events. The principal secured lotto funding to build a tennis wall on the sports grounds, which has been completed.

Inkwenkwezi High School, Khayelitsha, Western Cape, South Africa[11]

Inkwenkwezi High School, in the Lower Crossroads Township near Cape Town, was designed in 2008 by the Architects Noero Wolff. The school's architecture extends to and blends with the local Dunoon township community. Its facilities comprising its library, computing facilities and the main meeting area are all designed to be used by the local township community during and after school hours. The school is located within the township which it serves. Its design enables it respond to the informal settlement in which it is placed. This is helped by its symbolic local presence which is emphasised through the clear difference in the school's scale, both in height and overall form (see figure 5.3).

Figure 5.3 Dalweide School
Author's own image

Technical and design specifications

The school shows exemplary sustainable design features with water recycling and well-designed natural lighting for classrooms in place.[12]

The roofs allow for rainwater collection, critical in a township with limited access to services. The classrooms are made of two single-banked two-storey buildings. Both are designed to allow for the allowance of ample daylighting for classroom work purposes. The library block, which is open outside of school hours for community use, has been designed to be used independently of the school, which can be closed off for access control issues at the end of the school day.

Curriculum support

Inkwenkwezi follows the post-1994 South African School curriculum requirements. It was also designed to the principles of the Western Cape School Design process, with Noero Wolff architects successfully designing the School. The South African secondary school curriculum calls for shared use of school facilities with local communities and involving the community

Figure 5.4 Inkwenkwezi School, DuNoon, Cape Town, South Africa
Courtesy Wolff Architects

in the running of schools and other social infrastructure. This school fulfils these curriculum goals.

Community links

The combined use of the library by the community and their access to the school courtyard area and other spaces at certain times has proved very popular to the local township. The school itself is prominent in its location and the star logo, which emphasises the Xhosa meaning of the word *Inkwenkwezi*; (morning star) has been embraced by the local community where it has been described as an "optimistic epithet", and indeed a 'beacon of light' to the Khayelitsha township.[13]

East/Central African school case studies

The final two schools discussed are from East and Central Africa. The Aga Khan Academy Mombasa is a privately funded school in Kenya whilst the MASS schools in Rwanda are both designed by the US-based non-profit team MASS Design. The Aga Khan Academy has had historical roots in East

Contemporary school design case studies   107

Africa, but has had a recently built new school built in Mombasa, whilst the MASS team have been involved in a number of school buildings in Rwanda over the past decade. Both buildings take an environmental approach to design, with a focus on orientation and design to allow for passive cooling strategies. In the Aga Khan School complex, the architect uses screen walling to reduce direct glare, and also as an homage to Swahili architecture. The open-air auditorium also enables students to engage directly with the local climate, which is not often the case in African school design. The MASS schools also, despite being designed for a poorer student group, are focused on good orientation in relation to climate and site geography. The Rwandan schools also are designed with the incorporation of local building materials in the structure and fabric of the new schools.

The Aga Khan Academy, Mombasa, Kenya[14]

The Aga Khan Foundation (AKFN) is a non-profit NGO which promotes the objectives of the Aga Khan, based on the principles of Shi'a Islam. Its schools are fee-paying, although there are bursaries for poorer students who meet means test criteria The AKFN has been involved in education in East Africa since 1905, when it set up a girls' school in Zanzibar, Tanzania.

The Aga Khan's initial investment in African education was curtailed with the move towards mass education in Africa from the recommendations of the Phelps-Stokes Reports which the late colonial government policies, and international organisations such as UNESCO in the post-WW2 era, encouraged. This meant that private charities, including Christian missions and also the Aga Khan Foundation, had less involvement in school provision until the relaxation of national education policies following the neo liberalisation of education funding and provision from the 1980s. Tanzania's Arusha self-reliance policies from the 1960s meant that private education in that country was discouraged and only re-established when the country's involvement with socialism collapsed in the 1980s.

The Aga Khan Foundation developed a global educational network covering educational institutions from kindergarten to universities across the world. This has taken place from the 1980s in Africa after the aforementioned relaxation of restrictions of education funding by private non-state organisations. This had been with the 'blessing' of the main financial aid donors including the World Bank and other NGOs. The Mombasa School discussed here is representative of the contemporary design and development of Aga Khan Educational Foundation schools across Africa and worldwide.

The Aga Khan Academy in Mombasa was founded in 2003. It is located on Mombasa Island, and its campus delivers kindergarten through to secondary age education. This mini-campus is designed as an independent self-sustaining unit which educates a diverse range of students from different backgrounds in Kenya. It is fully fee-paying, with a means-based bursary model available as discussed earlier.

108 *Contemporary school design case studies*

Design and technology

The school campus has been purposefully designed by Aga Khan-commissioned architects to respond to the cultural context of coastal East Africa. Termed 'Swahili' architecture, the campus incorporates the use of Islamic-inspired facades and courtyards.[15] Classrooms are designed to make optimum use of passive methods of cooling via daytime cross-ventilation, and night time displacement cooling. The campus is 'state of the art'[16] in its incorporation of technology and innovative teaching methods, and it also has recreational facilities including its own swimming pool and sports grounds.

Curriculum support

Its students are enrolled onto the International Baccalaureate (IB) curriculum.

The school delivers the International Baccalaureate, an international qualification which separates its students from the national educational curriculum of Kenya, and is rather a globally recognised qualification, which not only qualifies its students to continue their academic careers in Aga Khan tertiary institutions but global universities throughout the world.

Community links

As a private school with few links to Kenya's educational infrastructure, the Mombasa Academy does have community initiatives where students are involved in donating books to local communities and also work on community development schemes. The school campus, however, has been designed as an independent secured space on Mombasa Island. It allows controlled access to only staff, students and parents who have occasion to visit the campus. Local outreach and engagement with the campus is only negotiable or possible on the Academy's terms.

Umbano (2007) and Mubugu (2014) primary schools, Rwanda

MASS Design[17]

In 2007, MASS Design designed a primary school to replace a disintegrating school in Umbano that existed on the site in the post-genocide landscape of Kigali, the capital city of Rwanda. This was one of the first international projects of this young US-based architectural team. It amassed considerable global interest, and was followed by a number of projects in Rwanda. The Mubuga school project in the Musanze district, also in Rwanda, completed in 2015, was designed by MASS as a prototype design for school classrooms across Rwanda. MASS Design use local materials and engaged local labour in the onsite construction of their projects which include health, education

Figure 5.5 Umbano School, Rwanda
Courtesy Iwan Baan Photography

and other social infrastructure projects in the USA, Africa and elsewhere in the emerging world.

Design and technology

Both Umbano and Mubugu schools use primarily local materials in their design. Conceptually, the architectural design of these schools respond to the basic needs of contemporary classroom design in the Rwandan context. This is for the development of a school network with classrooms robust enough to form the pedagogic infrastructural backdrop to the country's new nine-year primary education curriculum programme.

MASS Design's emphasis has focused on the use of local materials and engagement with local craftsmen and builders in school construction. Architectural form has responded to local landscapes. In the case of the Umbano Primary school, the tiered design is in direct conversation to the steep graded site location. The Mubugu prototype is less site-specific but focuses on the use of local materials and incorporation of local labour in all aspects of construction. The main materials used for both schools are stabilised earth, wooden window and clerestory frames, and the use of corrugated roofing sheets. Vierendeel trusses are used structurally for the roof to incorporate the clerestory lighting strips, but otherwise the one-storey stabilised earth structures do not need structural concrete, which is important as much of Rwanda is in a seismologically sensitive region. Environmentally, classrooms are designed to enable cross-ventilation and good daylighting with the use of clerestory lighting, which ensures top light penetration across the classroom to areas where local daylighting from windows would not reach.

Curriculum support

The Rwandan government's new education curriculum seeks to improve access to primary education for all Rwandan children, and also to improve the quality of the education delivered. The MASS schools are designed by the US team in connection with various charitable foundations including UNESCO. MASS also has become a major player in the design of social infrastructure in Rwanda, and with its experience with the Umbano Primary school has links to policymakers and seems well placed to have successfully interpreted the 2006 educational curriculum in its Mubugu school design prototype.

Community links

MASS Design engages local community in all its projects. The link to the schools with the local community, however, remains less clear. Students

Figure 5.6 Mubugu School, Rwanda MASS Design
Iwan Baan Studio

Contemporary school design case studies   111

clearly benefit from new schools, but the after-school time use of Umbano school seems limited as its functions were designed primarily for the needs of the school children and not the local community. The Mubugo school has a wider remit as an 'Advanced Education Centre' with other facilities planned, including a library and local sports facilities. Free access and use of these social facilities, when they are built, should endear their use to their local community; however, there is currently no mention of local community context in available literature on the school.

Analysis

From the range of schools examined in this chapter, it is evident that there is no common design approach or policy theme that informs contemporary school design. Across the African regions where case study schools were selected there were however a few key themes which provided the contextual background to the school design schemes described. These can be summarised as follows.

The effect of neoliberal funding approaches on educational provision

As discussed in earlier chapters, the overarching theme which has influenced contemporary school provision in Africa is the move from national education systems underpinned by strong education policy frameworks and international support from UNESCO, the World Bank and other large NGOs to a neoliberal approach to educational provision. This has affected all aspects of education provision from teacher management and school funding to school design. This new education market place has also provided the space in which various players and organisations have been able to compete with and sometimes succeed in the delivery of education systems, including new school design, more successfully than can national state education systems.

For lower-middle income status African countries which have some political and economic stability, this liberalisation of education has been better regulated by the experienced educational bureaucrats. These are those whose job it is to ensure national educational policies which are implemented across the country and extend to school design guidelines and curriculum aspirations. Thus in the case of Ghana and South Africa, NGOs and other educational bodies work with education policy specialists in collaboration with communities to develop and design new school buildings which respond to both government policy objectives and the needs of local communities.

In the case of the Western Cape Province in South Africa, this has been taken further with the involvement of South African architects in the design of schools for communities across the province. In Ghana, as in Nigeria, NGOs have to work with the Ministry of Education and local communities to deliver new schools which respond with ministry guidelines. In the Western Region of Ghana near Elmina, where the SABRE Trust has been

112   Contemporary school design case studies

involved in building schools it has worked collaboratively with the Ghanaian Ministry of Education to ensure that SABRE Trust schools were conceived and designed to respond to the pedagogic and physical design requirements of the new Ghanaian education curriculum.

The effect of NGO involvement in school provision

In countries with more fragile economies and governance structures in place, NGOs and the micro-economies which support these organisations have had a significant influence as major players in the provision of education, particularly in rural and disadvantaged areas in African countries where National Education systems have failed to do this.[18] Aside from providing teachers and administrative support for schools through the historic Peace Corps, VSO and other voluntary schemes, there have also been numerous school building programmes carried out by well-meaning NGOs. This has its successes, as evidenced by the MASS schools programme in Rwanda described here, and others elsewhere from Malawi to Sierra Leone. This approach, however, is not always successful where NGO interests have only a limited understanding of national education policies and wider contemporary global pedagogies.

Even where NGOs have a good appreciation of the wider contemporary socio-political context in which schools are being designed, this may not be enough to ensure that the schools built by expatriate teams will remain in use and stay well maintained once the programme team has designed the school building or classroom and left for home. There is often the need to acknowledge and incorporate the relevant historic context to school building programmes and also an appreciation of the specific cultural settings in which they have been designed in the past. Earlier chapters have documented that there have been clear guidelines on school design drawn up by international organisations such as UNESCO since the 1950s, and in some cases even earlier by missionaries and other historic education providers.[19] These groups had often identified appropriate local building materials methods and climatic responses needed for school design. Often today's NGOs seek to re-invent the wheel in their approach to design and community participation. Also, with limited continuity once schools are built, the much-publicised community participation and building innovation have limited support or simply disappears as the NGO teams move to their next development project.

The influence of contemporary approaches to 21st century learning

The most critical influence on future school design is how African education policies are going to respond to 21st century learning innovations. As explored elsewhere, it is likely that Africa's successful leapfrog into digital

Contemporary school design case studies 113

technologies in areas such as digital banking and telephony seems to be being replicated in digital learning.[20] The "*hole in the wall experiment*", though yet to be consistently replicated, suggests that remote digital learning is already possible in Africa.[21]

The effect which this might have on school design could be transformational. It has long been acknowledged that a key problem with educational provision in rural and poor areas is the difficulty in getting teaching personnel to commit to living in these remote or distant locations.[22] With digital education, the need for facilitators to enable students make use of digital materials becomes easier to fulfil, and also importantly the classroom might become the local learning space, open to all in the community and not just school children during the school day. The example of the Inkwenkwezi school design in Cape Town shows how schools can be flexibly designed to enable to local public use some areas; in this case, the classroom in out of school hours.

In such a future scenario, the need for the traditional classroom changes to a need for spaces in which self and peer-to-peer learning takes place. It could be that the traditional library model will in the future become a more appropriate learning space for certain school situations for rural and poor communities where the school has a more community accessible function. We cannot plan for such future scenarios as described; however, it is important to appreciate what possible game changers to education might take place in the not-too-distant future.

Conclusions

Since the late 20th century, African education and its schools have had to deal with the transition from the certainty of national education policies with the international funding that guaranteed the staffing, equipment and schools to the fragmented educational landscape of the neoliberal funding approach to the contemporary educational market. This chapter has sought to show this varied school design sector through the different case studies chosen with examples from the three major regions of sub-Saharan Africa.

As discussed, however, each case and situation is unique to its own context. The three themes explored – the effects of policies NGO-donor aid activities and relationships to local communities, and finally design engagement with future learning policies – are, however, crucial to the future success of all contemporary school or learning space design projects.

In all six case studies presented in this chapter, various aspects of these policies have been demonstrated. The range of school provision across the continent is also clearly shown. As might be expected, the Aga Khan private school is best designed to benefit from new pedagogies and technologies; however Inkwenkwezi, the state-run but independently designed state school in the south African township Khayelitsha, shows the possibilities good design can produce.

114 *Contemporary school design case studies*

The liberal strategic school planning and design framework of the Western Cape Region's educational division has been instrumental in driving this change in approach. This approach to school delivery and planning oversight is crucial for the public education sector. In Africa this is particularly important, as funds and good designers who can work within a community context can be difficult to find.

This chapter has attempted to give a limited but wide-ranging overview of the state and kinds of school design which give can be found in contemporary Africa. There are positive signs that there is the emergence of a new approach to school design which will grow with local architecture and communities involved in the delivering new schools in new neighbourhoods. In rural areas, however, as has been shown in the cases of both Mubugo and Dwabor schools (in Rwanda and Ghana, respectively) and is the case in other locations in rural Africa, the reliance on external contributors and funders of school provision suggests that alternative educational approaches which are less invested in replicating the traditional school building model and traditional learning pedagogies, which Chapter 6 examines, might be a means for better delivery and educational engagement in rural and also hard to reach urban communities.

Notes

1 Uduku, O. (2008b) *Designing Schools as Development Hubs for Learning*. Final Report. Bristol: University of Bristol.
2 World Bank (2007) *Education in Sierra Leone, Present Challenges, Future Opportunities*. https://openknowledge.worldbank.org/handle/10986/6653. Accessed April 2018; and World Bank (2010) *Liberia Country Status Report: Out of the Ashes Learning Lessons From the Past to Guide Education Delivery in Liberia*. http://documents.worldbank.org/curated/en/257321468057236139/Liberia-education-country-status-report-out-of-the-ashes-learning-lessons-from-the-past-to-guide-education-recovery-in-Liberia. Accessed April 2018.
3 This has, however, changed with the establishment of the University of The Gambia (f. 1999) and more recently of the private American International University West Africa Campus (f. 2011). See University of The Gambia homepage www.utg.edu.gm/. Accessed March 2018; and American International University of West Africa homepage www.aiu.edu.gm/. Accessed May 2017. However recent World Bank Status reports on the Gambia highlight the fragility of educational provision and infrastructure development in the city See, for example, World Bank (2014) *READ Project Report*. http://documents.worldbank.org/curated/en/869821468024280057/pdf/ISR-Disclosable-P133079-06-22-2016-1466635929267.pdf; and World Bank (2017) *Country Report*. www.worldbank.org/en/country/gambia/overview. Both accessed June 2017.
4 A selection of references is available for Dwabor school, including: ARUP (2010) *A Prototype Kindergarten for a Remote District of Ghana*. www.arup.com/projects/dwabor-kindergarten; Gryc, H. and da Silva, J. (2013) Global Engineers Thinking Locally: Creating Kindergartens for Africa. *Civil Engineering*, 166(CE3), ICE Proceedings. www.sabretrust.org/downloads/ICE_Proceedings_Aug13.pdf; and Sabre Report (2015) *Building a Brighter Future for Children in Ghana*. www.sabretrust.org/downloads/Sabre_AR_2015.pdf. All URLs accessed August 2017.

Contemporary school design case studies 115

5 Telephone interview with Dominic Bond, June 2017.
6 Article 25 (2014) New Prototype School for Sierra Leone. www.article-25.org/previous-projects/prototype-child-friendly-school/. Accessed April 2018.
7 Dalweide School plans: courtesy Western Provincial Education Department, 2008; Uduku, O. (2011) School Building Design for Feeding Programmes and Community Outreach: Insights From Ghana and South Africa. *International Journal of Educational Development*, 31, pp. 59–66.
8 Uduku (2008b).
9 South African Government (1998) *National Education Policy*.
10 The government scheme funds breakfast meals, the NGO funds lunch provision which is optional to South African schools. See also Uduku (2011).
11 See Uduku, O. (2015) Spaces for 21st Century Learning. In *Routledge Handbook on International Learning and Development*. London: Routledge, pp. 196–209.
12 South African Institute of Architecture (2007) *A Digest of South African Architecture*.
13 Slessor, C. (1995, March) The South Africa Issue. Special Edition Editorial. *Architectural Review*.
14 All information accessed from Aga Khan Foundation Schools website url: www.akdn.org/our-agencies/aga-khan-education-services/akes-east-africa. Accessed June 2017. But see also www.agakhanacademies.org/general/commitment-excellence-designing-aga-khan-academies for the Aga Khan Foundation view on the design of educational environments. Accessed June 2017.
15 From Aga Khan Mombasa School, Information Brochure. www.agakhanacademies.org/sites/default/files/AKA%20Mombasa%20brochure%202014.pdf. Accessed May 2017.
16 Ibid.
17 See MASS website. https://massdesigngroup.org/design?type=44&location=All&discipline=52, and further references including; Architectural Digest, Architectural Review (2014, 2015), Bernstein, F. A. (2016, October 20) This Nonprofit Architecture Firm Transformed a Rwandan School. *Architectural Digest*. www.architecturaldigest.com/story/mass-design-group-rwanda-school. Accessed December 2017. Also see Hirano, S. et al. (2011) Developing Rwanda's Schools Infrastructure Standards and Guidelines. *International Journal of Disaster Resilience in the Built Environment*, 2(1), pp. 30–46. There are also blog posts such as: Archdaily Blog Posts (2017, 2018) *Umubano Primary School / MASS Design Group*. www.archdaily.com/372709/umubano-primary-school-mass-design-group.
18 See, for example, World Bank blogs on improving technology in education in poor, rural and isolated communities, around the world: http://blogs.worldbank.org/edutech/education-technology-poor-rural or the UNICEF report on recent on water and sanitation initiatives in rural areas including schools, UNICEF (2014) *UNICEF Report on Water and Sanitation Initiatives in Rural Areas Including Schools*. www.unicef.org/publicpartnerships/files/2014_Annual_Results_Report_WASH.pdf. See also Hassel, B. C. and Dean, S. (2015) *ROCI Idaho*. www.rociidaho.org/wp-content/uploads/2015/03/ROCI_2015_RuralTech_Final.pdf. All accessed June 2017.
19 See Chapters 1 and 2 specifically.
20 Uduku (2015).
21 See official website: www.hole-in-the-wall.com/abouthiwel.html. Accessed June 2017; and Unwin, T. (ed.) (2009) Box Case Study: The Hole in the Wall or Minimally Invasive Education. In *ICT4D, Information and Communication Technology for Development*. Cambridge: Cambridge University Press, p. 340.
22 See Uduku (2015).

6 Conclusions
Education futures in Africa

In this final chapter, the themes examined in the historical and contemporary parts of this book are revisited. This highlights the significance and inter-relatedness of the critical issues which this volume has identified. It also seeks to focus on what contribution these have had to the continuing debate about what constitutes good or successful educational design in Africa in the 21st century. A critical appraisal of what school planning and design can contribute to local educational needs with further examples of where this has been achieved successfully in Africa and elsewhere is also discussed. This is situated within a wider discussion about the changing approach to education pedagogy, from early years to local community level, within different international contexts. This in effect highlights the need to appreciate that the new learning modes, technologies and concepts will need well-planned and innovatively designed spaces for learning.

Future education in Africa

The establishment of universal free basic education in Africa remains a key development goal which has yet to be achieved. Goal 2 to "achieve universal primary education" of the United Nations initial 2000–2015 Millennium Development Goals (MDGs) was a target set for African countries and those elsewhere in the emerging world.[1] However, by 2015, Goal 4 ('quality education') of the subsequent Sustainable Development Goals (SDGs) notes that despite there being significant progress in achieving universal free primary education in the world, "progress has been tough in some developing regions . . . while sub-Saharan Africa made the greatest progress in primary school enrolment among all developing regions, from 52% in 1990 to up to 78% in 2012, large disparities still remain.[2] Children from the poorest households are up to four times more likely to be out of school than those of the richest households. Disparities between rural and urban areas also remains high. This chapter seeks to explore the means by which to best ensure the spread of appropriately designed school classrooms, or learning spaces, across the continent. This is a critical aspiration two centuries since Africa's first encounter with Western education.

Although the African school classroom of the future will be expected to deliver the baseline fundamental educational experience expected of contemporary schools for its students, education and knowledge systems are likely to depend less on traditional textbook-based forms of study and teacher-directed learning. This is because interactive online systems will make remote learning more possible for most of the African continent. *Learning spaces*, the likely to be adopted catch-all for classrooms of the future, will exist but they predictably will inhabit non-traditional spaces; libraries and other communal places instead of traditional dedicated spaces within school buildings. Thus, as learning becomes less teacher directed and shifts towards peer-to-peer and remote learning formats, the physical design of the traditional classroom is set to become redundant.

Considering the vastness of the African continent and the remote country regions to which education has yet to make serious inroads, this may take some time to achieve. This is despite the numerous international and national education reports and goals since the last century, from the early 20th century Phelps-Stokes Reports to today's Sustainable Development Goals.[3] However, with the speed of penetration of the mobile phone and GSM networks in Africa, which are the main carriers and conveyors of the new 'e-learning' systems, timescales may be much faster than envisaged. There are a number of trial e-learning projects currently taking place across Africa, and ICT systems from the 'One Laptop per Child' projects to e-learning systems. However, the leap from the historic classroom 'chalk and talk' setting to a more distributed learning approach is inevitable, and is likely to produce a transformational change in the design of Africa's historical classrooms to contemporary learning spaces.

The context to previous school design history

The early chapters of this book have established that Africa's educational landscape has remained relatively unchanged since the mid-20th century when most countries became independent, established their own national education policies and adopted school design policies and standards. These were an amalgamation of earlier missionary and colonial design guidelines and the UNESCO standards. There has been only limited change to African school design and teaching in middle income country education, chiefly in South Africa and at independent private schools. The majority of Africa's schools remain designed to the mid-20th century guidelines, which do not challenge this historic status quo. These historic 'chalk and talk' classrooms have remained the standard design to be found throughout Africa to the present day. This is both for pragmatic reasons: their design and construction has required minimal innovation in material sourcing and delivery; and also for cultural reasons, as the historic school classroom design remains a recognisable symbol of the school and the educational presence, particularly

118   *Conclusions*

in rural and poorer urban communities, where social infrastructure is minimal or non-existent.

The child-centred learning movement that emerged in postwar Europe and America resulted in changed classroom design, particularly at kindergarten-nursery and primary level in the West, with the introduction of open classrooms and decentralised, informal classroom spaces.[4] Elsewhere in the world, there have been examples of schools which have been designed to respond better to the learning and teaching needs of their students.[5] These same policies which advocated this change in school design were introduced through the design guides produced by UNESCO and educational consultants working on 1960s in newly independent countries of the Global South, including Africa.[6] In reality, this new child-centred focus had limited adoption in much of the South. This is because, as earlier pointed out, official government policies were focused on the building of basic traditional school classroom blocks and ensuring their spread to rural areas, and the growing urban populations in informal settlements.

The new child-centred learning curriculum model was, however, adopted by some demonstration schools in Africa. These institutions were often university-based schools for the children of academic staff. These demonstration schools were also affiliated to education departments in African universities including the universities of Ibadan and Ife in Nigeria and KNUST, Kumasi and Legon universities in Ghana.[7] Private independent schools that work to international curriculums, such as the Aga Khan schools in East Africa, described in the Mombasa Academy case study in Chapter 5, the International Schools in West Africa and other privately run institutions in Africa are also more likely to have changed their curriculum and classroom designs to respond to contemporary education pedagogy. This advocates more liberal child-centred, experiential learning practices, particularly at junior years. It has resulted in many independent schools favouring the design of open multi-function space learning-play areas and appropriately scaled classroom features such as lower windows and child-sized furniture.

South Africa's emergence from its pre-1994, racial-specific or, *apartheid* education policy in effect enabled a national reorganisation and reconsideration of education policies at all levels.[8] This included the evolution of new school building design guidelines, named 'norms and standards'.[9] Such policies also had specific provincial-level interpretations. This is because each of South Africa's nine provinces have had historical autonomy in relation to their application of educational policies.[10] At the country level, South Africa was also one of the first countries in the world and in sub-Saharan Africa to adopt the child feeding programmes for kindergarten and early primary school children.[11] The design of post-apartheid primary schools across South Africa were radically changed to adapt to the needs of the school feeding programmes. These programmes needed not only more classrooms for the increased enrolment of children in many communities, but also the design

Conclusions   119

of kitchens and storage related to the cooking and storage of foodstuffs for these programmes.[12] In some schools, on-site farms were also incorporated within the school grounds. Examples of these schools include the Dalweide and Vukani schools, discussed in Chapter 5.

In this vein, the idea of the school as a community hub has evolved from its earlier historic links with early missionary infrastructure, which often included a combination of social infrastructure such as the dispensary/clinic, the church and the school, all comprising parts of the 'Mission'.[13] In the 21st century, the idea of the education or community hub, incorporating the school and other community functions, has also been identified and promoted by a number of policies and authors in different international contexts.[14] This ranges from the open schools advocated by the *escuela nueva* movement in Latin America[15] through to remote schools in Ladakh and the new high schools in South Africa such as Inkwenkwezi High school, as discussed.[16] This suggested potential for a broader multi-functional future for educational facilities within local communities is thus already being developed.

This chapter, however, seeks to explore how schools in the African sub-continent might engage with future trends in learning, and the need of national educational policymakers, to ensure that their school infrastructure is able to respond to the new, UN-backed Global Sustainable Development Goals for education and development.[17] In Africa and other continents whose nations depend heavily on support and funding from UN agencies the World Bank and other NGOs, this is especially crucial. This chapter considers future themes in educational development. It engages with and seeks to interpret current policies and material relating to the spread of communication and information technologies in educational development at local, national and international levels. The conceptual development, design and function of the 21st century classroom or learning space is also considered.

The contextual background to education in Africa: The 1980s–1990s

In African nations, as in those elsewhere in the emerging world, the mid-1990s heralded the end of the era of structural adjustment. This was after the period in the 1980s when the majority of African governments had to cut social spending in keeping with the austerity policies demanded by the World Bank and other major lenders who had bailed out these countries from their accrued debts incurred from the global downturn of commodity prices and subsequent collapse of national economies throughout the continent. At its end, however, education became less nationalised and more decentralised to regional levels.[18] Furthermore, the neoliberal reforms in financial spending, and subsequently educational aid, encouraged the development of private schools of all levels of funding; thus, the aftermath of the

120 Conclusions

structural adjustment era resulted in an uneven school landscape of often poorly funded state schools and a range of private schools of various funding means and expertise.[19]

This era also broadly coincided with the rapid spread of school theories related to child-centred learning as countries such as the UK embarked on upgrading their ageing school infrastructure in various nationally funded projects.[20] These theories did ultimately trickle down to school planning and design, but they were adopted mainly by independent schools and not by most national government school providers. Thus, the standards and norms for school design, as first established in the postwar era by UNESCO, remain the basis for school design standards and inspection in the majority of schools in African countries and those elsewhere in emerging world.

Thus, the new pedagogic theories of child-centred engagement with space settings in the classroom have ensured that schools in the West and those run by private providers elsewhere in the world, including Africa, have been able to develop more contemporary interpretations and design responses to the educational needs of the 21st century child. This gained further global coverage in the 1990s with the integration of education pedagogy at the end of the Cold War and the international push towards universal development as had been articulated first through world education conferences, the UN Millennium Development Goals and now the Sustainable Development Goals, where Goal 4 centres on the target of achieving accessible educational for all.

In contrast, most schools in Africa and elsewhere in the emerging world remain focused on the design and delivery of the historic post-WW2 UNESCO standard school norms of the 1950s and 1960s. This is exemplified by the classroom model where the 'teacher teaches – students listen', with classroom spaces designed for a notional 35–40 students at the maximum.[21] However, since the late 20th century, it has been acknowledged across the world including Africa in educational circles that new forms of learning will incorporate the use of digital computer-based technologies.[22] More recently, this has spread to recognising mobile telephone and tablet app internet technologies in the classroom.[23]

In the West, the investment into this emerging strand of learning and the increased funding it was seen to require was incorporated into school policy and the development of the educational curriculum. Exemplars of this included the UK BBC-Acorn Computer scheme for schools, and the involvement of Silicon Valley in the development of Californian education.[24] In the emerging world and in Africa, this development has been – and remains in most countries – aid-dependent. This means that donations of equipment, sometime already obsolete, has taken place from the early educational computing era of the 1990s to the present day, this donor-recipient situation having become an accepted norm.[25]

Post-2001 to the present . . .

With the United Nations' declaration of the Millennium Development Goals (MDGs) just prior to 2000, and the further realignment of geo-politics after the 2001 9/11 bombing, the global goal to achieve access to basic education for all was reinforced and backed by major international organisations including the World Bank, UNESCO and international governments.[26] Child-based learning, flexible classrooms and schools as a community resource have also re-entered the vocabulary of school provision, as has 'educational facilities management', formerly called school building programmes.[27] Examples of international schools designed with elements of child-based learning and more radical Latin American *escuela neuva*-focused pedagogical concepts[28] have been recorded in various publications, including architectural journals and educational development journals.[29]

Since the financial crash in 2007–2008, however, the realignment of the global financial markets has inevitably had an effect on investment in education, particularly capital-intensive infrastructure such as school buildings globally.[30] In the emerging world, the economic downturn has had less national effect on schools investment, in physical 'bricks and mortar' terms, as despite the global situation, local economies have continued to grow, and consequently there has been a significant investment in and spread of basic school building construction in emerging countries including those in Africa. However, despite this increased education coverage, the MDG goals for basic education were not reached in Africa by 2015, and this has now been rolled into Goal 4 of the new SDGs.[31]

Furthermore, at a global level, more strategic areas of capital investment in education in areas such as ICT (generally meaning the purchase of desktop computers for classroom computing labs) has had attracted less funding since the international financial crash of 2008. This has in turn resulted in the slowed investment and development of ICT programmes for schools on the African continent.[32] Thus, despite the knowledge that the future global educational landscape will need youths who have competencies in technology and ICT, most of Africa's state school network has been unable to invest in the infrastructure and teaching needed for this.

The aid sector

An area of increased development and external educational investment in Africa is the aid sector. Probably since the attainment of self-rule in the 1960s, few African nations have had the amount of aid and development interest in education as they have in the present day.[33] Some countries' economies are more dependent on direct or indirect NGO funding than

122   *Conclusions*

they are in actual state investment in education, particularly in the provision of basic education infrastructure such as classrooms, and often teachers, especially in remote rural areas.[34] School infrastructure provision, as in new school and classroom building, receives the most direct capital aid.[35] More recently, schools with classrooms designed to incorporate ICT education programmes and community development infrastructure have benefitted from significant tranches of this kind of specific technical aid as global ICT players such as the One Laptop per Child Programme and IBM have sought to invest in global ICT education.[36] Fewer large-scale operators have also developed well-meaning computer equipment donation programmes to schools for ICT learning in Africa and elsewhere in the emerging world. These smaller programmes often have more local, informal arrangements with local communities and sometimes education ministries.[37]

Thus these growing 'aid' initiatives and programmes are playing an increasingly important role in providing 21st century educational infrastructure, from the basic classroom through to fully specified ICT labs. In many countries, this 21st century educational 'aid pipeline' has been crucial in enabling post-conflict and post-disaster regions to have educational facilities built after the vicissitudes of socio-economic collapse, and absent political governance. However, in some countries and certain regions there seems to be local reliance on this NGO 'aid pipeline' to deliver school infrastructure in remote areas, with limited or no collaboration with national governments, who in turn a blind eye to these developments. This can lead to a situation in which the school and classroom design standards used within the aid context are often developed and produced by the aid body and do not necessarily tie in to existing design standards. This means that the 'pro-bono' built schools are therefore not integrated into national school infrastructure programmes where they exist.

An emerging area in educational infrastructure which is embracing IT provision is the design and establishment of educational facilities in settlements and camps for the children of refugees and Internally Displaced Persons (IDPs). The UNHCR, in association with the UNDP and other international agencies, is supporting educational programmes and initiatives that enable children and learners in these communities engage in online learning and acquiring critical IT skills to equip them with the skills needed to engage with work and life in the 21st century (see figure 6.1).[38]

Thus, the context to school design history over the post-WW2 years has been dominated by global policies and trends dictated by international bodies, the most influential being the World Bank and UNESCO. Increased access to education remains the main policy goal of all organisations, as despite the historic programmes including Education for All, the Millennium Development Goals and present SDGs, a significant proportion of school age children on the African continent remain out of school, and those in school are functionally illiterate at school completion.[39]

Figure 6.1 Refugees Using Tablets in Classroom
Courtesy UNHCR

Future school design programmes

At an international level, the interest and investment in Educational Facilities Provision (EFP), incorporating school design programmes, has fluctuated in parallel with global economies and markets. Often, as discussed, in both the West and emerging world, capital funding for school building projects is cut as the economy enters a downturn. There has, however, been near total acknowledgement amongst education practitioners of the need to develop the learning space to respond to contemporary educational needs and practice in which child-centred learning is promoted, as is the flexible use of the classroom for varied group and single-function activities. Exemplar schools from the emerging world and the West that demonstrate this design response to new learning space requirements and also the link of learning and the classroom to local communities abound in popular and academic writing.[40]

New learning concepts: ICT and learning . . .

As Prensky (2001) has noted, today's youth are now digital natives, and their facility and ability to not only communicate but exist in the digital world opens up channels of educational development.[41] The ubiquity and relative low cost of mobile telephone technology suggests that this medium has the most potential in future education expansion. There have already been a

124   *Conclusions*

number of digital education initiatives such as the earlier mentioned US-originated, but now wound-down, one laptop per child (OLPC) programme, which achieved some penetration in Latin America, Africa and Asia.[42] India and China have also been successful in creating bespoke online learning programmes, which however are reliant on access to power and functioning desktop computers.[43] A number of external mediated programmes aimed at giving access to learning to the disadvantaged in the emerging world have ranged from the donation of old computer equipment to schools and the 'upcycling' of old computers to the donation of new computers and ICT facilities within purpose-built classrooms or technology centres, or in some cases as container classrooms.[44] In the developed world, much of this digital provision and access has been provided through the creation of more flexible school campuses, and also the upgrading and design of new libraries that now function as learning centres giving access to digital learning to all local users, such as the 'Idea Store' libraries in London.[45]

The main issues with this traditional approach to ICT provision and learning in education are its cost and the infrastructure required to enable students engage with online learning. With adequate capital investment, ongoing investments in software upgrades and support for local technical and teaching staff support, this approach has proven to be successful, as is evidenced in some Indian cities and parts of urban South Africa.[46] For poorer, more rural and hard-to-access areas, this traditional ICT hardware provision approach is impossible, due both to the aforementioned cost limitations and also the paucity of fixed communication networks.

Models of digital learning based on using mobile phones as the main medium for learning medium are being developed and reported on. Being linked to a wider ecology of open access information sources and cloud-based wifi networks, possibly transmitted from central community buildings, means that access to and the use of this form of digital learning can be affordable, community located and flexible to access. Interestingly, this 'mobile learning' model has relevance in both learning 'worlds'; in the emerging world, this might be obvious due to the relatively low tech low maintenance and low-cost approach. In developed countries, however, its ability to enable flexibility of learning, and also in its ideal form be less tied to the scarce resource of good schools, teachers and equipment, makes it attractive to struggling locations and neighbourhoods. The approach also is particularly suited to rural neighbourhoods in more remote parts of the world, be this in the Scottish Islands or Central Africa, where regular communications infrastructure is non-existent or limited due to the location and the capital costs involved in linking these regions to conventional infrastructure networks.

Test projects already exist which have begun to explore the possibilities of this approach. Whilst today these may seem aspirational but as technology is set to continue to follow Moore's law,[47] and the ubiquity of the smartphone grows in new markets, manufacturers are pursing in the emerging world.

Furthermore, as with the music industry, access to open access books – particularly in this case learning materials – could be a disruptive technology. This could fundamentally change both the marketing model for learning, or more precisely learning media (traditional textbooks, and paper-based content) and also for its consumption; from learning being located in the traditional regulated school classroom environment, to the flexibility and accessibility of location and time of use of one's personal hand-held mobile phone device.[48]

This scenario, in turn, is likely to be a game changer for the conceptualisation and delivery of education worldwide, as has the spread and coverage of the mobile telephone. More importantly, this will have a direct influence on the ways in which learners engage with information. This, in turn, will challenge how 21st century learning spaces are conceived and designed.

How will learning evolve to respond to the incorporation of e-content on a pervasive scale? In certain situations where delivering traditional classroom-taught education is difficult, such as in war or natural disaster zones, the potential for near-100% e-education scenarios delivered via mobile devices becomes plausible. In such cases, the learning space might be secondary to ensuring there is a space able to provide a safe shelter to learners from outside danger, with only limited or mediated contact with a teacher-facilitator.

The flexibility of learning also currently being trialled now via the UCL schools experiment, could become the mainstream or norm, as the economic reality of children's lives in poorer emerging countries is recognised, or the needs of 'out of school' and 'excluded' children elsewhere are met via more consistent levels of educational delivery tailored to the student or student group and not to a dated conventional norm.

The accessibility of learning material online, the already discussed ubiquity of mobile phones and today's communications media has successfully shrunk major barriers to learning. Despite this, there is a lack of architects and designers with the organisational and logistical skills that are crucial to developing the design of future places and spaces for new forms of non-traditional class-based digital learning. This will be critical if we are to succeed in delivering the required range of transformational learning spaces. The education of a new breed of creative spatial thinkers will need to be trained and supported to help deliver the new 21st century spaces that are needed in all environments, contextually challenging or neutral, in both the West and the emerging world.

New learning spaces

School building programmes today, therefore, share many of the historic issues of the past. Particularly, there remains limited provision and poor access to schools and education in the most vulnerable communities. This section explores what future possibilities present themselves for contemporary

126   *Conclusions*

learning and teaching practice, utilising the technologies and media to support existing learning spaces that are now available globally, and create new ones.

Education researchers and commentators have investigated and discussed various ways in which education can be better integrated within local communities, engaging with contemporary education and sociological discourses focused on flexibility of learning, inclusivity of learners and widening access to all. As discussed earlier, the flexible classroom concept has been developed and embedded into school design since the 1980s, as has the idea of the school being a community resource with areas of shared access such as libraries and ICT learning areas.[49]

More radical ideas have also been explored such as the programme-based learning approach, doing away with the classroom altogether, the Chicago public schools strategy[50] or having learning centred around the teenage body clock, the UCL-London strategy.[51] Whilst there has also been a 'back to the traditional' trend amongst some (i.e., doing away with technology in classrooms and returning to more traditional modes of learning), future trends point to the increased incorporation and use of digital technologies for learning and as part of the future development of the 21st century learning environment.[52] This is explored further in the final Reflections section of this book.

Future learning networks for Africa . . .

For urban Africa, which is projected to increasingly be the birthplace of most of Africa's 21st century youth,[53] the ICT future just discussed is likely to make access to a good education considerably easier than it is today. How this will work out in parts of remote, rural Africa is less certain, despite many anecdotal case studies suggesting its potential, as recorded by the 'hole in the wall' experiment as translated from Ethiopia which might offer a glimpse of the possible.[54]

However, there is yet to be enough statistical evidence to confirm this. There are three key issues that we can examine as being likely to have a direct impact on how future learning at school level, and in community networks of learning or 'practice'. These are:

- new technologies,
- new learning spaces and
- the need to deliver evidence-based international outcomes.

New Technologies for learning, including the use of smartphone apps, to access digital information and learning have already been discussed in the previous section. Their importance to future African education is reinforced here, as this is the factor most likely to produce the leapfrog or 'disruptive' pedagogical element to classroom learning at all levels in Africa. Arguably, younger basic education students are more likely to benefit from new learning

Figure 6.2 'Hole in the Wall' Learning, India
Courtesy Professor Sugata Mitra

technologies, as even in remote parts of Africa the mobile phone is becoming ubiquitous.[55] Despite mobile phone access posing more of a challenge to potential students in remote villages in Africa, national mobile phone usage statistics suggest that even in rural areas, Mithra's thesis on mediated virtual peer-to-peer learning is likely to play a large role in ensuring that access to and the take up of virtual learning in rural areas will be achievable (see figure 6.2).[56]

A key aspect of these new 'e-technologies' and information formats is their relative cost. Unlike the past costs associated with textbooks, teachers and the supported spaces for learning (specialised classrooms), the 'e-learning' and digital material has limited costs; the hardware costs of a mobile phone as discussed is cheap and likely to become even cheaper as lower 'branded' equipment is designed and made for the masses in the emerging world.[57] Open source material online is also becoming 'free' for those who can successfully access this.

The relative autonomy that the use of the mobile phone as a personalised learning tool, and the likely spread of open source information and adapted Massive Online Open-learning Courses (MOOCs), suggests that the need to engage with the 'teacher' and the 'book' are likely to be bypassed in

128   *Conclusions*

the supported e-environment. The economic and practical costs of sending teachers out to remote rural areas across the world have never fully been resolved. In remote locations in countries such as Australia and Canada, the idea of the 'flying teacher' or traditional distance education, has historically been developed to respond to this problem of providing education to pupils in remote areas.[58] These rural regions in Africa and elsewhere in the emerging world have not had the financial means to develop similar programmes. The use of digital and the virtual material that is accessible online should significantly contribute to reducing the costs related to providing distance learning programmes.

Whilst this transformation is likely to take time, particularly because of the costs involved in ensuring GPS coverage to remote locations and poorer urban areas with low digital signal coverage, there is evidence to suggest that the outcomes of access to better digital coverage is already showing positive developmental results in Africa. Some of this success is related to the use of similar 'e-services' by health and disaster response networks, and the subsequent international funding of 'e- telecommunication' networks.[59]

The new learning spaces . . .

School buildings, classrooms and other educational facilities come second place in the future educational landscape. The need for dedicated mono-function learning spaces in the more digital learning world of the future will change significantly from the present. Already the current model, as still held up as the classroom standard and norm for much of Africa, has been challenged and changed significantly in the West. It is likely that with the adoption of more internet learning and the associated micro-technologies required for this (i.e., smartphones, tablets, etc.), the need for the traditional classroom will become challenged.

Already in some government schools, such as in South Africa, the classroom has been replaced by group learning spaces for certain subjects.[60] This change is also beginning to rapidly transform classrooms for primary/ kindergarten learning, which across Africa are beginning to adopt a more child-centred approach to learning, resulting in furniture being scaled to child size. Also, enlightened NGOs are able to reflect this change in their design, as evidenced by the Ghana Dwabor kindergarten case study. This spread is likely to increase as new thinking and designers are engaged in re-imagining the educational space in Africa. Part of this is likely to be integrated into a new understanding of and engagement with learning as being more of a community and not only child-based process. The re-emergence then of the social hub, from its historic earlier days as the mission, or community centre, is already becoming apparent.

This is evidenced by the use of communities such as the Dunoon community in Khayelitsha, Cape Town, where the library is a shared facility with the school and the community. This is equally true with David Adjaye's concept

Idea Stores in London,[61] as it is in South Africa. The concept, then, of the learning space may in time be as relevant – or more so – than the classroom, if facilities and support are to be best optimised in communities, particularly those where funding is particularly limited. This would not be a 'cut down' version of the traditional school concept which has historically been in place, but a reformulation or transformation of an educational model of wider relevance for the 21st century than arguably the non-workable model situated in the early 20th century.

No doubt, versions of the elite school will remain in place, for the old and nouveaux riche alike in Africa who can afford the costs and funding for this. Increasingly, however, at local level there is already the need to redefine development and the sustainable form which this can take.

Local/international outcomes, policies and programmes

This need to evaluate and produce new models of sustainable development for classroom and learning spaces design is the final factor which this chapter explores. Since the end of WW2, the failure of the past development goals to meet the universal education targets as set out by international bodies shows that there is the need to critically engage and examine which education-related programmes are most likely to deliver the outcomes that the now reformulated Sustainable Development Goals (SDGs) set out to achieve. A positive analysis of the new SDGs suggests that they do look for a more integrated development outcome than did their MDG predecessors. Considering this new 'joined-up' development focus, the idea of future educational buildings in Africa taking on a more integrated strategy is particularly apt.

Conceptually also, as discussed in school design and new forms of learning, there is the need to develop a significant shift from traditional educational delivery models to those with more open-ended or more outward-reaching, community focused goals. The policies and outcome that are now being championed would seem to support this. Longitudinal evidence-based assessments have been shown not always to be the best way to assess the qualitative success of using integrated learning strategies at community level. Furthermore, there are creative ways of assessing learning attainment across age cohorts being taught in dispersed non-traditional learning environments, as demonstrated in the already mentioned *escuela neuva* educational model.[62]

Local policies have also had to respond to the different financial climate in which they find themselves. Even when there is the political will to commit to the delivery of fully funded national educational policies, these are now often impossible to deliver in the current increasingly uncertain local and international economic climate. The likely continued involvement, therefore, of charities and 'aid' organisations also creates a new space in which policies and programmes need to be both realistic and pragmatic in their delivery aspirations. It is important that there is an integrated understanding by various

130 Conclusions

actors as to how they can best 'plug in' to agreed outcomes for development. To just build a classroom should not be enough as a charity organisation's goal. Charity-funded African school building projects should demonstrate their 'impact' and integration into a local development plan or scheme, defined and promoted by local stakeholders, who after all are in the best position to know what developmental needs are most critical to their community. Indeed, local recipient communities should be closely involved all aspects of the process, to ensure the afterlife sustainability of these school building projects.[63]

A similar form of rigorous impact consideration should take place when selecting building materials, deciding on construction processes and engaging with all aspects of the learning space delivery. The longevity of the typical rectangular, 'bricks and mortar classroom block' has been mainly due to the ease and cheapness of build, and the easy recognition factor of the typical classroom block. For African governments also, it is easy to quantify investment in education by recording the number of classroom blocks that have been built over a time period, with little reference to the overcrowded pupil conditions which are the norm in many schools.

The dominance of the typical classroom design is, however, now being challenged by more recent cost-effective and climate-responsive classroom design interpretations by architects and designers in countries as diverse as the work being done by architects such as Francis Kere in Gando, Burkina Faso, and Kunle Adeyemi in Lagos, Nigeria (see figure 6.3).[64]

Figure 6.3 Floating School Makoko Iagos
Courtesy Kunle Adeyemi Architects

Conclusions 131

Also, the transformation of spaces such as the ubiquitous shipping containers into new learning spaces demonstrates what possibilities there are when creative thought is employed into envisioning future learning space prototypes.[65] However, even in the most futuristic e-learning scenarios, it is clear that there will still be the need for spaces and places in which students are able to study, learn and absorb current and future knowledge and information. Only a very fortunate few African children have the benefit of access to well-designed environments where learning, teacher-led or self-led, can take place.

Most of Africa's classrooms and learning spaces remain sparse affairs with neither access to power nor the security needed to enable them to be viable spaces for study outside of the limited school day. In the future, traditional classroom spaces could become transformed to learning spaces which have the flexibility to work as spaces equipped appropriately to have lighting and access to online resources for children and other learners to use outside of the school day. This would be in addition to their continued use as daytime classroom spaces; the example of the Noero Wolff-designed Inkwenkwezi library in Cape Town, discussed in Chapter 5, demonstrates how this can be achieved.

Reflections

Schools and classrooms in the 21st century are already undergoing transformations in design which have enabled them engage with new learning policies and basic interventions such as the UN-supported primary school feeding programmes common across countries in Africa. Also, they have responded to technology-ICT driven projects such as the One Laptop Per Child Programme that was rolled out across Africa, from Ghanaian to South African primary schools. As we approach the third decade of the 21st century, this transformation is likely to become even more rapid as learning concepts, processes and technologies develop even further.

The likely decentralisation of learning involving more usage of distributed learning processes such as the now-ubiquitous 'MOOCs' and other online programme delivery forms, as discussed, will inevitably have a disruptive effect on traditional learning systems.[66] The way in which this will affect the physical transformation of the classroom, from its current traditional spatial design to a new learning space typology, is not yet certain. However, the possible re-interpretations of learning areas, spaces and communities of peer-to-peer-based learning is already a developing research area.[67]

For African schools and learners, this is likely to be one of the most significant changes to the educational landscape in its two centuries of development from the mission schools to the present day. It is a set challenge to re-evaluate the fundamental premise of traditional education systems across the entire continent – from the 'bricks and mortar' school construction to new funding models for future teaching that may take on different forms; dispersed, shared and remotely delivered to 21st

132 *Conclusions*

century learners, who themselves may no longer fit into traditional 'child cohort' categories.

It may be that these more liberal pragmatic education policies are mostly promoted by the international NGOs, which have historically regulated and advised education policy. Alternatively, they may be challenged by the new technology purveyors, such as the OLPC foundation, IBM, Apple or private education providers and successors. These players are already set to gain more ground in determining education provision, which is already the case in some parts of India and elsewhere in Asia.[68] Liberalised education policies have already had the effect of significantly widening in the range of private education partners who operate in countries such as Nigeria, Kenya and South Africa, with mixed results.[69]

For school buildings and infrastructure, this might be a positive move, as the regulatory school designs – as is typical of state education systems – are challenged by philanthropic providers who have more open, contemporary approaches to designing learning spaces, including the incorporation of child-centred learning practices, digital learning tools and the design of facilities for use outside of classroom hours.

Whatever the case, there is likely to be a change in future African school design and its provision, from this historical overview of relative stasis and limited gradual transformation over time, to learning spaces that are designed to respond to the rapid pace of technological developments from the late 20th century to the present day. Optimistically, the globalising nature and spread of new media and digital technologies in learning should enable African nations to 'leap forward' with their design and provision of educational infrastructure, for 21st century educational requirements, and in so doing significantly improve childhood learning environments. This should be transformational, not only for African school design, but for educational development across the continent.

Ultimately then, Africa's classrooms need to be reinvented and transformed to show they have the pragmatism of programme and flexibility of design to allow these learning spaces to fully engage with new forms of technology for pedagogy. Also, there remains the real need for learning spaces in Africa and emerging countries to respond to the need to accommodate the significantly larger class sizes found in most schools, considering also what learning settings are best able to respond to large group teaching approaches. Design sustainability in relation to buildings, climate material and socio-cultural context will also be critical to this. These characteristics are relevant for the delivery of the educational needs of 21st century learners, who may be individuals, classes and communities in their broadest definition, with radically diverse learning practices and needs.

This holistic view takes us back to the history of the initial missionary schools – whose ethos was aligned to the mission, encompassing education, health and a social commitment to religion. This call for better, more responsive design of learning spaces is grounded in this past history, but calls for a new, fundamental and relevant approach to learning spaces design which better reflects the more flexible and open uses learning spaces should aspire to in today's transformed educational landscape.

As we approach the mid-21st century, there will be no doubt a reckoning and assessment of classroom design and school delivery. What has become clear is that as these technologies change learning globally, Africa will not be left out. The continent stands to gain from this new diffusion of educational practice and the effect this will have on traditional school infrastructure, that has been synonymous with the long history of Africa's encounter with Western education, embodied in its school buildings and classrooms from the mid-19th century to the present day.

When compared to the contemporary school building design programmes elsewhere in the world, Africa unfortunately remains particularly poorly served. Since the heady pre- to early post-independence decades of the 1950s–1970s there have been few national school building programmes in Africa. The closest to this was the significant investment in education made by the post-apartheid state, as part of the ANC freedom manifesto pledge in the late 1990s. As discussed with Case studies of Vukani and Inkwenkwezi schools, described in Chapter 5, this did produce a distinct set of schools in some South African provinces where school design had been devolved to local architects. This unfortunately only managed to produce a few bespoke exemplar school projects, which rightly gained critical design acclaim, but alas were not replicated on a national scale, as had been the earlier case of the IDA schools projects in Nigeria in the 1970s and the earlier National School building projects in Ghana in the 1950s and 1960s.

In contrast, in the UK the Blair government (1997–2006) initiated an ambitious scheme called the City Academies framework in 2002 to build new schools and renovate existing schools. Most British schools had had little improvement or innovation since the spur of construction which last took place as a result of the Education Act of 1944 that raised the school leaving age and thus meant more classrooms and schools had to be built to accommodate the increased secondary school-age population.[70] The City Academy programme was superseded by the Building Schools for the Future (BSF) initiative which was a more wide-ranging initiative that involved renowned British architects being called to redesign schools considering issues such as sustainability, community engagement and also a re-interpretation of learning spaces and space standards to better reflect teaching practice and new technologies in the 21st century.

There have been a number of publications on school design in the United Kingdom, providing a retrospective to these school building programmes from the 1990s and early 2000s. Elsewhere in the West, Hille's 2011 book *Modern Schools: A Century of School Design* provides a broad sweep of contemporary education architecture, focusing mainly but not exclusively on North America. Other books and papers have also focused on understanding and analysing school design processes and the relationship of school design to learning.

134 Conclusions

What is lacking, however, is a similar retrospective design analysis of schools in the emerging world. Recent media sites such as *Dezeen* and *ArchDaily*, and established journals including *Architectural Review* and the *RIBA Journal*, do however highlight exemplar education design projects in Africa such as the Lagos Floating School (*ArchDaily*, 2013, *Architectural Review* 2014),[71] Inkwenkwezi (*Architectural Review* 2007)[72] and the Gando School Project (*Archnet*, 2002).[73]

This book has focused on producing an historical and contemporary retrospective of educational design in Africa, from a select regional and national context. Despite the select coverage of schools which have been examined in these chapters, the ambition of the text to fill this gap and engage with the themes related specifically to school design, policy and practice in various regions of Africa has been achieved. Its critical analysis of the contextual background to Western education in Africa, its history and current design development issues provides a basis from which to form an understanding of the ongoing issues related to education provision in Africa and also good practice where and how it exists. Most importantly, it is hoped that this will be a basis for further research development and the improved delivery of learning spaces for 21st century Africa.

Figure 6.4 Dwabor School
Courtesy D. Bond and Sabre Charitable Trust

Conclusions 135

Notes

1 United Nations (2000) *Millennium Development Goals*. www.un.org/millennium-goals/. Accessed June 2017.
2 UNDP (2015b) *Sustainable Development Goals*. www.undp.org/content/undp/en/home/sustainable-development-goals.html. Accessed June 2017.
3 For Phelps-Stokes Reports (1920 and 1924) see, Lewis, L. J. (ed.) (1962) *Phelps-Stokes Reports on Education in Africa*. London: Oxford University Press, Education in Africa Reports, and UNDP (2015b).
4 See Dudek, M. (2000) *The Architecture of Schools*. London: Routledge.
5 Ibid.; and Harrison, A. and Hutton, L. (2013) *Design for the Changing Architectural Landscape: Space, Place and the Future of Learning*. London: Routledge.
6 See, for example, Vickery, D. J. (1984, 1988) *Facilities Design Guide*. Paris: UNESCO, and Almeida, R. (1985, 1988) *Handbook for Educational Buildings Planning*. Paris: UNESCO.
7 Uduku, O. (2015) Spaces for 21st Century Learning. In *Routledge Handbook on International Learning and Development*. London: Routledge, pp. 196–209.
8 South African Government (1996) *South African Schools Act, 1996 (Act No. 84 of 1996)*. www.greengazette.co.za/acts/south-african-schools-act_1996-084. Accessed April 2018.
9 South African Government (2009) *Department of Education Notice, No. of 2009 The National Minimum Uniform Norms and Standards for School Infrastructure*.
10 Western Cape Government (2014) *Proposal for Elimination of Public School Infrastructure Backlogs in the Western Cape*. https://wcedonline.westerncape.gov.za/documents/NormsAndStandards/WCED-NS-infrastructureplan2015.pdf. Accessed April 2018, as identified through the regulations relating to minimum uniform norms and standards for public school infrastructure promulgated in terms of the South African Government (1996).
11 Uduku, O. (2011) School Building Design for Feeding Programmes and Community Outreach: Insights From Ghana and South Africa. *International Journal of Educational Development*, 31, pp. 59–66.
12 Ibid.
13 Uduku, O. (2000) The Colonial Face of Educational Space. In L. Lokko (ed.), *White Papers Black Marks*. London: Athlone Press, pp. 44–65.
14 Uduku, O. (2008b) *Designing Schools as Development Hubs for Learning*. Final Report. Bristol: University of Bristol; ARUP (2014) *Roadmap for Safer School*. Design Guidance, ARUP. www.arup.com/publications/research/section/roadmap-for-safer-schools?query=global%20program%20for%20safer%20schools. Accessed March 2017; World Bank Houses of Parliament (2017) *Sure Start Briefing*. http://researchbriefings.parliament.uk/ResearchBriefing/Summary/CBP-7257. Accessed March 2018.
15 See Psacharopoulos, G., Rojas, C. and Velez, E. (1993). Achievement Evaluation of Colombia's Escuela Nueva: Is Multigrade the Answer? *Comparative Education Review*, 37(3), pp. 263–276.
16 Ladakh schools case study in Uduku (2015); and see ARUP website: http://arupcommunity.org/projects/d/druk-white-lotus-school. Accessed June 2017.
17 UNDP (2015b).
18 See Uduku, O. (1994b) *Schools in Africa: Perspectives on a Viable Physical Ideal*. Centre for African Studies Cape Town Seminar Semester 2, 1994, African Studies Centre, Robinson College. Cambridge: University of Cambridge; and note 10.
19 World Bank (1988) *Education in Africa Report*. Washington, DC: World Bank.
20 See Building Schools for the Future Project (2003) http://webarchive.national archives.gov.uk/20130401151715/www.education.gov.uk/publications/eOrderingDownload/DfES%200134%20200MIG469.pdf. Accessed January 2018; and

136 *Conclusions*

    also: www.oecd.org/unitedkingdom/buildingschoolsforthefutureintheunitedking-dom.htm. Accessed June 2017.

21 Vickery, D. J. (1985) *Norms and Standards of Educational Facilities*. Paris: UNESCO.

22 Uduku (2015).

23 Ibid.

24 Lean, T. (2016) *Electronic Dreams: How 1980s Britain Learned to Love the Computer*. London: Bloomsbury; and Aspray, W. (2016) *Participation in Computing: The National Science Foundation's Expansionary Programmes*. Basel, Switzerland: Springer.

25 Uduku (1994b) lists a number of ICT computing 'labs' which were filled with obsolete donated IBM PCs.

26 See United Nations (2000).

27 See Woolner, P. (2010) *The Design of Learning Spaces*. London: Bloomsbury, there are on average more than thirty articles per month, in the *Architects Journal* on schools from the Building Schools for the Future 1990s era to date, also see report by Middlewood, D. and Parker, R. (2009) *Leading and Managing Extended Schools: Ensuring Every Child Matters*. London: Sage.

28 The *escuela nueva* teaching system was initiated in Latin America, and involved delivering mass education using peer-to-peer and non-conventional multi-year classes. It has been adapted for use in countries such as Cuba and Ecuador. See Uduku (2011) and Uduku (2015).

29 See, for example, Worldwatch Institute (2017) *EarthEd: Rethinking Education in a Changing Planet*. Washington, DC: Island Press; Kleymeyer, C. D. (1994) *Culture Expression and Grassroot Development: Cases From Latin America and the Caribbean*. Boulder, CO: Reinner; and Al Borde Architects: http://nykyinen.com/al-borde-architects-rural-school-in-ecuador/. Accessed June 2017.

30 In the West, in the UK for example, there was a cut in the funding of the Schools for the Future Programme, and a reduction in funding for the upgrading of school infrastructure. See Curtis, P. (2010, July 5) School Buildings Programme Scrapped in Latest Round of Cuts. *The Guardian*.

31 UNDP (2015b).

32 See, for example, UNESCO (n.d.c) *Information and Communication Technology (ICT) in Education in Sub-Saharan Africa: A Comparative Analysis of Basic E-Readiness in Schools*. www.uis.unesco.org/Communication/Documents/ICT-africa.pdf. Accessed June 2017; and also Farell, G. and Isaacs, S. (2007) Survey of ICT and Education in Africa. *infoDev*. www.infodev.org/infodev-files/resource/InfodevDocuments_353.pdf. Accessed June 2017.

33 See UNESCO (2015a) *The Investment Case for Education and Equity*. www.unicef.org/publications/files/Investment_Case_for_Education_and_Equity_FINAL. pdf. Accessed June 2017.

34 See note 31.

35 Volunteer VSO or 'Peace Corps' teachers and those from other NGOs are usually directly funded by the NGOs and therefore remuneration and investment is not quantifiable in the same way.

36 OLPC (One Laptop Per Child). *Weblog*. http://one.laptop.org/about/mission. Accessed June 2017.

37 See, for example, McLeod, S. et al. (2014) *The ICT Classroom Project*. www. blogs.hss.ed.ac.uk/after-development/2014/02/10/ict-classroom-project/. Accessed June 2017, working with the NGOs Learning Planet and Aleutia.

38 UNHCR Blog. www.unhcr.org/uk/protection/operations/5149ba349/unhcr-education-strategy-2012-2016.html?query=ICT%20education. Accessed August 2017.

Conclusions 137

39 UNESCO (1990) *Meeting Basic Learning Needs: A Vision for the 1990s.* http:// unesdoc.unesco.org/images/0009/000975/097552e.pdf. Accessed April 2014; and UNDP (2014) *United Nations Human Development Report.* www.undp. org/content/undp/en/home/librarypage/hdr/2014-human-development-report. html. Accessed April 2018.

40 See Hille, R. T. (2011) *Modern Schools: A Century of School Design.* London: Wiley, and Dudek, M. (2000) *Kindergarten Architecture.* London: Spon, for example.

41 Prensky, M. (2001) Digital Natives, Digital Immigrants. *On the Horizon* (MCB University Press), 9(5).

42 OLPC website http://one.laptop.org/ (no longer active).

43 Carr-Chellman, A. A. (ed.) (2004) *Global Perspectives on E-Learning: Rhetoric and Reality.* Thousand Oaks, CA; London: SAGE Publications; and Moore, M. G. and Kearsley, G. (2011) *Distance Education: A Systems View of Online Learning.* Belmont, CA: Wadsworth, Cengage Learning.

44 For the ethics of computer donations see: Iles, A.T. (2004, November) Mapping Environmental Justice in Technology Flows. *Global Environmental Politics*, 4(4), pp. 76–107. For upcycling, see Simmons, D. (2014) Keepod: Can a $7 Stick Provide Billions Computer Access? *BBC News.* www.bbc.co.uk/news/technology-27346567; Samsung Container School. www.samsungvillage.com/blog/2011/10/27/ samsungblog-solar-powered-internet-school-provides-new-opportunities-for-students-in-africa/; Learning Planet Computer Classroom. www.blogs.hss.ed.ac.uk/ after-development/2014/02/10/ict-classroom-project/.

45 Idea Store: Tower Hamlets (2009). *Idea Store Strategy 2009.* www.ideastore. co.uk/public/document s/PDF/IdeaStowStrategyAppx I CAB290709.pdf.

46 See Besilant, J. (2010) Getting Clever About Smart Cities: New Opportunities Require New Business Models. *Forrester.* http://193.40.244.77/iot/wp-content/ uploads/2014/02/getting_clever_about_smart_cities_new_opportunities.pdf.

47 Moore's law (Moore, G. [1965, April 19] Cramming More Components Onto Integrated Circuits. *Electronics Magazine*, 38(8)) suggests that the number of transistors or circuit boards doubles every year, which partly explains the rapid speed in the development of computing and mobile telephony.

48 Robinson, K. (2010) Case Study: Longman Introduces Mobile Reading to Nigeria. *Pyramid Research.* www.pyramidresearch.com/documents/IMPACTofMobile ServicesInNIGERIA.pdf. Accessed January 2018.

49 For example: Criticos, C. and Thurlow, M. (1987) *Design of Learning Spaces.* Durban: Media Resources Centre, Department of Education, University of Natal, and the National Archives Kew, UNESCO Building Report Series in the 1970s on School Design in South East Asia (Vickery, 1966), and Asian Regional Institute for School Building Research (1972), or earlier texts such as Nelson, H. B. (1953) The Community School. In *Yearbook of the Society for the National Study of Education.* Chicago, IL: Chicago University Press.

50 Since the late 1990s, Chicago public schools have operated a decentralised budget and policy structure, with autonomous SRI International. Humphrey, D. C. and Shields, P. M. (2009) High School Reform in Chicago Public Schools: An Overview. *SRI International.* https://consortium.uchicago.edu/sites/default/files/ publications/Overview.pdf. Accessed June 2017.

51 See Stepian, W. and Gallagher, S. (1993, April) Problem Based Learning: As Authentic as It Gets. *Educational Leadership*, 50(7), pp. 23–28; and Biggs, J. (1999) *Teaching for Quality Learning at University.* Buckingham, UK: Society for Research into Higher Education and Open University Press, for the Asian experience. For UCL schools approach, see The UCL Academy. *The Academy Day: Level 3*, www.uclacademy.co.uk/The-Academy-Day; and Bell, S. (2015) *Start Secondary School at 10am to Improve Learning.* www.british

138 *Conclusions*

scienceassociation.org/news/start-secondary-school-at-10am-to-improve-learning. Both accessed June 2017.

52 See notes 28 and 31.

53 UNDP (2017) *World Development Report*. Washington, DC: World Bank; also see Sommers, M. (2010) Urban Youth in Africa. *Environment and Urbanization*, 22(2), pp. 317–332. International Institute for Environment and Development (IIED); and Lall, S. V. et al. (2017) *Africa's Cities: Opening Doors to the World*. World Bank. https://openknowledge.worldbank.org/handle/10986/25896. Accesed April 2018.

54 See Mitra, S. (2006) *The Hole in the Wall*. New York. www.hole-in-the-wall. com/abouthiwel.html. Accessed June 2017; and Unwin, T. (ed.) (2009) Box Case Study: The Hole in the Wall or Minimally Invasive Education. In *ICT4D, Information and Communication Technology for Development*. Cambridge: Cambridge University Press, p. 340. For Ethiopia see Talbot, D. (2012) Given Tablets But No Teachers, Ethiopian Children Teach Themselves. *MIT Technology Review*. www.technologyreview.com/s/506466/given-tablets-but-no-teachers-ethiopian-children-teach-themselves/. Accessed June 2017.

55 UNDP (2017).

56 See note 51.

57 A $10 Indian Smartphone, was briefly marketed (*The Guardian* (2016, February 17) Indian Firm Launches £5 Smartphone, Thought to Be World's Cheapest. www. theguardian.com/technology/2016/feb/17/india-cheapest-smartphone-worlds-ringing-bells. Accessed April 2018.), whilst basic Nokia and Chinese manufactured feature phones already cost less than $30 in South Africa (*The Economist* (2015, April 25) Technology in Africa, the Pioneering Continent. www.econ omist.com/news/middle-east-and-africa/21649516-innovation-increasingly-local-pioneering-continent. Accessed April 2018.).

58 See Higgins, A. H. (1994, Spring) A Background to Rural Education Schooling in Australia. *Journal of Research in Rural Education*, 10(1), pp. 48–57.

59 Including open platforms such as 'Ushahidi', www.ushahidi.com/. Accessed June 2017.

60 See Westerfield College case study report, in Uduku, O. (1994a) *Factors Affecting School Design in South Africa*. Report, Centre for African Studies, University of Cambridge.

61 Idea Store (2009) *Idea Store Story*. www.ideastore.co.uk/idea-story.

62 See note 27.

63 The Sabre Charitable Trust-funded Dwabor school case study described in Chapter 5 demonstrates this strategy.

64 For example, the Gando School designed by the Burkinabe architect Francis Kere, www.kere-architecture.com/projects/. Accessed June 2017 and the *escuela nueva* schools discussed earlier on in this chapter (see note 27).

65 See note 36, McLeod et al. (2014).

66 See Uduku, O. (2016) *In the Notes on the Future of the Book in Africa Project Blog*. https://academicbookfuture.org/2016/04/05/academic-book-in-africa/. Accessed June 2017.

67 See Harrison and Hutton (2013), although particularly Western education-focused, Chapters 4, 'Schools' (pp. 60–107) and 8, 'A Conceptual Learning Landscape' (pp. 236–245), have universal relevance to school design. Also see the work of Western Cape architects, Noero Wolff and Albertyn Wessels, both discussed in Chapter 5.

68 There are a number of mobile learning initiatives in Asia, in India particularly. See International Development Office (IDO) (2016) How Mobile Learning Is Delivering Vital Resources to Teachers in India. *Open University Report*. www.open.

ac.uk/about/international-development/news/mobile-learning-week-tess-india. Accessed June 2017.

69 See UNESCO (2014) *Reading in the Mobile Era: A Study of Mobile Reading in Developing Countries*. http://unesdoc.unesco.org/images/0022/002274/227436e. pdf. Accessed April 2018, which discusses patterns of readership amongst students in Africa and elsewhere. Pearson Education also had an earlier 2009 programme of introducing reading at primary level to children using mobile phones; see Agabi, C. (2009) Nigeria: Longman Launches Mobile Reading Pilot for Children. *AllAFrica.com*. http://allafrica.com/stories/200907020025.html. Accessed June 2017.

70 See Hawkes, D. (2014) Historical Context, Chapter 2. In P. Clegg (ed.), *Learning From Schools: Feilden Clegg Bradley Studios*. London: Artifice, pp. 6–17. Also Wright, S. (2016) New Labour New Approach. In N. Michandani and S. Wright (eds.), *Future Schools Innovative Design for Existing and New Buildings*. London: RIBA, pp. 10–12.

71 *ArchDaily* (2013) Lagos Floating School. www.archdaily.com/344047/ makoko-floating-school-nle-architects, Architectural Review (2014) www.archi tectural-review.com/today/learning-from-lagos-floating-school-makoko-nigeria-kunl-adeyemi-nl/8652311.article. Accessed December 2017.

72 See also Low, I. (2010) Space and Transformation: Reflection on the New WCED Schools Programme. In E. Pieterse (ed.), *Countercurrents, Experiments in Sustainability in the Cape Town Region*. Johannesburg: Jacarana, pp. 202–215.

73 Archnet (2002) *Francis Kere's Gando School Won an Aga Khan Award in 2002–2004*. https://archnet.org/sites/4363. Francis Kere's Gando school won an Aga Khan award in 2002–2004, has since been extended and led to the architect designing the 2017 Serpentine Pavilion in London, Serpentine Pavilion (2017) *Serpentine Pavilion 2017 Designed by Francis Kéré, 23 June 2017 to 19 November 2017*. www.serpentinegalleries.org/exhibitions-events/serpentine-pavilion-2017-designed-francis-k%C3%A9r%C3%A9. Accessed December 2017.

Afterword

School Design in Africa: Critical Histories and 21st Century Challenges has been a long-drawn project. The writing process has been long, and with significant breaks and pauses. In some ways, it mimics the history of school design in Africa. The continent's schools have had a long evolutionary development over centuries. This has been uneven in its coverage, with significant differences across the continent.

The aspiration to produce a book that was comprehensive in all aspects of its coverage of school design in Africa was ambitious. This volume has ultimately achieved some – if not all – of this vision. Producing and writing it has been a journey of learning and discovery. I hope that the wide context and background of the book's subject matter, education in Africa, will help engender it to the reader. This is not the last word on this subject, but hopefully it does make a significant contribution both to our understanding of the long history of school design in Africa and the important challenges that today's schools on the continent now have to encounter.

The range of case studies discussed is also hoped to help concretise the history and reality of Africa's schools. They, of course, can only offer a snapshot in time, and in book format are only a selected sample of a much greater range and variation of schools to be found across Africa. The predominant focus of the book on Anglophone countries is also regretted, as discussed in the Preface. Again, this linguistic and regional focus relates back to the colonial legacies which create the 'silos' that critical research and writing in Africa are read within. There is clearly a future collaborative project in which scholars across these linguistic and other divides find common purpose to produce an integrated history of school design and infrastructure policy across Africa.

This comparative discourse and discussion is more apparent in the book's exploration of contemporary issues related to school design. E-learning and its infrastructure is transnational in its development, and the large urban conurbations such as Kinshasa-Brazzaville or the Lagos-Lome-Cotonou urban strip have created urban areas which are transnational in character. At a local level, Adeyemi's Makoko Floating School project[1] also challenges neat perceptions of local authority control, as the location of the school off

Afterword 141

the Lagos coastline meant local authorities could consider it outside of and in contravention to local government jurisdiction on schools.

The discussion of the new 'market' in education in Africa also echoes the fears of UNESCO as articulated in its most recent position publication, which calls for a return to a more humanist viewing of education as a common right and goal.[2] This does contradict with the mixed public free market approach to education found in most of Africa's cities. The dependence on 'aid-architecture' for school design in rural areas can be traced back to the reduced investment in rural education by state governments and the increasing aid-architecture economy. However, as discussed in Chapters 5 and 6, aid programmes devised to design schools in rural areas can be set up and run, but the staying power to convert these efforts into local impact is much more difficult to achieve. The success of the Sabre Charitable Trust schools programme in Ghana shows this can be done.

Future classrooms or school learning spaces design also seems secure. The mix of new digital learning, a better understanding of the spatial needs required for child-centred learning pedagogies and the acknowledgement of how classrooms can best to be configured to accommodate class sizes of more than eighty. There still, however, will need to be a long-term critical assessment of initiatives such as the "hole in the wall" digital learning programme.[3] The democratisation of education and the target of full access to education for all children – allowing "ensuring inclusive and equitable quality education and promoting lifelong learning opportunities for all"[4] and indeed the use of schools as not just containers for learning but as development hubs remains a future aspiration not so far away.

Further research writing and case study analysis of schools throughout Africa is clearly an area which needs more engagement. The text produced focuses near exclusively on educational design and policy in Anglophone Africa. The clear contextual and practical differences to the execution of educational policy in countries with different post-colonial histories will make this area of research of particular interest, as the contrasts between these regions should build a more complete picture of the past and contemporary issues in school provision and educational design in sub-Saharan Africa.

This book is ultimately dedicated to African children and the design of their formative learning spaces, which has formed the ultimate focus of this oeuvre. My hope is that the writing of this volume will help us all to better understand how good school design can contribute to ensuring that children have better learning experiences and successes in their encounters with the future educational landscape.

Planning and delivering these new learning spaces might not be cheap, but as has been said:

> If you think education is expensive, wait until you see how much ignorance costs in the 21st century.[5]
>
> U.S. President Obama

142 Afterword

Figure BM1.1 Africa ICT Project
Rendering courtesy: Shaun McLeod et al.

Notes

1 *See Architectural Review* (2014) www.architectural-review.com/today/learning-from-lagos-floating-school-makoko-nigeria-kunl-adeyemi-nl/8652311.article. Accessed December 2017; and *ArchDaily* (2013) Lagos Floating School. www.archdaily.com/344047/ makoko-floating-school-nle-architects.
2 UNESCO (2015), Rethinking Education: Towards a Global Common Good, Paris, UNESCO.
3 Mitra, S. (2006) *The Hole in the Wall*. New York. www.hole-in-the-wall.com/abouthiwel.html. Accessed June 2017. Also Note 2 p. 49.
4 UNDP (2015a) *Sustainable Development Goal (SDG) 4, Quality Education*. www.undp.org/content/dam/undp/library/corporate/brochure/SDGs_Booklet_Web_En.pdf. Accessed April 2018.
5 Twitterfeed: "If you think education is expensive, wait until you see how much ignorance costs in the 21st century." – President Obama #ABetterBargain, 24 July 2013. Accessed April 2018.

Bibliography

Achebe, C. (1958) *Things Fall Apart*. London: Heinemann.

Achebe, C. (2010) *The African Trilogy*. London: Everyman.

Achebe, C. (2012) *There Was a Country*. London: Penguin.

Adekunle, J. (2002) Nationalism Ethnicity and National Integration: An Analysis of Political History, in A. Oyebade (ed.), *The Transformation of Nigeria, Essays in Honour of Toyin Falola*. Trenton, NJ: Africa World Press, pp. 426–429.

Aderinoye, R. A. (2007) Expanding Access to Adult Basic Education in Nigeria: The Intervention of Open Distance Learning. *Adult Education in Nigeria*, 14, pp. 216–226.

Adesina, S. and Ogunsaju S. (eds.) (1984) *Secondary Education in Nigeria*. Ile-Ife: University of Ife Press.

African Development Bank (ADB) (2017) *Africa's Urban Population Projection Statistics*. www.afdb.org/fileadmin/uploads/afdb/Documents/Publications/Tracking_Africa%E2%80%99s_Progress_in_Figures.pdf. Accessed August 2017.

Aga Khan Foundation. *View on the Design of Educational Environments*. www.agakhanacademies.org/general/commitment-excellence-designing-aga-khan-academies. Accessed June 2017.

Aga Khan Foundation Schools. *Website*. www.akdn.org/our-agencies/aga-khan-education-services/akes-east-africa. Accessed June 2017.

Aga Khan Mombasa School. *Information Brochure*. www.agakhanacademies.org/sites/default/files/AKA%20Mombasa%20brochure%202014.pdf. Accessed May 2017

Agabi, C. (2009) Nigeria: Longman Launches Mobile Reading Pilot for Children. *AllAfrica.com*. http://allafrica.com/stories/200907020025.html. Accessed June 2017.

Ahmed, I. (2013) Northern Nigeria Launches Massive Literacy Campaign. *Voice of America*. www.voanews.com/a/northern-nigeria-launches-massive-literacy-campaign-for-400000/1812906.html. Accessed 15 December 2017.

Ajayi, J. F. A. (1965) *Christian Missions in Nigeria 1841–1891: The Making of a New Elite*. Evanston, IL: Northwestern University Press.

Ajibade, B., Ekpe, E. and Bassey, T. (2012, May) More than Fabric Motifs: Changed Meaning of the Nsibidi on the Efik Ukara Cloth. *Mediterranean Journal of Social Sciences*, 2(2), pp. 297–303. www.mcser.org/images/stories/2_journal/mjss_may_2012/babson_ajibade_ester_ekpe.pdf.

Alafe-Aluko, M. O. (1973) *The Historical Development of the Comprehensive High School Aiyetoro (f. 1963) Nigeria*. Ph.D. Thesis, Washington University, Graduate School of Education.

144 Bibliography

Al Borde Architects (2009) *Rural School in Ecuador*. http://nykyinen.com/al-borde-architects-rural-school-in-ecuador/. Accessed June 2017.

Almeida, R. (1985, 1988) *Handbook for Educational Buildings Planning*. Paris: UNESCO.

American International University of West Africa. *Homepage*. www.aiu.edu.gm/history.html. Accessed May 2017.

Archdaily Blog Posts (2017, 2018) *Umubano Primary School / MASS Design Group*. www.archdaily.com/372709/umubano-primary-school-mass-design-group.

Archnet (2002) *Francis Kere's Gando School Won an Aga Khan Award in 2002–2004*. https://archnet.org/sites/4363

ARUP (2010) *A Prototype Kindergarten for a Remote District of Ghana*. www.arup.com/projects/dwabor-kindergarten.

ARUP. (2012) *Druk White Lotus School*. http://arupcommunity.org/projects/d/druk-white-lotus-school. Accessed June 2017.

ARUP (2014) *Roadmap for Safer School*. Design Guidance, ARUP. www.arup.com/publications/research/section/roadmap-for-safer-schools?query=global%20program%20for%20safer%20schools. Accessed March 2017.

Ashby, E. (1965) A Contribution to the Dialogue on African Universities. *Higher Education Quarterly*, 20(1), pp. 70–89.

Aspray, W. (2016) *Participation in Computing: The National Science Foundation's Expansionary Programmes*. Basel, Switzerland: Springer.

Ayandele, E. A. (1966) *The Missionary Impact on Modern Nigeria 1842–1914: A Political and Social Analysis*. London: Longman Green and Co.

Aye, E. (1986) *Hope Waddell Training Institution Life and Work: 1894–1978*. Edinburgh: National Library of Scotland.

Baker, N. (1987) *Passive and Low Energy Building Design for Tropical Island Climates*. London: Commonwealth Secretariat.

Bell, S. (2015) *Start Secondary School at 10am to Improve Learning*. www.britishscienceassociation.org/news/start-secondary-school-at-10am-to-improve-learning. Accessed June 2017.

Bernstein, F. A. (2016, October 20) This Non-profit Architecture Firm Transformed a Rwandan School. *Architectural Digest*. www.architecturaldigest.com/story/mass-design-group-rwanda-school. Accessed December 2017.

Besilant, J. (2010) Getting Clever About Smart Cities: New Opportunities Require New Business Models. *Forrester*. http://193.40.244.77/iot/wp-content/uploads/2014/02/getting_clever_about_smart_cities_new_opportunities.pdf.

Biggs, J. (1999) *Teaching for Quality Learning at University*. Buckingham, UK: Society for Research into Higher Education and Open University Press.

Birmingham, D. (2016) *A Short History of Modern Angola*. Oxford: Oxford University Press.

Bond, M. (1968, March) A Library for Bolgatanga. *Architectural Forum*, CXXV111, pp. 66–69.

Bray, M. (1986) *New Resources for Education, Community Management and Financing of Schools in Less Developed Countries*. London: Commonwealth Secretariat.

Bray, M. (1988) *Double-Shift Schooling: Design and Operation for Cost Effectiveness*. London: Commonwealth Secretariat/Paris: UNESCO.

Bray, M. and Lillis, K. (1988) *Community Funding of Education: Issues and Policy Implications in Less Developed Countries*. London: Commonwealth Secretariat/Pergamon Press.

Bibliography   145

Brink, P. J. (1993) Studying African Women's Secret Societies: The Fattening Room of the Annang. In C. Renzetti and R. Lee (eds.), *Researching Sensitive Topics*. Newbury Park, CA: Sage.

Building and Construction Authority, Singapore Government. *Sustainable Built Environment*. www.bca.gov.sg/Sustain/sustain.html.

Building Schools for the Future Project (BSF) (2003) http://webarchive.national archives.gov.uk/20130401151715/www.education.gov.uk/publications/eOrdering Download/DfES%200134%20200MIG469.pdf. Accessed January 2018.

Carlson, A. (2003) *Nsibidi, Gender, and Literacy: The Art of the Bakor-Ejagham, Cross River State*. Ph.D. Thesis, Indiana University.

Carr-Chellman, A. A. (ed.) (2005) *Global Perspectives on E-Learning: Rhetoric and Reality*. Thousand Oaks, CA; London: Sage Publications.

Christopher, A. J. (1986) *Atlas of Apartheid*. London: Routledge.

Cairns Regional Council (2011) *Sustainable Tropical Building Design: Guidelines for Commercial Buildings*. www.cairns.qld.gov.au/__data/assets/pdf_file/0003/ 45642/BuildingDesign.pdf

Criticos, C. and Thurlow, M. (1987) *Design of Learning Spaces*. Durban: Media Resources Centre, Department of Education, University of Natal.

Cross, M. (2011) *An Unfulfilled Promise: Transforming Education in Mozambique*. Addis Ababa, Ethiopia: Organisation for Social Science Research in Eastern and Southern Africa.

Curtis, P. (2010, July 5) School Buildings Programme Scrapped in Latest Round of Cuts. *The Guardian*.

Davidson, B. (1977) *A History of West Africa 1000–1800*. London: Longman.

Davidson, B. (1998) *West Africa, Before the Colonial Era: A History to 1850*. London: Longman.

Denyer, S. (1978) *African Traditional Architecture*. London: Heinemann.

De Raedt, K. (2013) Shifting Conditions, Frameworks and Approaches: The Work of KPDV in Postcolonial Africa. *ABE Journal*, 4. http://journals.openedition.org/ abe/566?lang=en. Accessed January 2018.

De Raedt, K. (2014) Between True Believers' and Operational Experts: UNESCO Architects and School Building in Post Colonial Africa. *Journal of Architecture*, 19(1), pp. 19–42.

De Raedt, K. and Lagae, J. (2014) Building for L'Authencite, Architect Eugene Palumbo in Mobuto's Congo. *Journal of Architectural Education*, 68(2), pp. 178–189.

Dmchowski, Z. R. (1990) *Introduction to Traditional Nigerian Architecture. Volume 1: Northern Nigeria*. London: Ethnographica.

Dore, R. (1997) *The Diploma Disease*. London: Institute of Education.

Drew, J. and Fry, M., with introduction by I. Jackson (2014) *Village Housing in the Tropics* (reprint). London: Routledge.

Dudek, M. (2000) *The Architecture of Schools*. London: Routledge.

Dudek, M. (2000) *Kindergarten Architecture*. London: Spon.

Echeruo, M. J. C. (1977) *Victorian Lagos: Aspects of Nineteenth Century Lagos Live*. London: Macmillan.

The Economist (2015a, August) Learning Unleashed, Low Cost Private Schools. (Print Edition briefing). www.economist.com/news/briefing/21660063-where-governments-are-failing-provide-youngsters-decent-education-private-sector. Accessed April 2018.

146   Bibliography

The Economist (2015b, August) The $ a Week School. www.economist.com/print-edition/2015-08-01. Accessed April 2018.

The Economist (2015, April 25) Technology in Africa, the Pioneering Continent. www.economist.com/news/middle-east-and-africa/21649516-innovation-increasingly-local-pioneering-continent. Accessed April 2018.

The Economist (2017a, January 28) Could do better: Bridge International Academies Gets High Marks for Ambition but Its Business Model Is Still Unproven. www.economist.com/news/business/21715695-its-biggest-challenge-may-well-be-financial-bridge-international-academies-gets-high-marks. Accessed April 2018.

The Economist (2017b, January 28) Emerging Markets Should Welcome Low Cost Schools. www.economist.com/news/leaders/21715665-east-african-crackdown-bridge-international-academies-hopelessly-misguided-emerging. Accessed April 2018.

Fafunwa, B. (1974) *History of Education in Nigeria*. London: Allen and Unwin.

Falola, T. and Ezekwem, O. (eds.) (2016) *Writing the Nigeria-Biafra Civil War*. London: James Currey.

Farell, G. and Isaacs, S. (2007) Survey of ICT and Education in Africa. *infoDev*. www.infodev.org/infodev-files/resource/InfodevDocuments_353.pdf. Accessed June 2017.

Foreign Policy (2017) *US to Pull Out of UNESCO Again*. http://foreignpolicy.com/2017/10/11/u-s-to-pull-out-of-unesco-again/. Accessed December 2017.

Forsyth, F. (1969) *The Biafra Story*. London: Harmondsworth Penguin.

Freire, P. (1970) *Pedagogy of the Oppressed*. London: Penguin.

Fry, M. and Drew, J. (1948) *Village Housing in the Tropics*. London: Lund Humphries.

Fry, M. and Drew, J. (1964) *Tropical Architecture in the Warm Humid Zone*. London: Architectural Press.

Fyle, M. (1999) *Introduction to the History of African Civilisation. Volume 1: Pre-colonial Africa*. Lanham, MD: University Press of America.

Glendinning, M. (2008) *Modern Architect: The Life and Times of Robert Matthew*. London: RIBA.

Goldway, M. (1962) *Report on Vocational Education in Eastern Nigeria*. Lagos: Ministry of Education.

Graham, S. (1966) *Government Mission Education in Northern Nigeria, With Special Reference to the Work of Hans Vischer*. Ibadan: Ibadan University Press.

Greenhalgh, T. et al. (2007) Realist Review to Understand the Efficacy of School Feeding Programmes. *BMJ*, 335(7625): 858–861.

Gryc, H. and da Silva, J. (2013) Global Engineers Thinking Locally: Creating Kindergartens for Africa. *Civil Engineering*, 166(CE3), ICE Proceedings. www.sabretrust.org/downloads/ICE_Proceedings_Aug13.pdf.

The Guardian (2002) Michael Stern Obituary. www.theguardian.com/news/2002/aug/01/guardianobituaries.highereducation. Accessed December 2017.

The Guardian (2016, February 17) Indian Firm Launches £5 Smartphone, Thought to Be World's Cheapest. www.theguardian.com/technology/2016/feb/17/india-cheapest-smartphone-worlds-ringing-bells. Accessed April 2018.

Harrison, A. and Hutton, L. (2013) *Design for the Changing Architectural Landscape: Space, Place and the Future of Learning*. London: Routledge.

Harvard Graduate School of Education, and USAID (1966) *Harvard/AID Project Progress Report and Work Plan*. Comprehensive High School, Aiyetoro, Western Nigeria, 31st March 1966.

Bibliography 147

Hassel, B. C. and Dean, S. (2015) *ROCI Idaho*. www.rociidaho.org/wp-content/uploads/2015/03/ROCI_2015_RuralTech_Final.pdf. Accessed June 2017.

Hawkes, D. (2014) Historical Context, Chapter 2. In P. Clegg (ed.), *Learning From Schools: Feilden Clegg Bradley Studios*. London: Artifice, pp. 6–17.

Hawthorne, P. (1993) *Historic Schools of South Africa*. Cape Town, South Africa: Pachyderm.

Hentz, J. J. and Solomon, H. (2017) *Understanding Boko Haram: Terrorism and Insurgency in Africa*. Abingdon, Oxon; New York, NY: Routledge.

Herbert, G. (1978) *Pioneers of Prefabrication: The British Contribution in the Nineteenth Century*. Baltimore, MD: Johns Hopkins University Press.

Herskovits, M. J. (1959) Continuity and Change. In M. J. Herskovits and W. Bascom (eds.), *African Cultures*. Chicago, IL: Chicago University Press.

Higgins, A. H. (1994, Spring) A Background to Rural Education Schooling in Australia. *Journal of Research in Rural Education*, 10(1), pp. 48–57.

Hille, R. T. (2011) *Modern Schools: A Century of School Design*. London: Wiley.

Hilliard, F. H. (1957) *A Short History of Education in British West Africa*. London: Nelson.

Hirano, S. et al. (2011) Developing Rwanda's Schools Infrastructure Standards and Guidelines. *International Journal of Disaster Resilience in the Built Environment*, 2(1), pp. 30–46.

Hole in the Wall (n.d.) *Official Archived Website*. www.hole-in-the-wall.com/abouthiwel.html. Accessed June 2017.

Hubbard, J. P. (2000) *Education Under Colonial Rule: A History of Kastina College, 1921–1942*. Latham, NY: University Press of America.

Humphrey, D. C. and Shields, P. M. (2009) High School Reform in Chicago Public Schools: An Overview. *SRI International*. https://consortium.uchicago.edu/sites/default/files/publications/Overview.pdf. Accessed June 2017.

Hussey, E. R. J. (1945) Higher Education in West Africa. *Journal of African Affairs*, 44(177), pp. 165–170.

Idea Store (2009). *Idea Store Story*. www.ideastore.co.uk/idea-story. Accessed June 2017.

Idea Store: Tower Hamlets (2009). *Idea Store Strategy 2009*. www.ideastore.co.uk/public/document s/PDF/IdeaStowStrategyAppxICAB290709.pdf. Accessed June 2017.

Igwe, S. O. (1986) *Education in Eastern Nigeria 1847–1975*. London: Evans.

Iles, A.T. (2004, November) Mapping Environmental Justice in Technology Flows. *Global Environmental Politics*, 4(4), pp. 76–107.

Intergovernmental Panel on Climate Change (IPCC) (2014) www.ipcc.ch/. Accessed May 2017.

International Development Office (IDO) (2016) How Mobile Learning Is Delivering Vital Resources to Teachers in India. *Open University Report*. www.open.ac.uk/about/international-development/news/mobile-learning-week-tess-india. Accessed June 2017.

Isichei, E. A. (1997) *A History of African Societies to 1870*. Cambridge: Cambridge University Press.

Jackson, I. and Holland, J. (2014) *The Architecture of Maxwell Fry and Jane Drew*. London: Routledge.

Kallaway, P. (1996) Policy Challenges for Education in the New South Africa: The Case for School Feeding in the Context of Social and Economic Reconstruction. *Transformation*, 31, pp. 1–24.

148 Bibliography

Kallaway, P. (ed.) (2002) *The History of Education Under Apartheid 1948–1994: The Doors of Learning and Culture Shall Be Opened.* New York, NY: Peter Lang.

Kalu, O. U. (ed.) (1980) *Writing in Pre-colonial Africa: A Case Study of Nsibidi in African Cultural Development.* Enugu: Fourth Dimension Publishers.

Kere, F. (n.d.) *Gando School.* www.kere-architecture.com/projects/. Accessed June 2017.

Kleymeyer, C. D. (1994) *Culture Expression and Grassroot Development: Cases From Latin America and the Caribbean.* Boulder, CO: Reinner.

Koenigsberger, O. H. et al. (1973) *Manual of Tropical Building and Housing.* London: Thames and Hudson.

Kottek, M., Grieser, J., Beck, C., Rudolf, B. and Rubel, F. (2006) World Map of the Koppen-Geiger Climate Classification Updated. *Meteorol. X*, 15, pp. 259–263.

Laborde, G. (2017) Congratulations to Uruguay on the 10th Anniversary of its National OLPC Program, Plan Ceibal! Feature: Uruguay Marks 10 Years of Bridging Digital Divide. *One Laptop Per Child.* http://blog.laptop.org/2017/05/15/congratulations-to-uruguay-on-the-10th-anniversary-of-its-national-olpc-program-plan-ceibal-feature-uruguay-marks-10-years-of-bridging-digital-divide/#.WlUa YFSFj2Q. Accessed January 2018.

Lall, S. V. et al. (2017) *Africa's Cities: Opening Doors to the World.* World Bank. https://openknowledge.worldbank.org/handle/10986/25896. Accessed April 2018.

Lauglo, J. and Maclean, R. (2005) *Vocationalisation of Secondary Education Revisited.* UNESCO UNEVOC Book Series. New York, NY: Springer.

Lean, T. (2016) *Electronic Dreams: How 1980s Britain Learned to Love the Computer.* London: Bloomsbury.

Learning Planet Computer Classroom. www.blogs.hss.ed.ac.uk/after-development/2014/02/10/ict-classroom-project/ Accessed June 2017.

Le Roux, H. (2003, September) The Networks of Tropical Architecture. *Journal of Architecture*, 8, pp. 337–354.

Le Roux, H. (2004) The Post-colonial Architecture of Ghana and Nigeria. *Architectural History*, 47, pp. 361–392.

Lewis, L. J. (ed.) (1962) *Phelps-Stokes Reports on Education in Africa.* London: Oxford University Press.

Lovedale Missionary Institution (1904) *Report for Lovedale Missionary Institution 1903.* Alice, Eastern Cape, South Africa: Lovedale Press.

Low, I. (2010) Space and Transformation: Reflection on the New WCED Schools Programme. In E. Pieterse (ed.), *Countercurrents, Experiments in Sustainability in the Cape Town Region.* Johannesburg: Jacarana, pp. 202–215.

MacCormack, C. (1982) Ritual Fattening and Female Fertility. In T. Vaskilampi and C. MacCormack (eds.), *Folk Medicine and Health Culture: Role of Folk Medicine in Modern Health Care.* Conference Proceedings of the Nordic Research Symposium, 27–28 August, Department of Community Health, University of Kuopio, Kuopio, Finland.

MASS Design Material. *Website.* https://massdesigngroup.org/design?type=44&location=All&discipline=52. Accessed December 2017.

McLeod, S. et al. (2014) *The ICT Classroom Project.* www.blogs.hss.ed.ac.uk/after-development/2014/02/10/ict-classroom-project/. Accessed June 2017.

Middlewood, D. and Parker, R. (2009) *Leading and Managing Extended Schools: Ensuring Every Child Matters.* London: Sage.

Mitra, S. (2006) *The Hole in the Wall.* New York. www.hole-in-the-wall.com/abouthiwel.html. Accessed June 2017.

Bibliography 149

Molony, T. (2015) *Nyerere, the Early Years*. London: James Currey.

Moore, G. (1965, April 19) Cramming More Components Onto Integrated Circuits. *Electronics Magazine*, 38(8).

Moore, M. G. and Kearsley, G. (2011) *Distance Education: A Systems View of Online Learning*. Belmont, CA: Wadsworth, Cengage Learning.

Mwira, K. (1990, August) Kenya's Harambee Secondary School Movement: The Contradictions of Public Policy. *Comparative Education Review*, 34(3), pp. 350–368.

Nelson, H. B. (1953) The Community School. In *Yearbook of the Society for the National Study of Education*. Chicago, IL: Chicago University Press.

Nyerere, J. (1968) *Freedom and Socialism: A Selection From Writings & Speeches, 1965–1967*. Dar es Salaam: Oxford University Press.

Ochiagha, T. (2015) *Achebe and Friends at Umuahia*. London: James Currey.

OECD. *Building Schools for the Future in the United Kingdom*. www.oecd.org/unitedkingdom/buildingschoolsforthefutureintheunitedkingdom.htm. Accessed June 2017.

Oliver, P. (1976) *Shelter in African*. London: Barrie and Jenkins.

OLPC (One Laptop Per Child). *Mission*. http://one.laptop.org/about/mission. Accessed June 2017.

Onsomu, E. N. et al. (2004) *Community Schools in Kenya: Case Study on Community Participation in Funding and Managing Schools*. http://unesdoc.unesco.org/images/0013/001362/136278e.pdf. Accessed January 2018.

Orkidstudio. https://orkidstudio.org/. Accessed May 2017.

Overseas Building Notes, BRE, London, 50–73 1950–73 (Preceded by Colonial Building Notes 1–50, and Anteceded by Tropical Building Notes).

Oyebade, A. (ed.) (2002) The Transformation of Nigeria, Essays in the Honor of Toyin Falola. Trenton, NJ: Africa World Press.

Paracka, D. J. (2002) *The Athens of West Africa*. Ph.D. Thesis, Georgia State University, USA.

Prensky, M. (2001) Digital Natives, Digital Immigrants. *On the Horizon* (MCB University Press), 9(5).

Psacharopoulos, G. (2006, May) World Bank Policy on Education: A Personal Account. *International Journal of Education Development*, pp. 329–338.

Psacharopoulos, G., Rojas, C. and Velez, E. (1993). Achievement Evaluation of Colombia's Escuela Nueva: Is Multigrade the Answer? *Comparative Education Review*, 37(3), pp. 263-276.

Psacharopoulos, G. and Woodhall, H. (1986) *Education for Development: An Analysis of Investment Choices*. New York: Oxford University Press (for the World Bank).

Randall, P. (1982) *Little England on the Veld: The English Private School System in South Africa*. Johannesburg, South Africa: Ravan Press.

Rapoport, A. (1969) *House Form and Culture*. London: Prentice Hall.

Raufu, A. (2014) *Sects and Social Disorder*. London: James Currey.

Robinson, K. (2010) Case Study: Longman Introduces Mobile Reading to Nigeria. *Pyramid Research*. www.pyramidresearch.com/documents/IMPACTofMobileServicesInNIGERIA.pdf. Accessed January 2018.

Sabre Report (2015) *Building a Brighter Future for Children in Ghana*. www.sabretrust.org/downloads/Sabre_AR_2015.pdf. Accessed August 2017.

Samsung Container School. www.samsungvillage.com/blog/2011/10/27/samsungblog-solar-powered-internet-school-provides-new-opportunities-for-students-in-africa/. Accessed June 2017.

150 Bibliography

Schwerdtfeger, F. W. (1982) *Traditional Housing in Nigerian Cities: A Comparative Study of Houses in Zaria, Ibadan and Marrakech*. London: Wiley.

Serpentine Pavilion (2017) *Serpentine Pavilion 2017 Designed by Francis Kéré, 23 June 2017 to 19 November 2017*. www.serpentinegalleries.org/exhibitions-events/serpentine-pavilion-2017-designed-francis-k%C3%A9r%C3%A9. Accessed December 2017.

Sewell, J. P. (1975) Regeneration? Chapter 5. In *UNESCO and World Politics*. Princeton, NJ: Princeton University Press, pp. 199–278. http://unesdoc.unesco.org/images/0012/001211/121117e.pdf. Accessed August 2017.

Shaplin, J. T. (1961, May) Ashby Commission Report on Higher Education in Nigeria. *Higher Education Quarterly*, 15(3), pp. 229–237.

Shepherd, H. W. (1940) *Lovedale, South Africa: The Story of a Century 1841–1941*. Alice, Eastern Cape, South Africa: Lovedale Press.

Simmons, D. (2014) Keepod: Can a $7 Stick Provide Billions Computer Access? *BBC News*. www.bbc.co.uk/news/technology-27346567

Skapski, A. (1962) *The Development of Technical Education and Its Relation to the Education System in Western Nigeria*. A Report Commissioned by the Government of Western Nigeria.

Skapski, A. (1966) *Report of the Comparative Technical Education Seminar Abroad and Recommendation for a National Plan of Vocational and Technical Education in the Republic of Nigeria*. Lagos: Federal Ministry of Education.

Slessor, C. (1995, March) The South Africa Issue. Special Edition Editorial. *Architectural Review*.

Smit, W. and Hennessy, K. (1995) *Taking South African Education out of the Ghetto. An Urban-Planning Perspective*. Cape Town: UCT Press Buchu Books.

Smith, M. G. (2015) *Boko Haram: Inside Nigeria's Unholy War*. London: I. B. Tauris.

Smith, R. (2016) *Education Citizenship and Cuban Identity*. London: Palgrave.

Sommers, M. (2010) Urban Youth in Africa. *Environment and Urbanization*, 22(2), pp. 317–332. International Institute for Environment and Development (IIED).

South African Government (1953) *Bantu Education Act* (No. 47).

South African Government (1996) *South Africa Schools Act, 1996 (Act No. 84 of 1996)* www.greengazette.co.za/acts/south-african-schools-act_1996-084. Accessed April 2018.

South African Government (1998) *National Education Policy*.

South African Government (2009) *Department of Education Notice, No. of 2009 The National Minimum Uniform Norms and Standards for School Infrastructure*.

South African Institute of Architecture (2007) *A Digest of South African Architecture*.

Stepian, W. and Gallagher, S. (1993, April) Problem Based Learning: As Authentic as It Gets. *Educational Leadership*, 50(7), pp. 23–28.

Stone, H. (2009) Schools Buildings in Developing Countries. *Practical Action, Technical Brief*. https://practicalaction.org//docs/technical_information_service/school_buildings_in_developing_countires.pdf. Accessed January 2018.

Strayer, R. W. (1973) The Making of Mission Schools in Kenya. *Comparative Education Review*, 17(3), pp. 313–330.

Talbot, D. (2012) Given Tablets But No Teachers, Ethiopian Children Teach Themselves. *MIT Technology Review*. www.technologyreview.com/news/506466/given-tablets-but-no-teachersethiopian-children-teach-themselves/. Accessed May 2017.

Bibliography 151

Taylor, W. H. (1996) *Mission to Educate: A History of the Educational Work of the Scottish Presbyterian Mission in East Nigeria 1846–1960*. London: Brill.

Theyuenk, S. (2009) *School Construction Strategies for Universal Primary Education in Africa: Should Communities Be Empowered to Build their Schools?* Washington, DC: World Bank.

Thompson, N. (2014) *A Study of Early Corrugated Buildings in Scotland*. www.arct. cam.ac.uk/Downloads/ichs/vol-3-3097-3116-thompson.pdf. Accessed 2017.

Turner and Townsend (2017) *International Construction Market Survey*. www. turnerandtownsend.com/media/1518/international-construction-market-survey-2016.pdf. Accessed May 2017.

The UCL Academy. *The Academy Day: Level 3*. www.uclacademy.co.uk/The-Academy-Day. Accessed June 2017.

Uduku, O. (1993a) *Factors Affecting School Design in Ghana*. Report, Centre for African Studies, University of Cambridge.

Uduku, O. (1993b) *Factors Affecting School Design in Nigeria*. Ph.D. Thesis, University of Cambridge.

Uduku, O. (1994a) *Factors Affecting School Design in South Africa*. Report, Centre for African Studies, University of Cambridge.

Uduku, O. (1994b) *Schools in Africa: Perspectives on a Viable Physical Ideal*. Centre for African Studies Cape Town Seminar Semester 2, 1994, African Studies Centre, Robinson College. Cambridge: University of Cambridge.

Uduku, O. (1994c) Wusasa, Where the Future Acknowledges the Past. *Habitat International*, 18(4), pp. 67–79.

Uduku, O. (2000) The Colonial Face of Educational Space. In L. Lokko (ed.), *White Papers Black Marks*. London: Athlone Press, pp. 44–65.

Uduku, O. (2002) The Socio-Economic Basis of a Diaspora Community, Igbo bu'ike. *Review of African Political Economy*, 29(92), pp. 301–311.

Uduku, O. (2003a) Educational Design and Modernism in West Africa. *Docomomo Journal* (28 March), pp. 76–82.

Uduku, O. (2003b) Video Recorded interview with Michael Grice. London: Architectural Association.

Uduku, O. (2005) Architecture scolaire et éducation: en Afrique anglophone. *XIXe-XXe siècles de l'éducation*, no. 102, mai 2004 (parution: mars 2005).

Uduku, O. (2006, December) Modernist Architecture and 'the Tropical' in West Africa: The Tropical Architecture Movement in West Africa. *Habitat International*, 30(3), pp. 396–411.

Uduku, O. (2008a) *Bolgatanga Library, Adaptive Modernism in Ghana, 40 Years On*. Presented at the Refereed Proceedings of the 10th Docomomo Conference, 13–20 September, Rotterdam, The Netherlands, 'The Challenge of Change' (ed. D. Van Heuvel), T-U Delft.

Uduku, O. (2008b) *Designing Schools as Development Hubs for Learning*. Final Report. Bristol: University of Bristol.

Uduku, O. (2010) *Tropical Ivory Towers: A Critical Evaluation of Design Symbolism and Practical Aspirations of the West African University Campuses in Their Fifth Decade*. Docomomo, 11th International Conference, Mexico City, 12 pp.

Uduku, O. (2011) School Building Design for Feeding Programmes and Community Outreach: Insights From Ghana and South Africa. *International Journal of Educational Development*, 31, pp. 59–66.

152 Bibliography

Uduku, O. (2014) *Village Housing in the Tropics*, With Special Reference to West Africa: Jane Drew, Maxwell Fry, and Harry L. Ford Humphries, 1947, 134 pages, and *Fry, Drew, Knight, Creamer: Architecture*: Stephen Hitchins Lund Humphries, 1978 160 pages. *Journal of Architectural Education*, 68(2), pp. 265–266.

Uduku, O. (2015) Spaces for 21st Century Learning. In *Routledge Handbook on International Learning and Development*. London: Routledge, pp. 196–209.

Uduku, O. (2016) The UNESCO-IDA School Building Programme in Africa: The Nigeria 'Unity' Schools, Chapter 14. In J. Willis and K. Darien-Smith (eds.), *Designing Schools, Space, Place and Pedagogy*. London: Taylor and Francis, pp. 175–187.

Uduku, O. and Criticos, C. (eds.) (1994) *Learning Spaces in Africa Conference*. Durban: University of KwaZulu Natal.

UNDP (2014) *United Nations Human Development Report*. www.undp.org/content/undp/en/home/librarypage/hdr/2014-human-development-report.html. Accessed April 2018.

UNDP (2015a) *Sustainable Development Goal (SDG) 4, Quality Education*. www.undp.org/content/dam/undp/library/corporate/brochure/SDGs_Booklet_Web_En.pdf. Accessed April 2018.

UNDP (2015b) *Sustainable Development Goals*. www.undp.org/content/undp/en/home/sustainable-development-goals. html. Accessed June 2017.

UNDP (2017) *World Development Report*. Washington, DC: World Bank.

UNDP Report (2016) *Country Profiles for Botswana*. http://hdr.undp.org/en/countries/profiles/BWA; and Gabon http://hdr.undp.org/en/countries/profiles/GAB respectively. Both Accessed August 2017.

UNESCO (1990) *Meeting Basic Learning Needs: A Vision for the 1990s*. http://unesdoc.unesco.org/images/0009/000975/097552e.pdf. Accessed April 2014.

UNESCO (2008) *Inclusive Dimensions of the Right to Education*. Paris: UNESCO.

UNESCO (2014) *Reading in the Mobile Era: A Study of Mobile Reading in Developing Countries*. http://unesdoc.unesco.org/images/0022/002274/227436e.pdf. Accessed April 2018.

UNESCO (2015a) *The Investment Case for Education and Equity*. www.unicef.org/publications/files/Investment_Case_for_Education_and_Equity_FINAL.pdf. Accessed June 2017. p 49 box 10, 'The hole in the wall experiment'.

UNESCO (2015b) *Rethinking Education for a Global Common Good*. http://unesdoc.unesco.org/images/0023/002325/232555e.pdf. Accessed December 2017.

UNESCO. (n.d.a) *Architecture for Education*. www.unesco.org/education/pdf/BAT0029.PDF. Accessed August 2017.

UNESCO. (n.d.b) *History*. www.unesco.org/new/en/unesco/about-us/who-we-are/history/. Accessed May 2017.

UNESCO (n.d.c) *Information and Communication Technology (ICT) in Education in Sub-Saharan Africa: A Comparative Analysis of Basic E-Readiness in Schools*. www.uis.unesco.org/Communication/Documents/ICT-africa.pdf. Accessed June 2017.

UNHCR Blog. www.unhcr.org/uk/protection/operations/5149ba349/unhcr-education-strategy-2012-2016.html?query=ICT%20education. Accessed August 2017.

UNICEF (2014) *UNICEF Report on Water and Sanitation Initiatives in Rural Areas Including Schools*. www.unicef.org/publicpartnerships/files/2014_Annual_Results_Report_WASH.pdf.

United Nations (1948) *Universal Declaration of Human Rights, Article 26*. www.un.org/en/universal-declaration-human-rights/. Accessed May 2017.

Bibliography 153

United Nations (2000) *Millennium Development Goals*. www.un.org/millenniumgoals/. Accessed June 2017.

United Nations (2017) *Population 2050 Projections*. www.un.org/sustainable development/blog/2017/06/world-population-projected-to-reach-9-8-billion-in-2050-and-11–2-billion-in-2100-says-un/. Accessed August 2017.

University of Bristol (2008) *EdQual Project*. www.edqual.org/research.html.

University of The Gambia. *Homepage*. www.utg.edu.gm/. Accessed January 2018.

Unwin, T. (ed.) (2009) Box Case Study: The Hole in the Wall or Minimally Invasive Education. In *ICT4D, Information and Communication Technology for Development*. Cambridge: Cambridge University Press, p. 340.

US Congressional Serial Set (1961) issue 12554, p. 495.

Ushahidi. www.ushahidi.com/. Accessed June 2017.

Van Straaten, J. F., Richards, S. J. and Lotz, F. J. (1967). *Ventilation and Thermal Considerations in School Building Design*. Pretoria: CSIR.

Vickery, D. J. (1984, 1988) *Facilities Design Guide*. Paris: UNESCO.

Vickery, D. J. (1985) *Norms and Standards of Educational Facilities*. Paris: UNESCO.

Waddell, H. M. (1863) *The Diaries of H.M. Waddell and the Calabar Mission*. Edinburgh: National Library of Scotland Archives/Centre for Special Collections University of Edinburgh.

Waddell, H. M. (1863) *Twenty Nine Years in the West Indies and Central Africa: A Review of Missionary Work and Adventure*. London: T. Nelson and Sons.

Western Cape Government (2014) *Proposal for Elimination of Public School Infrastructure Backlogs in the Western Cape*. https://wcedonline.westerncape.gov.za/documents/NormsAndStandards/WCED-NS-infrastructureplan2015.pdf. Accessed April 2018.

White, H. (2004) *Books, Buildings and Learning Outcomes: An Impact Evaluation of World Bank Support to Basic Education in Ghana*. Washington, DC: World Bank.

Williams, D. (2001) *A History of the University College of Fort Hare South Africa: The 1950s the Waiting Years*. Ontario: The Edwin Mellen Press.

Woolner, P. (2010) *The Design of Learning Spaces*. London: Bloomsbury.

World Bank (1988) *Education in Africa Report*. Washington, DC: World Bank.

World Bank (2007) *Education in Sierra Leone, Present Challenges, Future Opportunities*. https://openknowledge.worldbank.org/handle/10986/6653. Accessed April 2018.

World Bank (2010) *Liberia Country Status Report: Out of the Ashes Learning Lessons From the Past to Guide Education Delivery in Liberia*. http://documents.worldbank.org/curated/en/257321468057236139/Liberia-education-country-status-report-out-of-the-ashes-learning-lessons-from-the-past-to-guide-education-recovery-in-Liberia. Accessed April 2018.

World Bank (2014) *READ Project Report*. http://documents.worldbank.org/curated/en/869821468024280057/pdf/ISR-Disclosable-P133079-06-22-2016-1466635929267.pdf. Accessed June 2017.

World Bank (2017) *Country Report*. www.worldbank.org/en/country/gambia/overview. Accessed June 2017.

World Bank (2017) *History Page*. www.worldbank.org/en/about/history. Accessed May 2017.

World Bank Blogs. *Promising Uses of Technology in Education in Poor, Rural and Isolated Communities, Around the World*. http://blogs.worldbank.org/edutech/education-technology-poor-rural.

154 *Bibliography*

World Bank House of Parliament (2017) *Sure Start Briefing*. http://researchbriefings.parliament.uk/ResearchBriefing/Summary/CBP-7257. Accessed March 2018.

World Bank – IBRD Archive Papers Online. www.worldbank.org/en/about/archives/history. Accessed August 2017.

Worldwatch Institute (2017) *EarthEd: Rethinking Education in a Changing Planet*. Washington, DC: Island Press.

Wright, S. (2016) New Labour New Approach. In N. Michandani and S. Wright (eds.), *Future Schools Innovative Design for Existing and New Buildings*. London: RIBA, pp. 10–12.

School Prospectuses and URLs

Aga Khan Academy, Mombasa, Kenya. *Financial Assistance*. www.agakhanacademies.org/mombasa/financial-assistance. Accessed May 2017.

American International School of Lagos. *AISL'S History*. www.aislagos.org/about-aisl/aisls-history-50-years-of-the-american-international-school-lagos. Accessed May 2017.

Atlantic Hall School, Nigeria. *Scholarships*. http://atlantic-hall.net/admissions-aids/scholarships/. Accessed May 2017.

Bishops Diocesan College, Cape Town. www.bishops.org.za/. Accessed August 2017.

Hillcrest International School, Kenya. *Our History*. www.hillcrest.ac.ke/hillcrest-history/. Accessed August 2017.

Loyola Jesuit College, Abuja. www.loyolajesuit.org/. Accessed August 2017.

Waterford Khambala webpage for History. www.waterford.sz/about/history.php.

Online Collections & Archives

1882 The Church Missionary Intelligencer. https://archive.org/stream/1882TheChurchMissionaryIntelligencer/1882_The_Church_Missionary_Intelligencer#page/n1/mode/2up.

Canmore [Scottish] National Record of the Historic Environment Archive Collection. Reference no. 561 357/2. Category All other, Robert Matthew Johnson-Marshall and Partners Collection c. 1965–1986. http://canmore.org.uk/collection/1178029. Accessed April 2018.

William Cooper's catalogue. https://archive.org/stream/IllustratedCatalogueOfGoodsManufacturedAndSuppliedByW.c.SperLtd/IllustratedComplete_djvu.txt, gives a clear description of what prefabricated buildings his company can 'ship' to the colonies, India and South Africa.

The New College Archive collection

This contains images of Schools near to Calabar, southeastern Nigeria, where the missionaries Mary Slessor and H. M. Waddell and had both worked.

Files: GB 0237 Edinburgh University Library Gen. 766/6 and GB 0237 Edinburgh University New College Library MSS CALA and MSS BOX 52.5.1–6, respectively.

Bibliography 155

National Archives Kew

Asian Regional Institute for School Building Research, 1972.
Colonial Building Notes (1900–1950) (specifically) *Colonial Building Note 57, Schools in the West Indies.*
DO 167/3, Ashby Commission Report on Higher Education in Nigeria, 1960/61.
Files on Colonial Welfare Development Funding Related to Education Funding in West Africa.
UNESCO (1961) Conference for African States on the Development of Education in Africa Addis Ababa Leading to the Outline of a Plan for African Educational Development or *Addis Ababa Declaration.*
UNESCO Building Report Series in the 1970s on School Design in South East Asia (Vickery, 1966).
UNESCO Design Guidelines, Paris, UNESCO 1966–88.
UNESCO had regional school building research offices in Bangkok, Dakar, and Beirut. www.unesco.org/education/pdf/BAT0029.PDF. Accessed August, 2017.
UNESCO (1990) *Meeting Basic Learning Needs, A Vision for the 1990s.* http://unesdoc.unesco.org/images/0009/000975/097552e.pdf. Accessed April 2014.

AA School Archives 1966

The AA Committee Minutes from 1960–1966 note the activities of the tropical studies unit, culminating in the formation of the Tropical School linked to the Kwame Nkrumah University of Science and Technology (KNUST) in Ghana.

Architectural Association Committee minutes in 1963

Wakely – AA archives 1966 School designs (1966) AA archives.

Journals

West African Builder and Architect (1963) Vol. 3, no. 1, pp. 8–12. Fourah Bay College Article, Frank Rutter.
West Africa Builder and Architect (1963) Vol. 5, no. 6, pp. 108–112. International School, Ibadan (Design Group) Phase 1.
West Africa Builder and Architect Vol. 2, no. 4, pp. 77–79. Factors Governing School Building Programmes Harris and White, West African Building Research Institute Accra.
West Africa Builder and Architect Vol. 8, no. 1. Art & Architecture in Nigeria, Editorial on IDA Schools in Nigeria.
Architectural Review (2014) www.architectural-review.com/today/learning-from-lagos-floating-school-makoko-nigeria-kunl-adeyemi-nl/8652311.article. Accessed December 2017.
ArchDaily (2013) Lagos Floating School. www.archdaily.com/344047/makoko-floating-school-nle-architects.

Personal communications

Uduku, O. (2003) Video Recorded interview with Michael Grice, Architectural Association, London.

156 *Bibliography*

Uduku, O. (2004) Personal interview with Max Bond, New York.
Uduku, O. (2017) Telephone interview with Dominic Bond, June 2017.

Exhibitions and conferences

Forms of Freedom: African Independence and Nordic Models, Exhibition on Scandinavian Architecture and Aid in East Africa, National Museum Nairobi, in collaboration with the National Museum of Art Oslo, November 2016–January 2017.
The Millennium Development Summit (2000) Anteceded by the Millennium Development Goals.
Space Group (2014) *Forms of Freedom: African Independence and Nordic Models*. The 14th International Architecture Biennale, The Nordic Pavilion, Venice, 7th June–23rd November 2014.
Uduku, O. (2016) *In the Notes on the Future of the Book in Africa Project Blog*. https://academicbookfuture.org/2016/04/05/academic-book-in-africa/. Accessed June 2017.
Uduku, O. and Le Roux, H. (2003) *The AA in Africa Exhibition*. Exhibition, 17 January–14th February 2003, The Architectural Association, London.
Uduku, O., Le Roux, H., Collins, M. et al. (2013) Alan Vaughan Richards Archive.

Twitter Feed

Obama, B. (2013) "If you think education is expensive, wait until you see how much ignorance costs in the 21st century." – President Obama #ABetterBargain. Accessed April 2018.

Websites

Africa Insight. http://westafricainsight.org/articles/view/126. Accessed 10 January 2015
Aga Khan Foundation (2017) *Education Overview*. www.akdn.org/our-agencies/aga-khan-foundation/education/education-overview. Accessed August 2017.
Archnet. http://archnet.org/collections/385/publications/1340. Accessed 10 January 2015.
Article 25 (2014) *New Prototype School for Sierra Leone*. www.article-25.org/previous-projects/prototype-child-friendly-school/. Accessed April 2018.

Index

Page numbers in italic indicate a figure on the corresponding page.

Achimota College 8, *8*, 29, 52
Adisadel College 6, 59–60, *60*
Aga Khan Development Network
   (AKDN) 40, 65, 68
Aga Khan Schools 14, 68, *69*,
   107–108, 118
aid sector 121–122
Architectural Association (AA) 10, 31,
   80, 83
assessment x, 44, 93–94, 129, 141; in
   the 1980s 14; and SDGs 89
attendance 10

Barewa College 31

Calabar 7; Hope Waddell College 5, 19,
   47n8, 51–55
Cape Town 7, 20, 41; Bishop's
   College 15; Dalweide Primary
   school *101*, 103–104; Diocesan
   College 69; Dunoon community
   128; Inkwenkwezi High School
   104–106, *106*, 113, 131; Project
   for the Study of Alternative
   Education in South Africa 87;
   University of Cape Town 9; Vukani
   School 87, 103
Christianity 3–7, 22n2, 38, 112, 117,
   119; *see also* missionary schools
classroom *see* learning spaces
colonial administration xi, 39, 84,
   107; and basic primary schools
   37; and design 28–31, 33–34, 70,
   117; and educational provision
   95n22; and national schools 9–11,
   10; post-WW2 58–59; *see also*
   missionary schools

colonial schools 7–8, *8*; government
   colleges 52–53, 57–58; post-WW2
   58–59; three Rs
curriculum 11; *see also* colonial
   administration
Commonwealth Education
   Secretariat 12
conferences 12–14
Council for Scientific and Industrial
   Research (CSIR) 34–35, 66

Dalweide School *101*, 103–104, 119
delivery 44, 71–72, 93, 114, 131–133;
   and contextual background to
   education 120; and environmental
   design 28; and ICT 125; and
   neoliberal funding approaches 111;
   and policies 129–130; and SDG4
   10, 18–19, 88; in South Africa
   70; traditional 92; and Western
   education 22; *see also* design
Department of Education and Training
   (DET) schools 19, 51, 66, *66*
deregulation *see* regulation
design xi–xii, 16–21, 43–46, 51,
   70–73, 93–94, 131–134; conceptual
   design concerns 91–92; and
   contemporary approaches 112–113;
   and contemporary schools 40–42,
   97–98; design guides 33–36, 47n10;
   and development goals 89–90;
   early case studies *27*, 52–58, *54*,
   56, *58*; East/Central Africa case
   studies 106–111, *109*; economic and
   socio-political factors for 36–39;
   and environment 27–32; and future
   schools 43, 116–117, 123; history

158　*Index*

of 117–122; of national schools 9–11, *10*; and neoliberal funding approaches 111–112; and NGO involvement 112; in the 1980s 14–15; and policy themes 80–85, 87–88, 129–131; post-1960s 64–66, *66*; post-WW2 case studies 58–64, *60, 63*; and private schools 67–70, *68, 69*; South Africa case studies *101*, 102–106, *106*; and technology 15–16, 88, 123–125, *123*; in the 21st century 77–78, 112–113; West Africa case studies 98– *100*; and the World Bank 12; *see also* colonial schools; *madrasas*; missionary schools
design guides *see under* design
displacement 91
Drew, Jane 9, 31–32, *59*, 62, 80–82; *see also* Fry, Max
Dwabor schools 98–101, *99*, 114, 128, *134*

East/Central Africa *see under* design; *see also specific schools*
economics 36–38
Educational Facilities Provision (EFP) 123
environment x–xi, 18, 26–36, 45, 48n32; assessment and 94; case studies 53–55, *54*, 101–102, 106, 109–110; and policy 85, *86*; and technology 132
environmental science 30, 47n10

Federal Government College 31, 60–64, *63*
feeding programs *42*
forced migration 90–91
Fry, Max 9, 10, 31–32, *33*, 59–60, 64

Ghana 4, 7–12, *8*, *10*, 20, 32, 77; child-centred learning curriculum model in 118; funding for schools in 37; Fry-Drew schools 19, 51, 62, 64; National School Buildings Programmes in 38, 41–42, 59, 133; NGOs in 112; One Laptop Per Child 16, 131; school design in 47n10, 82, 83, 92; UNESCO in 34; schools in rural areas in 141; *see also* Achimota College; Adisadel College; Dwabor schools; Mawuli School; Wakely, Pat
Government Technical College *10*

Hole in the Wall Learning 113, 126, *127*, 141
Hope Waddell College 5, *5*, 52–55
human rights 10, 79

Inkwenkwezi School 104–106, *106*, 113, 113, 119
International Bank for Reconstruction and Development (IBRD) 12, 60, 64–65, 79
International Development Agency (IDA) 19, 39, 41, 51, 60, 61, 133
International School *68*
International Technology Development Group (ITDG) 35
Islam 3–4, 6, 44, 87, 107; *see also madrasas*
Islamic schools *see madrasas*

Katsina College 6, *30*
Kings College 29, 52, 57–58, *58*

Lagos 7, 15, *27*, 46n4, 49n42, 61, 64; Ansar Ud Deen School 10; Atlantic College 14; e-learning in 140; Kings College 8, 52–53, 57–59, *58*; Kunle Adeyemi 130; Lagos Floating School 134, 141; St Gregory's College 28
learning spaces x–xiii, 38, 43–44, 132–133; development goals and 89; and future education 116–117, 125–126, 128–129, 141; and sustainable development 129–131; and technology 125; *see also* design; environment
libraries 12, 31–32, *32*, 124
lifelong learning x, 44, 50n60, 88
London School of Tropical Hygiene and Medicine (LSTM) 31
Lovedale College 55–57, *56*

madrasas 3–4, 87
Makoko Floating School 20, *130*
MASS design 35, 45, 106, 108–110
Mawuli School 64, *81*
migration *see* forced migration
Millennium Development Goals (MDGs) *see* Sustainable Development Goals
missionary schools xi, 4–7, 18–19, 43–44, 71, 132; case studies 52–60, *54, 56, 60*; and classroom design

70; and economic factors 37, 48n22; opportunity costs of 38; and school design 27–30, *27, 29,* 33–34; and school provision 107
Mombasa *5, 7;* Aga Khan School 68, *69,* 107–108, 118
Mubugu schools 108–110

national schools 8–11, *10*
neoliberalism 14–15, 111–112
Nigeria 19, 38, 65, 72, 82, 83; challenges in 44, 87–88; IDA-UNESCO school design programme in 41; indigenous education practices in 1–3, *2;* Islamic schools in 3–4, *3;* NGOs in 112; private education in 98, 132; school building programmes in 9, 34, 37; tuition in 40, 59; TVIs in 11; University of Ibadan 9, 32, 67–68, 118; Universal Primary Education project in 70; the World Bank in 12; *see also* Calabar; colonial schools; Hope Waddell College; Katsina College; Lagos; missionary schools; Sokoto; Wusasa College
NGOs 35, 112; *see also specific NGOs*
Nigerian National Education Policy 11
Noraid School 82, *82*
Nyerere, Julius 41, 65, 70, 82

One Laptop Per Child (OLPC) 15, 25n56, 43, 117, 122, 124, 131
opportunity costs 26, 38–39
Overseas Building Notes 9, 34

Paarl *see* Cape Town
policy 39–43, 78–88, 129–131
private schools 67–70, *68, 69,* 71, 72, 86–87, 108

regulation 14, 33, 35, 45, 67, 71, 86

school planning *see* design
schools 1–4, *2, 3; see also* colonial schools; *madrasas;* missionary schools; national schools; private schools
Sokoto 31, 60–64, *63*
South Africa 9, 45–46, 72–73, 132; DET schools of 19; education policies in 40–41; elite status religious

colleges in 15; environmental design guides in 34–36; new learning spaces in 128–129; new national education programme in 17; NGOs in 112; OLPC programme in 17; opportunity costs in 39; school design in 64–66, 70, 86–87, 92, 117–119; segregated education in 11–12, 85; subject teaching in 52; *see also* Cape Town; colonial schools; Delweide School; Department of Education and Training Schools; Lovedale College; missionary schools
Southern Africa *see under* design; *see also specific schools*
St Gregory's College 15, 28, *29,* 57
Sustainable Development Goals (SDGs) x, xii, 20, 77, 88–90, 93; and the aid sector 122; and development 129; and educational investment 14; and future education 116; and human rights 79; and school design 43–44, 46

Tanzania: Aga Khan School in 68, 107; *Ujaama* schools in 18, 41, 65, 70, 82–84
teachers x; and contemporary concepts of teaching 92; and environment 26; in future schools 43; in Ghana 99–100; and global education polices 39–40; and government schools 59, 62; and *madrasa* schools 4; and missionary schools 7, 52–53, 57; and NGOs 112; and policy 80–82; and private schools 67; and regulations 14–15; in South Africa 103; teacher-directed learning 117, 120; teacher education 13–14, 72; and technical education 12; and technologies 44, 125, 127–128
technical education 11–12
technology x–xiii, 16–17, 44–46, 119–121, 131–134; and access 88; adoption of new 90, 97; costs of 38; e-learning 43; and future learning networks 126–128; ICT 123–125, *142;* influences for 112–113; in Kenya 107–108; in new learning spaces 125–126, 128; in post-apartheid South Africa 72, 103; in Rwanda 108–110; and school choice 14; and school design 32; and virtual learning environments 15–16

160　*Index*

Ujaama 18, 41, 65, 70, 82–84
Umbano schools 108–111, *109*
United Nations Educational Social and Cultural Organisation (UNESCO) 12–13, 45, 67, 84, 120; and Federal Government College 61–62; and policy themes 79–82; and post-1960s school design 64–66; school design guides of 33–34
University of Science and Technology 9
USAID 11

vocational education *see* technical education
Vukani School *36*, 87, 103, 119, 133

Wakely, Pat 83, *83*
West Africa *see under* design; *see also specific schools*
World Bank 12–14; and global education policies 39–41; and schools provision 80, 83
Wusasa College 29

Zambia 82, *82*